T0311593

Accounting Ethics Education

Accounting education ought to prepare future professionals to enter a principles-based, rules-oriented field of activity wherein technical knowledge of accounting standards (principles, rules and decision procedures) and ethical awareness (the capacity to discern moral issues and resolve ethical dilemmas) are crucial. Accounting education is best performed by the accountant's adherence to the principles of the accounting profession and by individuals and firms following the appropriate rules, act according to the codes of conduct adopted by their profession, exercise clear judgment whenever they address financial transactions and consider/assess the state of a given business.

Accounting Ethics Education: Making Ethics Real gathers a diversity of contributions from invited well-known experts and other specialists. It promotes comprehensive reflection around key trends, discussing and highlighting the most updated research on accounting ethics education, being an essential and useful reference in the field. In the performance of accounting tasks, the accountant should be educated and supported in skills development and habit formation to solve accounting problems, recognize moral issues and resolve ethical dilemmas that will be encountered in their special tasks. Also, this book provides a moral map for identifying and acting on values when difficult situations arise.

Examining multiple perspectives, this book improves the scholarly debate by providing cutting-edge and insightful research vital for all those interested and immersed in these matters. It will be of great value to academics, students, researchers and professionals in the fields of accounting, accounting education and ethics.

Alberto J. Costa, Ph.D., is Professor at the University of Aveiro (Institute of Accounting and Administration, ISCA–UA), where he has been teaching ethics and deontology for several years now. He also teaches accounting and management control and is the head of the master's degree in accounting and management control. He is a full researcher of GOVCOPP (Research Unit on Governance, Competitiveness and Public Policies, University of Aveiro), on the Systems for Decision Support research group. He is a certified accountant, in Portugal, since 1997 and a member of GRUDIS – Portuguese Network of Accounting Research – since 2006. He develops research in the fields of financial accounting and management accounting and, particularly, in the areas of ethics and deontology. He has published papers in national and international journals.

Margarida M. Pinheiro, Ph.D., is Professor at the University of Aveiro (Institute of Accounting and Administration, ISCA–UA) and a full researcher at the Research Centre Didactics and Technology in Education of Trainers (CIDTFF), on the Policies, Evaluation and Quality research group. She is currently a member of the School Council. She was also a member of the Scientific Council and President of the Pedagogical Council of ISCA–UA. Margarida has been publishing in the areas of learning and teaching methodologies, quality of education, knowledge construction and internationalization of universities. She serves on the editorial board of the *Journal of Higher Education Pedagogies* and is a passionate researcher engaged in education at the higher education level.

Routledge Studies in Accounting

Corporate Environmental Reporting
The Western Approach to Nature
Leanne J. Morrison

Cost Management for Nonprofit and Voluntary Organisations
Zahirul Hoque and Tarek Rana

Multinational Enterprises and Transparent Tax Reporting
Alexandra Middleton and Jenni Muttonen

Accounting for M&A
Uses and Abuses of Accounting in Monitoring and Promoting Merger
Edited by Amir Amel-Zadeh and Geoff Meeks

Interventionist Research in Accounting
A Methodological Approach
Edited by Vicki Baard and Johannes Dumay

Accounting Ethics Education
Teaching Virtues and Values
Edited by Margarida M. Pinheiro and Alberto J. Costa

Auditor Going Concern Reporting
A Review of Global Research and Future Research Opportunities
Marshall A. Geiger, Anna Gold and Philip Wallage

Accounting Ethics Education
Making Ethics Real
Edited by Alberto J. Costa and Margarida M. Pinheiro

For more information about this series, please visit: www.routledge.com/ Routledge-Studies-in-Accounting/book-series/SE0715

Accounting Ethics Education

Making Ethics Real

Edited by Alberto J. Costa
and Margarida M. Pinheiro

Routledge
Taylor & Francis Group

NEW YORK AND LONDON

First published 2021
by Routledge
605 Third Avenue, New York, NY 10158

and by Routledge
2 Park Square, Milton Park, Abingdon, Oxon, OX14 4RN

Routledge is an imprint of the Taylor & Francis Group, an informa business

© 2021 Taylor & Francis

Library of Congress Cataloging-in-Publication Data
Names: Costa, Alberto J., editor. | Pinheiro, Margarida
 M., 1961– editor.
Title: Accounting ethics education : making ethics real / edited by
 Alberto J. Costa and Margarida M. Pinheiro.
Description: New York, NY : Routledge, 2021. | Series: Routledge
 studies in accounting | Includes bibliographical references and
 index.
Identifiers: LCCN 2020056917 (print) | LCCN 2020056918 (ebook) |
 ISBN 9780367857974 (hardback) | ISBN 9781003017509 (ebook)
Subjects: LCSH: Accounting—Study and teaching. | Accounting—
 Moral and ethical aspects. | Accountants—Professional ethics.
Classification: LCC HF5630 .A432 2021 (print) | LCC HF5630 (ebook) |
 DDC 174/.96570711—dc23
LC record available at https://lccn.loc.gov/2020056917
LC ebook record available at https://lccn.loc.gov/2020056918

ISBN: 978-0-367-85797-4 (hbk)
ISBN: 978-1-032-01999-4 (pbk)
ISBN: 978-1-003-01750-9 (ebk)

Typeset in Sabon
by Apex CoVantage, LLC

To all who believe in a better world and are willing to build it
Alberto J. Costa

To my son Pedro, who, as a financial analyst, has the responsibility to act ethically

To my daughter Laura, who, as a psychologist, has ethical responsibilities towards others
Margarida M. Pinheiro

Contents

PART 1
Ethical Training: Preparing From the Inside

Figures

Tables

Exhibits

Contributors

Richard A. Bernardi, Professor of Accounting at Roger Williams University, is a retired Air Force lieutenant colonel who flew the B-52 and FB-111 aircraft. He has also been Professor of National Security Affairs at the US Naval War College. Dr. Bernardi has published over 120 journal articles and received three Teaching Excellence Awards from both Roger Williams University (2) and the State University of New York (1).

Samantha A. Bilinsky graduated from Roger Williams University with a double major in accounting and finance. In her junior year, her Analytics team was placed second in the National AIS Student Chapter National Competition. She is a member of Beta Alpha Psi. Currently, Samantha is an audit associate at a Big-4 accounting firm.

Margaret N. Boldt, Ph.D., is Associate Professor of Accounting at Southeastern Louisiana University, USA. Her research and teaching interests include managerial decision-making and pedagogical advances.

Robert L. Braun, Ph.D., is Department Head and Phil K. Livingston Professor of Accounting at Southeastern Louisiana University. He has published in leading academic, pedagogical and practitioner journals. His teaching and research interests are ethics and auditing.

Callie H. Chase graduated from Roger Williams University with a degree in accounting; she also studied international studies abroad in Florence, Italy. She was a member of the Women's Field Hockey team and was named captain in her senior year. She is a member of Beta Alpha Psi. Currently, Callie is an audit associate at a regional accounting firm specializing in nonprofits, manufacturing and construction.

Alberto J. Costa, Ph.D., is Professor at the University of Aveiro (ISCA–UA), where he teaches ethics and deontology for several years now. He also teaches accounting and management control and is the head of the master's degree in accounting and management control. He is a full researcher of GOVCOPP (Research Unit on Governance,

Competitiveness and Public Policies, of the University of Aveiro) on the Systems for Decision Support research group. He is a certified accountant, in Portugal, since 1997 and member of GRUDIS – Portuguese Network of Accounting Research. He develops research in the fields of financial accounting and management accounting and, particularly, in the areas of ethics and deontology. He has published papers in national and international journals.

Christopher J. Cowton is Emeritus Professor at the University of Huddersfield, where he served as Professor of Accounting (1996–2016), Dean of the Business School (2008–2016) and Professor of Financial Ethics (2016–2019). He is currently Associate Director (Research) at the Institute of Business Ethics in London. He is a Chartered Governance Professional and a former member of the Ethics Standards Committee of the Institute of Chartered Accountants in England and Wales.

Lisa D. Giannini graduated from Roger Williams University with a double major in accounting and finance. She was a member of the Women's Rugby team throughout her college career and is a member of Beta Gamma Sigma Honor Society and Delta Sigma Pi. Currently, Lisa is an audit associate at a Big-4 accounting firm specializing in banking and capital markets with industry knowledge in foreign exchange, currency services and commodities trading.

Michael Kraten is Professor of Accounting and Chair of Accounting, Economics, and Finance programs at Houston Baptist University in Houston, Texas, USA. He is a member of the Executive Committee of the Sustainability Investment Leadership Council and an officer of the Public Interest Section of the AAA. He authors a professional and academic blog entitled Save the Blue Frog.

Joan Lee is Professor of Accounting in the Dolan School of Business, Fairfield University, where she teaches courses in financial and managerial accounting, accounting ethics and business ethics. She has published numerous articles in the areas of accounting ethics and pedagogy.

Samantha A. MacWhinnie graduated from Roger Williams University with a degree in accounting; she studied abroad in the Netherlands at the University of Amsterdam. She was a member of the Women's Rugby team throughout her college career. She currently works as an accountant in the food and beverage industry. Samantha is an honorary boatbuilder at The Landing School, where she assisted in building a 17 feet carbon fiber kayak.

Dawn W. Massey is Professor of Accounting in the Dolan School of Business, Fairfield University, where she teaches graduate courses in accounting ethics, communication and research. She has published numerous articles in the areas of accounting ethics and pedagogy.

William F. Miller, CPA, CGMA, is Professor of Accounting at the University of Wisconsin, Eau Claire. William's primary research interest is accounting ethics. He has authored or co-authored over 20 publications and has won the Institute of Management Accountants Carl Menconi Ethics Case writing competition three times (2011, 2012 and 2015), as well as the AAA's Public Interest Section best contribution to teaching award in 2015.

Steven M. Mintz is an emeritus professor from the California Polytechnic State University, San Luis Obispo. He has authored or co-authored over 30 publications and received the Accounting Exemplar award from the Public Interest Section of the AAA. Dr. Mintz is the lead author of the accounting ethics textbook *Ethical Obligations and Decision Making in Accounting: Text and Cases*.

Lars Jacob Tynes Pedersen earned his Ph.D. from the Norwegian School of Business and Economics, Bergen, Norway. He is now Associate Professor there in the Department of Accounting, Auditing and Law. He teaches business ethics and accounting ethics and does research on corporate sustainability. He is an active public speaker and strategic advisor for business organizations. His research has been published in management science and the *Journal of Business Ethics* and by several publishers, including Palgrave Macmillan, Edward Elgar and Wiley.

Margarida M. Pinheiro, Ph.D., is Professor at the University of Aveiro (ISCA-UA) and a full researcher at the Research Centre Didactics and Technology in Education of Trainers (CIDTFF) on the Policies, Evaluation and Quality research, group. She is currently member of the School Council. She was also a member of the Scientific Council and President of the Pedagogical Council of ISCA-UA. Margarida has been publishing in the areas of learning and teaching methodologies, quality of education, knowledge construction and internationalization of universities. She serves on the editorial board of the *Journal of Higher Education Pedagogies*. She is a passionate researcher engaged in education at the higher education level.

James E. Rebele retired as Professor of Accounting from Robert Morris University in 2017. Rebele received his Ph.D. from Indiana University, Bloomington, and he previously served as a faculty member at Lehigh University, Rutgers University, the University of Kansas, the University of Rhode Island and Santa Clara University. He served as Editor-in-Chief for the *Journal of Accounting Education* from 1998 until 2010. He also served as President of the American Accounting Association's (AAA) Teaching and Curriculum Section for 1999–2000 and as a member of the AAA Executive Council from 1998 to 2001. In May 2007, Rebele received a Lifetime Achievement Award from the British Accounting Association's Special Interest Group on Education.

Tara J. Shawver, CMA, is Department Chair and Professor of Accounting at King's College in Wilkes-Barre, PA. Tara is an active member of the AAA and the Institute of Management Accountants. She has authored or co-authored over 40 articles on topics of financial reporting, whistle-blowing, fraud, accounting ethics education and collaborative learning.

E. Kent St. Pierre is Professor and the Sutula Chair of Accounting at St. Joseph's University in Philadelphia, PA. He previously served as Editor-in-Chief of the *Journal of Accounting Education* and *Issues in Accounting Education* for 18 years and as a faculty member and department head at four different universities for over 40 years. He served as President of the AAA's Teaching and Curriculum Section and as President of the AAA Accounting Program Leadership Section. St. Pierre was inducted into the AAA Teaching and Curriculum Section Hall of Honor in 2016.

Iris Caroline Stuart, Ph.D. in Accounting, University of Iowa, holds appointments in accounting at the Norwegian School of Business, Bergen, the University of Agder, Kristiansand, Norway, and the University of Stavanger, Stavanger, Norway. She publishes in accounting ethics and auditing and teaches courses in accounting ethics, fraud and auditing. She mentors Ph.D. students in accounting and auditing.

Bruce Wayne Stuart, Ph.D. in American Studies, University of Minnesota, is retired from the History Faculty of the University of Bergen, Bergen, Norway. He has been a lecturer in accounting ethics at the Norwegian School of Business and Economics, Bergen, Norway. He specialized in lectures on the traditions of moral philosophy and their application to the practical ethics of accounting decision-making. He has published books on accounting ethics, and he consults with graduate students and faculty on issues of English academic writing.

Martin T. Stuebs, Jr. has served as Associate Professor in Accounting at Baylor University for 15 years and currently holds the R. E. and Marilyn Reamer Professorship in Accounting. He primarily teaches accounting ethics and managerial accounting courses, and his research interests include topics that span accounting ethics and professionalism. This work includes several award-winning accounting ethics cases and articles.

Acknowledgments

Editing and publishing a book is always a demanding process that requires patience, dedication and rigor. To complete this task, we needed a lot of effort and persistence and, in this way, it is important to highlight who was essential for us to reach the 'top of the mountain'.

Our first acknowledgment goes to Routledge, an outstanding publisher with a superb team, that believed, supported, encouraged and cherished this project from the beginning, 'giving birth' to a series of two books – this is the second. Few books have been published on accounting ethics education; therefore, we applaud Routledge's foresight in publishing such books.

We also offer our heartfelt appreciation to all the authors who were generous enough to share their knowledge and valuable time in adding very relevant contributions to the field of accounting ethics education and research. We feel extremely honored for having them on board and sincerely grateful for believing in this project.

Alberto J. Costa and Margarida M. Pinheiro

I am very appreciative of Margarida's enduring and unfailing support and for working with me to produce this book.

My most passionate thank you goes to my wife, Rosa, who inspires, supports, encourages and loves me every day and for being one of the most ethical human beings I know. Together with our children, Anita, Duarte and Alice, they remind me constantly that as long as we have each other, we have everything.

Finally, to my parents, for their example of love and for being always present.

Alberto

I thank Alberto for the partnership developed and for contributing to make this project a fluid and gratifying path.

I also want to thank my parents, for everything they have taught me throughout my life and for their ever-present optimism.

Margarida

This work is financially supported by national funds through FCT – Fundação para a Ciência e a Tecnologia, I.P., under the projects UIDB/CED/00194/2020 (CIDTFF – Research Centre on Didactics and Technology in the Education of Trainers) – and UIDB/04058/2020 (GOVCOPP – Research Unit on Governance, Competitiveness and Public Policies).

Foreword

I feel honored to write the Foreword for this book on accounting ethics education research. At the outset I would like to thank the editors for putting this book together and the authors for their extraordinary contributions. I am delighted to write this Foreword because I believe deeply in the value of ethics education. As a teacher, I believe education has no boundary on getting accounting students to think about ethical issues or help sharpen their ethical intelligence. Few experiences are more gratifying than the learning that comes with students' enlightened awareness of their moral power and the skills that enable them to take a firm stand in difficult situations. I personally believe that accounting ethics education can help shape students' character and caliber.

I have no doubt that our students go about their daily lives with compassion, healthy friendships and limitless empathy that guide them to be gentle human beings. However, in a wider world, it is also naïve to assume that our students will never face the ethical dilemmas that are ubiquitous in the world of business and accounting. It is not enough to expect that empathy, intuition or good intention is adequate to deal with the problems our students will face in practice. Inadequate preparation for professional practice underestimates the scholarly preparation to graduate competent accountants. I do not hesitate to sell the benefits of ethics education ranging from an enhanced ability to recognize issues that may otherwise go unnoticed through to making informed behavioral choices. In my view, ethical competence should not be an optional extra; learning how to be a professional should be mandatory and on par with learning the technical aspects of accounting. I for one appreciate the sincerity and genuineness of the calls for ethics education.

The accounting profession receives universal respect in society for the services it provides to the public. However, in practice the accounting profession is met with criticism in the wake of high-profile corporate collapses. The media drawing attention to highly publicized media cases of ethical transgressions arouses the public's interest in the ethical judgments and behavior of accountants. When media attention is high, public confidence in accounting and auditing is low. However, the public do not question the profession's technical competence but their behavioral choices stemming from a perceived breakdown in ethical standards. When accountants are seen or perceived to behave badly, it invites questions about the role of education to graduate ethical accountants. Support for ethics interventions stems from the premise that ethical awareness and decision-making can be enhanced through the educational process.

Notwithstanding the conflicting views on whether ethics should be taught, and conflicting expectations on how it might affect ethical decision-making or behavior, there is a long tradition of research to assess the impact of ethics education on the ethical attitudes of accounting students, often with mixed results. In many cases, accounting students fare unfavorably with comparable student groups questioning the efficacy of accounting education to develop ethical accountants. Broaching this sensitive topic may sometimes distance faculty from addressing this issue to avoid the negative news that may arise. However, in this book, two chapters address the issue of classroom cheating and its implications.

Boldt and Braun (Chapter 6) highlight the changing nature of accounting education in a technological age where staff–student interaction is increasingly distant and separated. They examine the implications on classroom cheating in the transition from traditional modes of teaching to online learning and assessment. In a survey of accounting students, Boldt and Braun (Chapter 6) found that 59% believed that the opportunity to cheat is greater in an online learning environment and almost half of the sample population believes that cheating was more common after the transition to online learning. The authors call for ethics education to bring moral leadership into accounting education.

The chapter by Bernardi et al. (Chapter 1) is premised on the assumption that classroom cheating is present. The authors investigate ways to reduce it from the perspective of the student. The results of a survey of accounting students provide a mix of suggestions to decrease classroom cheating or alternatively to deter cheating by increasing the propensity to blow the whistle. What emerged from the results are two notable findings: professors need to be more diligent when giving classroom tests and students must be assured of confidentiality if a professor expects them to report observations of cheating on an examination.

The chapter contributed by Rebele and Pierre (Chapter 2) questions the qualifications of accounting faculty and whether they possess the requisite knowledge or training to competently teach ethics. The authors examined doctoral training programs and found limited opportunity to pursue interests in ethics education, suggesting that the opportunity and motivation for teaching ethics do not come from teacher training but from a self-motivated pursuit, not a guided pursuit. The lack of teacher training not only makes the task of teaching ethics difficult but could also lead to deficient teaching.

Pedagogies for teaching ethics are both vast and diverse; for example, narratives that include books, movies and biographies with complex plots raise students' imaginative consciousness, creating personal moral conflict and the capacity to enhance their moral capacity. In this book, the Stuarts and Pedersen (Chapter 3) propose a framework of ethics education in an auditing course, integrating both technical expertise and ethical sensibility. The authors advocate the case-based approach to help students understand what it means to be a professional accountant through the application of virtue ethics and character formation. Enhancing students' virtues is expected to strengthen student's commitment to professional duty and public service.

In a parallel theme, Miller and Shawver (Chapter 7) adopt the curriculum on Giving Voice to Values (GVV) developed by Mary Gentile. GVV emphasizes how students may effectively act on their values. Where virtue ethics used in the Stuarts and Pedersen (Chapter 3) emphasizes character, GVV adopts an action-oriented approach to values-driven behavior. In an illustration and reflection on the application of GVV in a course on advance financial accounting, Miller and Shawver (Chapter 7) tout its many benefits. The authors emphasize how GVV increases confidence in students to deal with ethical issues and the likelihood that students will act on their values using the principles of GVV. Student engagement and participation were greatly enhanced using GVV.

People not involved in teaching ethics might think that ethical decision-making is about teaching the code of ethics and rules of independence in the belief that it will help students develop more sophisticated moral decision-making skills, thereby increasing their capacity to avoid unethical behavior. This approach to ethics education is focused on the rules of behavior, professional pronouncements and respect for the law, but it does very little to teach ethical systems of analysis and introduce skills to deal effectively with ethical challenges. Two chapters in this book address the issue of ethical decision-making by examining ways students can structure and improve their behavioral choices.

Highlighting the deficiencies of existing ethical decision-making models, Mintz and Miller (Chapter 8) propose the application of the PLUS model alongside case studies to understand the psychological processes and organizational systems that contribute to ethically questionable behavior. The acronym PLUS (Policies, Legal, Universal, Self) refers to the filters that bring ethical considerations and implications to ethical decision-making. Mintz and Miller (Chapter 8) illustrate the application of the PLUS model to evaluate the unethical actions of accountant Betty Vinson who made fraudulent entries in the books of WorldCom. The chapter explores how Vinson may have acted differently faced with alternative choices offered and delineated using the PLUS ethical decision-making model.

Lee and Massey (Chapter 9) similarly base their chapter on ethical decision-making models by reviewing the existing literature and proposing an alternative model labeled 'RADAR' (Research, Analyze, Decide, Act, Reflect). The RADAR model helps users to navigate ethical problems in accounting and when used in education, it enhances students' preparedness to address ethical issues. It is a comprehensive model particularly useful in the case approach to ethics education, leading students to make behavioral choices and reflecting back on the process and outcome to improve the handling of future ethical situations.

Educators teach with enthusiasm to develop a generation of ethically aware accounting professionals. However, program designers promoting ethics education face a significant barrier in overcoming the constraints imposed by the accreditation guidelines that emphasize the depth and breadth of technical accounting knowledge. Course content constructed around regulation leaves little room to devote to the softer sciences such as ethics, squeezed out in favor of accounting pronouncements. Cowton (Chapter 4) revisits the issue of professional accreditation and its constraining effect on the implementation and spread of ethics in the accounting curriculum. Professional accreditation aims to set the benchmark for acceptable standards of education, but in practice, it defines the content of accounting education by prescribing what should be taught. Cowton (Chapter 4) claims that the impetus to spread ethics education more widely is absent and in need of significant intervention. Paradoxically, he also claims that the very factor that constrains the development of ethics education, professional accreditation, is also the impetus that can grow ethics education.

Noting the narrowness of content in accounting education, Kraten and Stuebs (Chapter 5) call for the inclusion of corporate sustainability and corporate social responsibility, claiming that the underlying dimensions are on par with the ethics and responsibilities of professional accountants working toward sustainable outcomes. Being socially responsible is not only being ethical, but it underpins the ethics and moral development of sustainable professionals.

I hope that this book will become a premier reference for educators and researchers, helping to understand, teach and practice the art of accounting ethics education. The chapters in this book address different issues but are premised on one key theme: accounting ethics education helps to develop ethical dispositions and behavior in accounting students and provides a framework for good leadership and an ethical accounting profession.

There is no single best book on accounting ethics education; the praise for this book will depend heavily on the reader's interest. But I do believe this book provides a useful range of evidence for designing, implementing and evaluating a program of ethics education. Nothing will make me more happy than to learn that the book has been used widely by many scholars.

In all, this book clearly deserves to have a very wide readership. I think it should be carefully read by any faculty who has an interest in ethics education and the students they mentor.

It would be remiss if I failed to give credit to the editors and the many scholars involved in the development of this book and its sister book, *Accounting Ethics Education: Teaching Virtues and Values*, edited by Pinheiro, M. M. and Costa, A. J. (2020). On behalf of me, colleagues, past, present and future students: Thank you!

Steven Dellaportas
Professor of Accounting
University of Nottingham
Nottingham University Business School, Ningbo, China
Co-Editor, Accounting Section, Journal of Business Ethics

Preface

This book is the result of hard work, commitment and the ability to believe in an idea. If hard work is the result of commitment and this, in turn, is the result of dedication to a cause, only the ability to believe leads us to participate and to the act of actually doing something.

This book is the result of our faith in accounting ethics education. The proposal presented to Routledge proved to be strong enough to attract several specialists in the field, which led us to edit not one but two books on the subject. This is the second one.

This book comprehends a careful reflection not only around what ethical training means and how are we preparing our students from the inside but also around the process of making ethics real by giving voice to values. As an essential and useful instrument, this book cannot be read as a recipe for being ethical. Instead, it must be understood as a tool to foster reflection and motivation on how ethics can be taught to accounting students and how they should be motivated to act ethically. If students achieve so, the accounting profession will be enriched and dignified, and they will excel at being responsible professionals with high technical standards and superior ethical sensibility.

Alberto J. Costa and Margarida M. Pinheiro

Part 1

Ethical Training

Preparing From the Inside

1 Decreasing Cheating and Increasing Whistle-Blowing in the Classroom

A Replication Study

Richard A. Bernardi, Samantha A. Bilinsky, Callie H. Chase, Lisa D. Giannini & *Samantha A. MacWhinnie*

1. Introduction

Ameen, Guffey and McMillan (1996) and Bernardi, Baca, Landers and Witek (2008) found that over 60% of the students sampled feel that cheating has a direct relationship with the intense competition for grades. Ameen et al. (1996) also found that an increased emphasis on comprehending material, instead of focusing on getting an 'A', would create an environment where students would be less likely to cheat. Students who work hard to earn their grades do not want to see others get away with cheating (Malgwi & Rakovski, 2009). However, many students are hesitant to whistle-blow on classmates due to concerns about anonymity and that whistle-blowing is pointless as nothing is done about cheating (Burton & Near, 1995). Bernardi, Larkin, LaBontee, Lapierre and Morse (2012a) found that other reasons for not whistle-blowing included concerns about losing a friend, their reputation at school, and the belief that cheating does not affect them or that reporting cheating is not their responsibility. Given the increased level of cheating in college, it is not surprising that Bernardi et al. (2012a) also found that students did not whistle-blow because they too had cheated (i.e., a feeling of being a hypercritic).[1]

The current research is a continuation and replication of Bernardi, Landry, Landry, Buonafede and Berardi's (2016) and an extension of Bernardi et al.'s (2008). Lindsay (1995, p. 35) suggests that replication studies are a "crucial test of the reliability and validity . . . [which] leads, when successful, to generalizable" results; Burman, Reed and Alm (2010, p. 789) support Lindsay's suggestion adding that replication "shows the original article's findings are robust and substantial extensions over time".[2] Of the 187 students surveyed in this research, 78 students provided suggestions for reducing cheating and 1221 for increasing whistle-blowing in the classroom. However, five of the students' suggestions for reducing cheating and three of the suggestions for increasing whistle-blowing in the classroom had significant differences in response rates by students' cheating category.

2. Literature Review

Our literature review examines the findings associated with cheating and whistle-blowing in the classroom. We formatted our literature review on cheating using Little and Handel's (2016) adaptations of Albrecht, Albrecht, Albrecht and Zimbelman's (2020) fraud triangle. Little and Handel (2016) indicate that their cheating triangle's three conditions are similar to those present when fraud exists (Albrecht et al., 2020). They further adapt their cheating triangle into a solutions triangle to combat student cheating. We follow this section with a second section that reviews the literature associated with whistle-blowing.

2.1. Classroom Cheating

2.1.1. The Cheating Triangle

When fraud occurs, the Auditing Standards Board (American Institute of Certified Public Accountants, 2003, p. 1722) indicates that three conditions are typically present:

> First, management or other employees have an *incentive* or are under *pressure*, which provides a reason to commit fraud. Second, circumstances exist – for example, the absence of controls, ineffective controls, or the ability of management to override controls – that provide an *opportunity* for a fraud to be perpetrated. Third, those involved are able to *rationalize* committing a fraudulent act.

These conditions are referred to as the fraud triangle (Albrecht et al., 2020). Several studies (e.g., Becker, Connolly, Lentz & Morrison, 2006; Burke & Sanney, 2018; Choo & Tan, 2008; Little & Handel, 2016) have used the fraud triangle to examine students' cheating behavior.[3] For example, whereas Choo and Tan (2008) and Becker et al. (2006) found that each of the three conditions in the fraud triangle influenced students' cheating behavior, Choo and Tan (2008) found that all three conditions acted jointly when predicting cheating.

Little and Handel (2016) indicate that the fraud triangle's three conditions are similar to the conditions present when students cheat. They refer to the cheating triangle's conditions as the pressure for grades, poor control over the testing environment and students' belief that 'everyone cheats' (i.e., cynical attitude (Ameen et al., 1996; Bernardi & Adamaitis, 2007; Salter, Guffey & McMillan, 2001)). Wells (2005) suggests a fraud scale that adapts the conditions of the fraud triangle. This scale predicts the highest probability of cheating when situational pressures (i.e., pressure for high grades) and opportunities (i.e., lack of control of the testing environment) are high, whereas concurrently personal integrity is low.

Day, Hudson, Dobies and Waris (2011) and Van Yperen, Melvyn, van der Klauw and van der Klauw (2011) report that grade-oriented students (i.e., satisficing (Schwartz et al., 2002)) are more likely to cheat than students who focus on mastering the subject material (i.e., maximizing (Schwartz et al., 2002). Ballantine, Guo and Larres (2018, p. 247) define mastering the subject matter as "relating and structuring ideas, thinking creatively, weighing relevant evidence and critically evaluating knowledge". Schwartz et al. (2002) indicate that maximizing occurs when students are willing to put forth a significant effort to attain 'high-standard goals'; however, these authors indicate that satisficing occurs when students put in only a minimum effort to attain 'good-enough goals'. Elias (2019) found that students who scored higher on a measure of maximizing tendencies (Lai, 2010) perceived cheating (Simha, Armstrong & Albert, 2012) as being more unethical.

Tyson (1989) found that, whereas male students had higher attitudes related to questions pertaining to competition, female students had higher attitudes related to self-satisfaction and hard work (Gneezy, Niederle & Rustichini, 2003). In a replication study of Tyson (1989), Landry and Bernardi's (2015) students reported lower averages on questions dealing with work attitudes than those in Tyson's (1989) sample. However, whereas not wanting to work as hard as the students in Tyson's (1989) sample, Landry and Bernardi (2015) also found that their students expected higher grades than the students in Tyson's (1989) sample.

Maeda (2019), McCabe, Treviño and Butterfield (1999) and Rettinger and Jordan (2005) noted that cheating on examinations resulted from the desire to excel, parental pressure for higher grades and the need to get a job. Faulkender et al. (1994) indicated that students cheat when they believe the material is too difficult, did not attend class or were too busy to study. Additionally, when students observe unethical business behavior on the nightly news (i.e., negative reinforcement), they are more likely to feel that unethical behavior in an academic setting is acceptable. Examples of negative reinforcement that students are exposed to include the "misuse of . . . funds, insider trading, and accusations of plagiarism and other forms of dishonesty by national leaders" (Welsh, 1993, p. 6). Recent corporate scandals include Volkswagen's tampering with emission testing and Valeant Pharmaceuticals' significant price increase of prescription drugs (IG, 2018).

In an international study of cheating in Australia, China, Ireland and the United States of America, Bernardi et al. (2008) found that the ways students cheated could be grouped into three methods: writing, visual/oral communication and other methods. Whereas the writing methods included crib notes and writing on one's body/cloths, visual/oral methods included copying another student's exam, asking for answers and having another student take your exam. The other methods included using programmable calculators and cell phone and hiding notes in a bathroom, many of which were also reported by Smith, Davy, Rosenberg and Haight (2002). Finally, Bernardi et al. (2008) noted that students from all four countries provided similar responses.

Peer behavior influenced student cheating (Bernardi et al., 2016; Cicognani, 2019; Bernardi & LaCross, 2004). MacGregor and Stuebs (2012) found that students rationalize their cheating when there is some doubt about whether cheating is permitted or when they believe their peers have an unfair advantage over them by cheating (i.e., a cynical attitude – everyone cheats) (Ameen et al., 1996; Bernardi & Adamaitis, 2007; Salter et al., 2001). Ameen et al. (1996) found that, whereas 88% of students had witnessed a peer cheating, less than 16% of students believed that cheating was a serious problem. In a large European sample, over half the sample reported having cheated in college and that cheaters were more likely to know another student who cheated (Cicognani, 2019). Not only is academic dishonesty learned from observing peers but such peer behavior may create an attitude that cheating is an acceptable way of competing in an academic environment (McCabe, Treviño & Butterfield, 2001). Smyth and Davis (2003) found that 54% of students believed that cheating was acceptable behavior. Bernardi, Banzhoff, Martino and Savasta (2012b) found that students who observed other students cheating in college were more likely to cheat, which suggests the need to emphasize ethical behavior throughout a student's academic experience in college. Lawson (2004) noted that students' propensity to cheat in college associates with attitudes toward unethical behavior in the business.

2.1.2. The Solutions Triangle

Little and Handel (2016) also suggested a solutions triangle that parallels the three conditions of their cheating triangle. The solutions triangle proposes three methods that address cheating on examinations by suggesting an effective institutional integrity policy, closely controlling the testing environment, and effectively investigating and addressing cheating incidents. In another adaptation of Albrecht et al.'s (2020) fraud triangle, Bujaki, Lento and Sayed's (2019) components of their opportunity-and-prevention triangle closely parallel the components in Little and Handel's (2016) solutions triangle.

An institution's academic integrity programs and policies, such as honor codes, can have a significant influence on students' behaviors (McCabe et al., 2001). For example, students become aware of ethical behavior when institutions have high standards of integrity and faculty indicate the seriousness of cheating to their students (McCabe et al., 2001). Additionally, Eccles (1999) indicated that motivation can be personal or influenced by outside forces such as speeches, family, friends or major events; students may also be capable of inspiring themselves and others to perform various tasks (Clark, 2003). Malgwi and Rakovski (2009) suggest that faculty could reduce cheating and might create an environment where students perceive cheating as a socially unacceptable behavior. Almost 92% of graduates indicated their business professors' actions had the most impact on them (David Anderson & Lawrimore, 1990).

Smith, Davy and Easterling (2004) believe that instructors should circulate around the room and watch students during an in-class examination. Methods to reduce cheating also include having an empty seat between students, assigning seats, distributing different forms of the same test, having students put all books and personal belongings away (i.e., not readily accessible) and giving essay-type examinations (Smith et al., 2004; Faulkender et al., 1994). Wajda-Johnston, Handal, Brawer and Fabricatore (2001) indicate that a reduction in cheating could be accomplished by (percent reduction in parentheses) closely monitoring students during tests (65.0%), using assigned seating (49.4%) and frequently changing tests (36.6%).

Ameen et al. (1996) data indicated that, of the 33% of students who admitted to cheating, only 6% of these students reported that they had been caught cheating. In fact, Simkin and McLeod (2010, p. 447) found that "the risks involved (and the attendant fear of penalties)" are not factors that affected a student's rationale about cheating. Elias (2008) indicated that accounting faculty should increase the levels of socialization and commitment with their students prior to graduation because cheating in college associates with dishonest behavior in the workplace (Lucas & Friedrich, 2005). However, Keith-Spiegel, Tabachnick, Whitley and Washburn (1998, p. 224) noted that 71% of the professors they sampled indicated that "confronting cheating students is one of the most negative aspects of the teaching". Some professors feared retaliation (McCabe, 1993) if they accused a student of cheating (i.e., retaliation in the form of bad teaching evaluations (Keith-Spiegel et al., 1998)). Consequently, professors may overlook cheating because of the lack of evidence, the effort involved and/or the professor's lack of courage (Keith-Spiegel et al., 1998). Given the findings in prior research for addressing the incidence of cheating in the classroom, our first research question is:

RQ1: What measures can faculty use to decrease the probability of students cheating during an in-class examination?

2.1.3. Cheating History

Bernardi and Adamaitis (2007) found that a student's intent to cheat in the future associated with their history of cheating in the past, the testing environment and his/her cynicism (i.e., belief that 'everyone cheats'). Bernardi et al. (2016) found that having cheated on a minor examination positively associated with having cheated on a major examination; this finding is consistent with Baack, Fogliasso and Harris' (2000) slippery slope theory. This theory suggests that ignoring minor unethical actions leads to a reduction in an individual's level of ethical sensitivity to a point where the individual accepts larger unethical actions as being acceptable. Bernardi et al. (2016) also noted that a student's intent to cheat in the future positively associated with their history of cheating in the past and knowing or observing another/other student(s) cheating. Whereas Bernardi et al. (2008) provided ways to reduce cheating, they did not group these suggestions by students' prior history of cheating. Given Baack et al.'s (2000) slippery slope theory, one could posit that, as students' histories of cheating vary, their suggestions for reducing cheating would also vary, and our second research question is:

> *RQ2:* Do the measures provided by students to decrease the probability of cheating during vary by a students' history of cheating?

2.2. Whistle-Blowing

2.2.1. Definition

Near and Miceli (1985, p. 4) provide the following definition of corporate whistle-blowing as employees reporting "illegal, immoral, or illegitimate practices under the control of their employees, to persons . . . able to effect action". Paraphrasing Near and Miceli's (1985) definition, Bernardi, Banzhoff, Martino and Savasta (2011, p. 167) defined whistle-blowing in the classroom as "a student (students) informing his/her instructor and/or appropriate dean that another student (other students) has (have) cheated".

2.2.2. Institutional Values

When institutions emphasize their core values, students tend to embrace these values and carry them into their careers (Nonis & Swift, 2001). The Ethics Resource Center (2018, p. 9) found that an essential component "of effective ethics and compliance programs is the extent to which organizations value the reporting of concerns and suspected wrongdoings". For example, the Ethics Resource Center's (2018) report noted that 76% of the employees who witnessed wrongdoings reported them; however, 53% of the reporters experienced retaliations. Students prefer not to turn in a classmate who they observed cheating (Malgwi & Rakovski, 2009); only 9.2% of college students would report cheating even though 92.8% of students had witnessed another/other student(s) cheating (Bernardi et al., 2011). Whereas Bernardi et al. (2012a) and Elias (2008) found that students are less likely to whistle-blow due to the potential of retaliation, Bernardi, Goetjen and Brax (2013) found that students who whistle-blew were perceived as being brave.

Rennie and Crosby (2002) reported that 65% of students felt uncomfortable challenging a fellow student's integrity. Still, one should question why only 9.2% of students are willing to whistle-blow when 92.8% indicate that they observe other students cheating (i.e., a tenfold difference). One obvious reason is that it would be hypocritical to blow the whistle on another student when the potential whistle-blower was also guilty of cheating (Bernardi et al., 2012a). Another reason is that whistle-blowers are often perceived as traitors (Grant, 2002), snitches (Bernardi et al., 2013), or sneaks and backstabbers (Rennie & Crosby, 2002). Nitsch, Baetz and Hughes (2005) found that students who attended schools where breaches of the code of conduct went unreported were more likely to disregard dishonesty in the workplace. Likewise, when students did not recognize academic integrity in college, they did not recognize integrity in their workplace or their personal lives as well (Nonis & Swift, 2001). Elias (2008) emphasized the need to increase students' ethical awareness so that it will carry over into their professional careers.

Burton and Near (1995) found that students who did not report cheating indicated that they felt that it could not be done anonymously. Students in Bernardi et al.'s (2011) study reported that their classmates badgered whistle-blowers when the identities of students who had reported the cheating became known. Bernardi et al. (2016) reported that one of the means to increase whistle-blowing was to assure the confidentiality of the whistle-blower(s). Ayers and Kaplan (2005) noted that the potential perceived personal costs (i.e., retaliation) were much lower when reporting was anonymous. Increasing confidentiality could promote whistle-blowing by reducing the 'snitches get stitches' syndrome (Bernardi et al., 2012a, 2013). Increasing whistle-blowing could also be achieved by providing incentives (i.e., either bonus points or cash rewards), assuring the confidentiality of the whistle-blower or reducing the punishment for cheating (Bernardi et al., 2016). Given the suggestions in prior research for increasing the rate of whistle-blowing in the classroom, our third research question is:

> *RQ3:* What measures can faculty use to increase the probability that students will whistle-blow when they observe cheating in the classroom?

2.2.3. Cheating History

Bernardi et al. (2011) found that the number of reasons students provided for not whistle-blowing associated with their having cheated on a minor examination and having observed other students cheat. They also found that the reasons given by students for not whistle-blowing varied significantly with students' prior cheating history. Bernardi et al. (2013) found that the number of perceptions of whistle-blowers students provided associated with their having cheated on a major examination.

Additionally, the number of students responding by perception category varied by a students' cheating history. Bernardi et al. (2016) also found that students' suggestions for increasing whistle-blowing varied significantly with the students' prior cheating history. Our final research question is:

> RQ4: Do the measures provided by students to increase the probability of whistle-blowing when students observe cheating vary by students' history of cheating?

3. Methodology

3.1. Participants

Table 1.1 provides the demographic data for the 187 students (98 men and 89 women) enrolled in introductory accounting classes at a private university located in the Northeast region of the United States of America. The sample composition by class level was 126 (67.4%) sophomores and 61 (32.6%) juniors. The data indicate that 129 of the 187 (62.9%) students in this sample have cheated on a minor or major examination in college.[4] This rate of cheating is similar to the self-reported cheating rates from prior research: 67.0% (Burton & Near, 1995), 66.4% (Bernardi et al., 2004), 62.1% (Bernardi & Adamaitis, 2007) and 64.7% (Bernardi et al., 2011).

Table 1.1 Sample Demographics

Category	Men	Women	Total
Gender	98	89	187
Age	19.4	19.3	19.4
College Level			
Sophomore	71	55	126
Junior	27	34	61
Overall GPA	3.1	3.3	3.2
College Cheating			
Never	25 (25.4)	33 (37.1)	58 (31.0)
Minor Exams	18 (18.4)	22 (24.7)	40 (21.4)
Major Exams	3 (3.1)	5 (5.6)	8 (4.3)
Both Types	52 (53.1)	29 (32.6)	81 (43.3)
College Cheating Both Types	Number (percent of total) by gender and total sample Students who had cheated on both minor and major examinations		

3.2. Survey Questionnaires

Our survey included a two-part questionnaire; the first part (Appendix A) is a background questionnaire that requested information on age, gender, major, graduation year, overall GPA and home country. We asked questions on age and home country so that we did not include adult students and international students in our research. The reason for these exclusions is that neither the adult students nor the international students from specific countries had a large enough sample size for analysis as separate variables. The second part (Appendix B) included two questions from Ameen et al. (1996), Salter et al. (2001) and Bernardi and Adamaitis' (2007) questionnaires on cheating. Whereas prior research used survey questions with yes/no questions, we suggest that some of the information content of these questions was lost using yes/no questions. Consequently, the two questions that dealt with having cheated on minor or major examinations used an 11-point Likert scale where zero represented 'Never' and 10 represented '10 or more' times. The students were also asked to suggest possible actions that their university could take to increase whistle-blowing and/or reduce cheating in the classroom.

3.3. Survey Administration

Given the nature of the survey questions, we asked the instructors of the classes that participated in our research not to be present in their classrooms while their students were filling out the survey. For consistency purposes, the individuals who passed out the survey used scripted instructions and told the participants that the researchers would only be provided with an Excel file that contained the survey data (i.e., so that students' anonymity would be preserved). Consistent with prior research, the participants were advised not to write their name on the questionnaire so that their responses would be anonymous. Students were told that, whereas their surveys were numbered, we did this so that if there were any questions, we could refer to the specific survey. Finally, we told the students that the research team had randomly assigned the surveys to each section (i.e., no sequential numbering) so that even sections could not be identified.

4. Analysis

4.1. Overview

Of the 187 students in our sample, 46 students provided 78 suggestions on how to decrease cheating, whereas 80 students provided 122 suggestions on how to increase whistle-blowing (i.e., approximately half of the students provided suggestions in both categories). Table 1.2 provides a breakout of 75 students who did not provide any suggestions to Question 3 by the cheating category. The number of students who did not respond to this question differed significantly ($p < 0.01$) by cheating category.

Table 1.2 Provided No Suggestions for Reducing Cheating or Increasing Whistle-
blowing

Panel A: non-responders by gender

			Men	*Women*	
Sample size	(187)	*n*	98	89	
		%	52.4	47.6	
No comments provided	(75)	*n*	46	29	
		%	61.3	38.7	N/S

Panel B: non-responders by self-reported cheating history in college

			Never Cheated	*Only Minor*	*Both Types*	*Prob > ChiSq*
Sample size	(187)	*n*	58	48	81	
		%	31.0	25.7	43.3	
No comments provided	(75)	N	16	15	44	
		%	21.3	20.0	58.7	< 0.01

Both Types	Combination of cheated on only major examinations and cheated on both minor and major examinations.
N/S	Not Significant

Whereas there were more male students (46) who did not respond to Question 3 than female students (29), the percentages for male and female students did not vary significantly from the percent representation in the overall sample. The data in Panel B indicate that the students who reported having not cheated responded at a rate higher rate to Question 3 than their proportion in our sample of 187 students. The students who reported having cheated on only minor examinations responded at a higher rate to Question 3 than their proportion in the sample. Interestingly, students who reported having cheated on both types of examinations were significantly ($p < 0.01$) less likely to provide suggestions on how to reduce cheating or increase whistle-blowing.

4.2. Suggestions for Reducing Cheating (RQ1&2)

We analyzed our participants' suggestions for reducing the incidence of cheating in the classroom. After entering the data from the students' responses, we separated these responses into groups that provided similar or identical responses. Six of these suggestion groups (Table 1.3) for

Table 1.3 Suggestions for Reducing Cheating in the Classroom

Panel A: sample data on cheating suggestions

			Never Cheated	Only Minor	Both Types	Prob > ChiSq
Sample size	(187)	n	58	48	81	
		%	31.0	25.7	43.3	
Sample commenting	(46)	n	26	13	7	
		%	56.5	28.3	15.2	<0.001
Suggestions provided	(78)	n	30	17	31	
		%	38.5	21.8	39.7	<0.001

Panel B: suggestions for decreasing cheating

Suggestions			Never Cheated	Only Minor	Both Types	Prob > ChiSq
Professor awareness	(20)	n	9	2	9	
		%	45.0	10.0	45.0	<0.001
Bags and phones	(14)	n	5	0	9	
		%	35.7	0.0	64.3	<0.001
Change grading/testing	(12)	n	7	2	3	
		%	58.3	16.7	25.0	<0.001
Honesty policy	(8)	n	2	5	1	
		%	25.0	62.5	12.5	<0.001
Separate students	(8)	n	3	0	5	
		%	37.5	0.0	62.5	<0.001
Different tests	(5)	n	1	1	3	
		%	20.0	20.0	60.0	ISS
Other	(11)	n	3	7	1	
		%	27.3	63.6	9.1	NT

Both Types	Combination of cheated on only major examinations and cheated on both minor and major examinations.
ISS	Insufficient Sample Size
NT	Not Tested due to various different responses

decreasing cheating were relatively easy to identify; the 'other' category is a compilation of 11 suggestions that we could not separate into individual groups as these groups would contain only one or two suggestions. Panel A of Table 1.3 presents a breakdown of the 78 suggestions provided by the 46 students who responded to Question 3 (Appendix B) request to indicate ways to reduce cheating in the classroom by self-reported cheating category.

The percent of students by cheating category differed in both the sample commenting and the number of suggestions, as shown in Panel A of Table 1.3. The sample data for self-reported cheating category do not approximate the number of persons responding in each category ($p <$ 0.001); the percentages by cheating category also differed between the sample commenting and the number of suggestions received for each category ($p < 0.001$). In our testing for differences, we used the number of suggestions in each category in Panel A as our expected response rate for the data in Panel B. The current group of students provided suggestions for reducing cheating (RQ1) that were similar to Bernardi et al. (2008) and other prior research. Additionally, the number of suggestions for decreasing cheating varied significantly with students' prior history of cheating (RQ2).

Five of the six categories of the suggestions had sufficient sample sizes for statistical testing purposes. All five of the categories containing suggestions for decreasing cheating in Panel B indicated significant differences ($p < 0.001$) among the expected percentages and the actual response percentages by the cheating group. As an example, for the 'Bags and Phones' stored in the front of the classroom (i.e., not readily accessible) suggestion, one would have anticipated an expected (actual) rate of 38.5% (35.7%) for the never-cheated group, 21.8% (0.0%) for the cheated-on-minor-examinations-only group, and 45.0% (64.3%) for the cheated group. As shown in Panel B, the actual percent for the students in the cheated-on-minor-examinations-only group and the cheated-on-both-types group was significantly different from the expected percent.

4.3. Suggestions for Increasing Whistle-Blowing (RQ3&4)

We analyze our participants' suggestions for increasing the level of whistle-blowing in the classroom. When grouping students' suggestions for increasing whistle-blowing, we used the same sorting procedures as described earlier. Panel A of Table 1.4 presents a breakdown of the 122 suggestions provided by the 80 students who responded to Question 3 (Appendix B) request to indicate ways to increase whistle-blowing in the classroom by self-reported cheating category. The current group of students provided suggestions for increasing whistle-blowing (RQ3) that were similar to Bernardi et al. (2016) and other prior research. The number of suggestions for increasing whistle-blowing varied significantly with students' prior history of cheating (RQ4).

Table 1.4 Suggestions for Increasing Whistle-blowing in the Classroom

Panel A: sample data on whistle-blowing suggestions

			Never Cheated	Only Minor	Both Types	Prob > ChiSq
Sample size	(187)	n	58	48	81	
		%	31.0	25.7	43.3	
Sample commenting	(80)	n	30	24	26	
		%	37.5	30.0	32.5	<0.050
Suggestions provided	(122)	n	40	43	39	
		%	32.8	35.2	32.0	NS

Panel B: suggestions for increasing whistle-blowing

Suggestions			Never Cheated	Only Minor	Both Types	Prob > ChiSq
Provide incentives	(58)	n	18	20	20	
		%	31.0	34.5	34.5	NS
Not my business	(14)	n	5	4	5	
		%	35.7	28.6	35.7	NS
Anonymous reporting	(24)	n	10	8	6	
		%	41.7	33.3	25.0	<0.050
Ask students to W/B	(12)	n	6	3	3	
		%	50.0	25.0	25.0	<0.001
Less punishment	(6)	n	1	1	4	
		%	16.7	16.7	66.6	<0.001
Professor responsible	(4)	n	0	3	1	
		%	0	75.0	25.0	ISS
Other	(4)	n	0	4	0	
		%	0	100.0	0	NT

Both Types	Combination of cheated on only major examinations and cheated on both minor and major examinations.
ISS	Insufficient Sample Size
N/S	Not Significant
NT	Not Tested due to various different responses

The sample data for self-reported cheating category do not approximate the number of persons responding in each category ($p < 0.05$). However, the percentages by cheating category did not differ between the commenting sample and the number of suggestions received for each category as shown in Panel A of Table 1.4. We used the number of suggestions in each category in Panel A as our expected response rate for the data in Panel B. Two of the suggestion groups had insufficient sample sizes (ISS) – 'professor responsible' and 'other' groups. Three of the five groups we tested had significant differences (i.e., highlighted data) between the expected and the actual response rates among the three cheating categories (Panel B). Whereas the 'anonymous reporting' suggestions were significant ($p < 0.05$), 'asking students to whistle-blow' section and 'less punishment for cheating' sections were also significant ($p < 0.001$) in terms of differences between expected and actual results.

5. Conclusions

Our study replicated Bernardi et al. (2016) and extended the work of Bernardi et al. (2008) by examining methods to increase whistle-blowing and decrease cheating. In this study, we analyzed the suggestions from a sample size of 187 about ways to decrease cheating as well as suggestions to increase whistle-blowing. Of our findings, two are especially important to note: professors need to be more diligent when giving classroom tests to prevent cheating and students must be assured of confidentiality if a professor expects them to report anyone observed cheating on an examination.

Of the suggestions for deterring cheating on examinations in Bernardi et al.'s (2008) research, the current sample provided three similar suggestions (Bernardi et al. (2008) (suggestions in parentheses): professor awareness (i.e., increased supervision of testing), separating students (i.e., spreading the students out) and different tests (i.e., do not use the same test each semester).[5] It should be noted that, whereas the current sample was from the United States of America, Bernardi et al.'s (2008) sample came from Australia, China, the Republic of Ireland and the United States of America. Of the six suggestions for increasing whistle-blowing in the classroom in Bernardi et al.'s (2016) research, the current sample provided four similar suggestions: provide incentives (i.e., provide incentive points and/or cash rewards), anonymous reporting (i.e., confidentiality) and the professor is responsible (i.e., not my responsibility). Given the similarity with Bernardi et al.'s (2008, 2016) research, we suggest that our research fulfills Burman et al.'s (2010, p. 789) suggestion that replications "shows the original article's findings are robust . . . over time" results as well as Lindsay's (1995, p. 35) belief that replications are a "crucial test of the reliability and validity . . . [which] leads, when successful, to generalizable". Additionally, the current suggestion of the 'professor is responsible' is similar to the 'mind your own business' comment in Bernardi et al.'s (2013) research on students' perceptions of whistle-blowers.

We used Little and Handel's (2016) adaptation of Albrecht et al.'s (2020) fraud triangle to frame our literature review on cheating. Our results (Table 1.3) indicate that the suggestion of 'changing grading/ testing' suggests a way of reducing the pressure inherent in examinations (i.e., condition 1 – the pressure for grades). The suggestions provided by students of 'professor awareness', 'separating students', 'different tests' and 'bags and phones' up front address the need to control the testing environment (i.e., condition 2 – poor control over the testing environment). Additionally, the suggestions of it is 'not my business' and the 'professor is responsible' (Table 1.4) for increasing whistle-blowing also address the need for faculty to control the testing environment. Whereas our results (Table 1.3) did not provide any suggestions for changing students' belief that 'everyone cheats', one could speculate that, if the suggestions for controlling the testing environment were effectively implemented, students' belief that 'everyone cheats' would gradually be reduced as classroom cheating decreased.

The most frequent suggestion of how to decrease cheating was to increase professors' awareness of the testing environment. Interestingly, the same number of these suggestions came from the never-cheated group and the cheated-on-both-types-of-examinations group (i.e., nine of this suggestion from each group – Table 1.3). Consequently, when teachers sit in the front of the room and grade papers or look at their phones when students are taking their examination, it makes it easier to cheat rather than when professors walk around or continuously scan the room. If students are still listing this as a suggestion, then faculty are not adjusting their classroom behavior, given consistent research findings suggesting that professors need to be more diligent in observing student behavior during an in-class examination.

Only three of the suggestions about how to increase whistle-blowing by the cheating group had significant differences (i.e., anonymous reporting, asking students to whistle-blow and less punishment). Of the three suggestions, anonymous reporting and less punishment for cheaters match the ways to increase whistle-blowing suggested in Bernardi et al. (2016) – increased confidentiality and lower punishment. The largest group of students in the current research (Bernardi et al., 2016) who suggested anonymous reporting (increasing confidentiality) were the students who reported that they have never cheated. Following Malgwi and Rakovski's (2009) research, these are the honest students who work hard to earn their grades and do not want to see others get away with cheating. In the current research, 66.6% of the students suggesting the lower punishment method were from the group of students who had cheated on 'Both Types' of examinations.

There were no significant differences in the response rates by the cheating group for providing incentives to whistle-blowing; however, given the large number of students who suggested this method (i.e., 58 of the 122 (47.5%)), we believe that a further discussion is warranted. The students in Bernardi et al.'s (2016) sample suggested two types of methods for increasing whistle-blowing – incentive points ($n = 99$) and cash rewards ($n = 41$). If one combines these groups, then 140 of the 286 (49.0%) suggestions indicated some kind of incentive for whistle-blowing. The finding of an equal distribution of the suggestion (i.e., approximately one-third of the sample in each cheating group) among the cheating groups in the current research differs significantly from Bernardi et al.'s (2016). In Bernardi et al.'s (2016) sample ($n = 140$), the never-cheated and cheated-on-minor-examinations-only groups accounted for approximately 75.0% of the suggestions, whereas the cheated-on-both-types group accounted for 25.0% of the suggestions. In the current sample, the cheated-on-both-types group is not only willing to cheat whenever they choose, but they are also willing to whistle-blow on other students who are cheating for the right price. They want to cheat plus get additional incentive points or cash for whistle-blowing on other students.

Our sample has two apparent limitations. First, the data were collected from one university in the Northeast region of the United States of America and as such may not be generalizable to the overall population of students; consequently, if this research is replicated in the future, there should be a wider base of institutions. Second, whereas we included sophomores and juniors in our sample, future research should also include samples comprised of freshmen and seniors to examine shifting beliefs in colleges. Our study also noted that 18% of students made suggestions indicating that cheating could be reduced by requiring students to put their phones and bags in the front of the room (i.e., not accessible to the student). Future research could look further into this aspect to see if cheating is becoming easier or more common because of the increased access students have to technology.

Acknowledgments

The authors would like to thank Briana Silveira for her assistance in early stages of this research.

Notes

1. Whereas their sample was limited in size and from Indonesia, Herdian, Nuraeni and Septiningsih (2019) found that teachers admitted to having cheated on examinations and their theses.
2. Bracketed data added to the original words cited from the authors.
3. Whereas Becker et al. (2006) provide a list of activities that they indicate constitute academic fraud, this research focuses on cheating on academic examinations.

4. Because there were only eight students (i.e., 4.3% of our sample) who reported cheating on only major examinations, we combined the suggestions of these students with those of the students who reported cheating on both minor and major examinations (i.e. Both Types).
5. Prior research (Bernardi et al., 2008; Smith et al., 2004; Wajda-Johnston et al., 2001) and this research clearly indicate that professors need to be more diligent (Table 1.3) when giving classroom tests to prevent cheating. Bernardi et al. (2008) indicate that classroom examinations warrant increased supervision by professors; Smith et al. (2004) suggest that instructors should circulate around the room and watch students. Wajda-Johnston et al. (2001) indicate that a 65.0% reduction in cheating could be accomplished by closely monitoring students during in-class examinations.

References

Albrecht, W. S., Albrecht, C. O., Albrecht, C. C., & Zimbelman, M. F. (2020). *Fraud Examination* (6th ed.). Boston, MA: Cengage.

Ameen, E., Guffey, D. M., & McMillan, J. J. (1996). Accounting Students' Perceptions of Questionable Academic Practices and Factors Affecting Their Propensity to Cheat. *Accounting Education, 5*(3), 191–205.

American Institute of Certified Public Accountants. (2003). Consideration of Fraud in a Financial Statement Audit (Section 316). *Statement on Auditing Standards No. 99*, 1719–1769. Retrieved May 25th, 2020, from www.aicpa. org/Research/Standards/AuditAttest/DownloadableDocuments/AU-00316.pdf

Ayers, S., & Kaplan, S. E. (2005). Wrongdoing by Consultants: An Examination of Employees' Reporting Intentions. *Journal of Business Ethics, 57*(2), 121–137.

Baack, D., Fogliasso, C., & Harris, J. (2000). The Personal Impact of Ethical Decisions: A Social Penetration Theory. *Journal of Business Ethics, 24*(1), 39–49.

Ballantine, J. A., Guo, X., & Larres, P. (2018). Can Future Managers and Business Executives Be Influenced to Behave More Ethically in the Workplace? The Impact of Approaches to Learning on Business Students' Cheating Behavior. *Journal of Business Ethics, 149*(1), 245–258.

Becker, D., Connolly, J., Lentz, P., & Morrison, J. (2006). Using the Business Fraud Triangle to Predict Academic Dishonesty Among Business Students. *Academy of Educational Leadership Journal, 10*(1), 37–55.

Bernardi, R. A., & Adamaitis, K. L. (2007). Data Contamination by Social Desirability Response Bias: An International Study of Students Cheating Behavior. *Research on Professional Responsibility and Ethics in Accounting, 11*, 159–176.

Bernardi, R. A., Baca, A. V., Landers, K. S., & Witek, M. B. (2008). Methods of Cheating and Deterrents to Classroom Cheating: An International Study. *Ethics & Behavior, 18*(4), 373–391.

Bernardi, R. A., Banzhoff, C. A., Martino, A. M., & Savasta, K. J. (2011). Cheating and Whistle-Blowing in the Classroom. *Research on Professional Responsibility and Ethics in Accounting, 15*, 165–191.

Bernardi, R. A., Banzhoff, C. A., Martino, A. M., & Savasta, K. J. (2012b). Challenges to Academic Integrity: Identifying the Factors Associated With the Cheating Chain. *Accounting Education: An International Journal, 21*(3), 247–263.

Bernardi, R. A., Goetjen, E. S., & Brax, J. M. (2013). Whistle-Blowing in the Classroom: The Influence of Students' Perceptions of Whistle-Blowers. In S.

Mintz (Ed.), *Accounting for the Public Interest: An International Perspective on Accounting to Society* (pp. 247–271). Dordrecht, Netherlands: Springer Science Press.

Bernardi, R. A., & LaCross, C. C. (2004). Data Contamination by Social Desirability Response Bias in Research on Students' Cheating Behavior. *Journal of College Teaching and Learning, 1*(8), 13–25.

Bernardi, R. A., Landry, A. C., Landry, E. E., Buonafede, M. R., & Berardi, M. C. (2016). What Actions Can Be Taken to Increase Whistle-Blowing in the Classroom? *Accounting Education: An International Journal, 25*(1), 88–106.

Bernardi, R. A., Larkin, M. B., LaBontee, L. A., Lapierre, R. A., & Morse, N. C. (2012a). Classroom Cheating: Reasons not to Whistle-Blow and the Probability of Whistle-Blowing. *Research on Professional Responsibility and Ethics in Accounting, 16*, 203–233.

Bernardi, R. A., Metzger, R. L., Scofield-Bruno, R. G., Wade-Hoogkamp, M. A., Reyes, L. E., & Barnaby, G. H. (2004). Examining the Decision Process of Students' Cheating Behavior: An Exploratory Study. *Journal of Business Ethics, 50*(4), 397–414.

Bujaki, M., Lento, C., & Sayed, N. (2019). Utilizing Professional Accounting Concepts to Understand and Respond to Academic Dishonesty in Accounting Programs. *Journal of Accounting Education, 47*, 28–47.

Burke, D. D., & Sanney, K. J. (2018). Applying the Fraud Triangle to Higher Education: Ethical Implications. *Journal of Legal Studies Education, 35*(1), 5–43.

Burman, L. E., Reed, W. R., & Alm, J. (2010). A Call for Replication Studies. *Public Finance Review, 38*(6), 787–793.

Burton, B. K., & Near, J. P. (1995). Estimating the Incidence of Wrongdoing and Whistle-Blowing: Results of a Study Using Randomized Response Technique. *Journal of Business Ethics, 14*(1), 17–30.

Choo, F., & Tan, K. (2008). The Effect of Fraud Triangle Factors on Students' Cheating Behaviors. *Advances in Accounting Education, 9*, 205–220.

Cicognani, S. (2019). Dishonesty Among University Students. In A. Bucciol & N. Montinari (Eds.), *Dishonesty in Behavioral Economics* (Chapter 2.4). London: Academic Press.

Clark, R. E. (2003). Fostering the Work Motivation of Individuals and Teams. *Performance Improvement, 42*(3), 21–29.

David, F. R., Anderson, L. M., & Lawrimore, K. W. (1990). Perspectives on Business Ethics in Management Education. *SAM Advanced Management Journal, 55*(4), 26–32.

Day, N. E., Hudson, D., Dobies, P. R., & Waris, R. (2011). Student or Situation? Personality and Classroom Context as Predictors of Attitudes About Business School Cheating. *Social Psychology of Education: An International Journal, 14*(2), 261–282.

Eccles, J. (1999). The Development of Children Ages 6 to 14. *The Future of Children, 9*(2), 30–44.

Elias, R. Z. (2008). Auditing Students' Professional Commitment and Anticipatory Socialization and Their Relationship to Whistle-Blowing. *Managerial Auditing Journal, 23*(3), 283–294.

Elias, R. Z. (2019). The Relationship between Emotional Intelligence, Maximizing Tendencies and Business Students' Perceptions of Cheating. *Journal of Ethical and Legal Issues, 12*, 1–14.

Ethics Resource Center. (2018). *2018 National Business Ethics Survey: Workplace Ethics in Transition.* Retrieved May 25th, 2020, from https://www.ethics.org/knowledge-center/2018-gbes-2/

Faulkender, P. J., Range, L. M., Hamilton, M., Strehlow, M., Jackson, S. B., Blanchard, E., & Dean, P. (1994). The Case of the Stolen Psychology Test: An Analysis of an Actual Cheating Incident. *Ethics & Behavior,* 4(3), 209–217.

Gneezy, U., Niederle, M., & Rustichini, A. (2003). Performance in Competitive Environments: Gender Differences. *The Quarterly Journal of Economics,* 118(3), 1049–1074.

Grant, C. (2002). Whistle-Blowers: Saints of Secular Culture. *Journal of Business Ethics,* 39(4), 391–399.

Herdian, H., Nuraeni, N., & Septiningsih, D. S. (2019). Teachers' Past Academic Dishonesty in Their College. *International Journal of Psychoanalysis and Education,* 11(1), 51–58.

Investors Gold (IG). (2018). *Top 10 Biggest Corporate Scandals and How They Affected Share Prices.* Retrieved May 25th, 2020, from www.ig.com/en/news-and-trade-ideas/top-10-biggest-corporate-scandals-and-how-they-affected-share-pr-181101

Keith-Spiegel, P., Tabachnick, B. G., Whitley, B. E. Jr., & Washburn, J. (1998). Why Professors Ignore Cheating: Opinions of a National Sample of Psychology Instructors. *Ethics & Behavior,* 8(3), 215–227.

Lai, L. (2010). Maximizing Without Difficulty: A Modified Maximizing Scale and Its Correlates. *Judgment and Decision Making,* 5(3), 164–175.

Landry, A. C., & Bernardi, R. A. (2015). Students' Grade Expectations and Work Ethic in College: Evidence of the Entitlement Generation. *The Accounting Educators' Journal,* 25, 1–24.

Lawson, R. A. (2004). Is Classroom Cheating Related to Business Students' Propensity to Cheat in the 'Real World'? *Journal of Business Ethics,* 49(2), 189–199.

Lindsay, M. (1995). Reconsidering the Status of Tests of Significance: An Alternative Criterion of Adequacy. *Accounting, Organizations and Society,* 20(1), 35–53.

Little, J., & Handel, S. (2016). Student Cheating and the Fraud Triangle. *Business Education Forum,* February, 37–44.

Lucas, G. M., & Friedrich, J. (2005). Individual Differences in Workplace Deviance and Integrity as Predictors of Academic Dishonesty. *Ethics & Behavior,* 15(1), 15–35.

MacGregor, J., & Stuebs, M. (2012). To Cheat or Not to Cheat: Rationalizing Academic Impropriety. *Accounting Education: An International Journal,* 21(3), 265–287.

Maeda, M. (2019). Exam Cheating among Cambodian Students: When, How and Why It Happens. *Compare: A Journal of Comparative and International Education,* 1–19.

Malgwi, C. A., & Rakovski, C. C. (2009). Combating Academic Fraud: Are Students Reticent About Uncovering the Covert? *Journal of Academic Ethics,* 7(2), 207–221.

McCabe, D. L. (1993). Faculty Responses to Academic Dishonesty: The Influence of Student Honor Codes. *Research in Higher Education,* 34(5), 647–658.

McCabe, D. L., Treviño, L. K., & Butterfield, K. D. (1999). Academic Integrity in Honor-Code and Non-Honor-Code Environments: A Qualitative Investigation. *Journal of Higher Education,* 70(2), 211–234.

McCabe, D. L., Treviño, L. K., & Butterfield, K. D. (2001). Cheating in Academic Institutions: A Decade of Research. *Ethics & Behavior, 11*(3), 219–232.

Near, J. P., & Miceli, M. P. (1985). Organizational Dissidence: The Case of Whistle-Blowing. *Journal of Business Ethics, 4*(1), 1–16.

Nitsch, D., Baetz, M., & Hughes, J. C. (2005). Why Code of Conduct Violations Go Unreported: A Conceptual Framework to Guide Intervention and Future Research. *Journal of Business Ethics, 57*(4), 327–341.

Nonis, S., & Swift, C. O. (2001). An Examination of the Relationship Between Academic Dishonesty and Workplace Dishonesty: A Multi-Campus Investigation. *Journal of Education for Business, 77*(2), 69–77.

Rennie, S. C., & Crosby, J. R. (2002). Students' Perceptions of Whistle Blowing: Implications for Self-Regulation: A Questionnaire and Focus Group Survey. *Medical Education, 36*(2), 173–179.

Rettinger, D. A., & Jordan, A. E. (2005). The Relations Among Religion, Motivation, and College Cheating: A Natural Experiment. *Ethics & Behavior, 15*(2), 107–129.

Salter, S. B., Guffey, D. M., & McMillan, J. J. (2001). Truth, Consequences and Culture: A Comparative Examination of Cheating and Attitudes About Cheating Among U.S. and U.K. Students. *Journal of Business Ethics, 31*(1), 37–50.

Schwartz, B., Ward, A., Lyubomirsky, S., Monterosso, J., White, K., & Lehman, D. R. (2002). Maximizing vs. Satisficing: Happiness Is a Matter of Choice. *Journal of Personality and Social Psychology, 83*(5), 1178–1197.

Simha, A., Armstrong, J. P., & Albert, J. F. (2012). Who Leads and Who Lags? A Comparison of Cheating Attitudes and Behaviors Among Leadership and Business Students. *Journal of Education for Business, 87*(6), 316–324.

Simkin, M. G., & McLeod, A. (2010). Why Do College Students Cheat? *Journal of Business Ethics, 94*(3), 441–453.

Smith, K. J., Davy, J. A., & Easterling, D. (2004). An Examination of Cheating and Its Antecedents among Marketing and Management Majors. *Journal of Business Ethics, 50*(1), 63–80.

Smith, K. J., Davy, J. A., Rosenberg, D. L., & Haight, G. T. (2002). A Structural Modeling Investigation of the Influence of Demographic and Attitudinal Factors and In-Class Deterrents on Cheating Behavior Among Accounting Majors. *Journal of Accounting Education, 20*(1), 45–65.

Smyth, M. L., & Davis, J. R. (2003). An Examination of Student Cheating in the Two-Year College. *Community College Review, 31*(1), 17–33.

Tyson, T. (1989). Grade Performance in Introductory Accounting Courses: Why Female Students Outperform Male Students. *Issues in Accounting Education, 4*(1), 153–159.

Van Yperen, N. W., Melvyn, R. W., van der Klauw, H., & van der Klauw, M. (2011). To Win, or Not to Lose, at Any Cost: The Impact of Achievement Goals on Cheating. *British Journal of Management, 22*(1), 5–15.

Wajda-Johnston, V. A., Handal, P. J., Brawer, P. A., & Fabricatore, A. N. (2001). Academic Dishonesty at the Graduate Level. *Ethics & Behavior, 11*(3), 287–305.

Wells, J. T. (2005). *Principles of Fraud Examination*. Hoboken, NJ: John Wiley & Sons, Inc.

Welsh, J. F. (1993). *Student Academic Dishonesty in Higher Education: Social Context and Institutional Response*. Unpublished Report, Kansas Board of Regents, Topeka, USA.

Appendix A
Demographic Data

Gender (circle one):   Male   Female
Age: _____
Home Country: _____
Year in College: _____ Overall GPA: _____
Major: _____

Appendix B
Background and Beliefs

Using the scale below as a guide, please write the upper number to the left of each question that best reflects your response.

0	1	2	3	4	5	6	7	8	9	10
Never										10 or more

____ 1. How many times have you cheated on an exam worth 20% or more of the final grade in college?

____ 2. How many times have you cheated on an exam worth 20% or more of the final grade in college?

3. Please suggest possible actions that this university could be taken to increase whistle-blowing and/or reduce cheating in the classroom:

    1. _____

    2. _____

    3. _____

    4. _____

2 Barriers to Teaching Accounting Ethics

Accounting Faculty Qualifications and Students' Ability to Learn

James E. Rebele & E. Kent St. Pierre

1. Introduction

Position statements on accounting education (Albrecht & Sack, 2000; American Institute of Certified Public Accountants (AICPA), 2018; Accounting Education Change Commission (AECC), 1990; AICPA & AAA, 2012; Arthur Andersen et al., 1989) have consistently identified ethics or ethical awareness as a necessary competency for accounting graduates and, therefore, as an important competency for accounting education programs to develop. Integrating ethics education into the accounting curriculum is not new, and accounting students have long been exposed to the importance of ethical behavior for accounting professionals (Mastracchio, 2005; McNair & Milam, 1993). High-profile accounting scandals both in the United States of America and internationally have negatively impacted accounting's long-standing reputation for being a highly ethical profession. Recognizing that the financial health of the accounting profession depended on restoring and maintaining its reputation led to calls for a renewed emphasis on teaching ethics to accounting students. More focus on teaching ethics in accounting education programs will supposedly develop graduates who will become ethical accounting professionals.

All of us would agree that accounting professionals should act ethically, but there are several important reasons to question the role that accounting education can play in enhancing the ethical awareness of students. One concern is that developing accounting students' ethical awareness as a learning objective has not been clearly or universally defined. For example, the AICPA (2018) includes "Behave in a manner bound by Ethical Principles for the protection of society" under its Ethical Conduct competency. A framework for accounting education developed by a joint Institute for Management Accountants (IMA) and American Accounting Association (AAA) task force (Lawson et al., 2014) included 'Ethics and Social Responsibility' as a broad management competency and not as an accounting competency. After more than 40 years of integrating ethics into accounting education, we do not have clarity and agreement on what we are trying to accomplish. How reasonable is it to expect that today's graduates of accounting education programs are more ethical than past graduates – that is, how reasonable is it to expect that efforts to teach ethics to accounting students have been successful?

There is also a question as to what role education, as opposed to parental or cultural influence, can play in graduating more ethical accounting students. Students arrive at universities with different life experiences and different ideas as to what is or is not ethical. Can a student with questionable ethical standards and behavior be changed by a few accounting courses that integrate ethics? Would an accounting student with an already-developed strong ethical compass become a more ethical accounting professional by, for example, completing some cases on accounting ethics? Can accounting faculty reliably assess the effectiveness of ethics education, or must we accept on faith that our efforts are having the desired, positive effect? John Delaney, former Dean at the University of Pittsburgh, noted how companies still experience problems with unethical behavior more than 25 years after business schools started teaching ethics (Korn, 2013), which raises the question as to how effective efforts to teach ethics have been.

Developing so-called soft skills, such as ethics and critical thinking, may not be as straightforward as teaching technical accounting material; so, it is reasonable to question whether accounting faculty are themselves qualified to teach ethics. Simply telling faculty members to emphasize, or at least include, ethics in their classes may be inadequate. Where do accounting faculty members receive training to teach ethics, what is the nature of this training and what support or resources do faculty members have to teach ethics? It is also important to question:

1) Can students be taught ethics in the college classroom?
2) Do accounting faculty members fulfill their professional responsibilities in an ethical manner, or do we preach to students that they should act ethically when fulfilling their professional requirements when some of us might not be ethical in our own professional situations?

We will not argue against accounting education programs attempting to teach ethics, as we recognize the fundamental importance of ethics to the accounting profession and the need for graduates who will behave ethically as professionals. We also recognize, however, that there are many challenges to teaching ethics and that these challenges have largely been ignored. One paper cannot address all of these challenges, so we limit our discussion to the question of whether accounting faculty members are qualified to teach ethics and whether students can 'learn' ethical behavior in the college classroom. 'Qualified faculty' will be interpreted here as any training and support that accounting faculty receive to teach ethics and whether accounting faculty members act ethically when fulfilling their professional responsibilities.

The following section discusses accounting faculty members' qualifications to teach ethics. Because specific training to teach ethics is rare, we focus on formal training to simply teach under the assumption that being more qualified to teach makes one more qualified to teach ethics. We also consider resources available to teach ethics to accounting students, including cases and guidance provided by the American Accounting Association (AAA) and the European Accounting Association (EAA). Included in our discussion of faculty qualifications is accounting faculty members' ethics, including mechanisms in place to promote ethical behavior and to deal with unethical behavior. The concluding section of the chapter provides recommendations, which follow from our observations about faculty qualifications and support. We provide recommendations that we believe are practical ways to improve faculty qualifications and the ethics education provided to accounting students.

2. Faculty Training and Support to Teach Ethics

Accounting doctoral programs focus on developing students' research skills, and relatively little attention is given to helping future faculty members become effective teachers (Dunn, Hooks & Kohlbeck, 2016). Admitting students to doctoral programs is based primarily on their potential to do research and not, in a significant way, on the expectation that they will be effective teachers. A review of websites for accounting doctoral programs of different academic reputations revealed the following statements: "Our faculty selects students based on outstanding intellectual ability and a strong commitment to a career in research" (IU, 2020); "Our program is oriented toward training students to take academic jobs at research universities" (UCONN, 2020); and "Our program offers broad based interdisciplinary training that prepares students for a career in academic research institutions" (UF, 2020). We are not suggesting that accounting faculty members who are strong researchers cannot also be effective teachers. Instead, our point is that most accounting doctoral programs focus on preparing students for careers as researchers and not as teachers.

If accounting doctoral programs are not focused on specifically preparing students to teach, then what training and guidance do future faculty members receive in this area? Most accounting faculty members may have taught classes in the doctoral program in exchange for receiving tuition support or stipends. Department syllabi might be available and large introductory courses generally have a faculty coordinator. Few of us, however, likely received much help with preparing lecture notes or exams, with assessment or with using technology in the classroom. The reality often is that accounting faculty members are generally trained researchers but self-taught teachers (Dunn et al., 2016).

There are exceptions that indicate a few accounting doctoral programs make more formal efforts to train students for their teaching responsibilities. As one example, Callahan, Spiceland, Spiceland and Hairston (2016) describe a two-semester teaching practicum that accounting doctoral students complete in their first year. The practicum includes seminars on teaching, practice teaching opportunities and faculty mentoring for doctoral students teaching their first course. This example appears unusual at best.

The AAA and the EAA are the two major accounting education professional associations. We therefore looked at what these two associations are doing to assist accounting faculty with their development as teachers. The AAA publishes *Issues in Accounting Education* (*IAE*) and has a section, Teaching Learning and Curriculum (TLC), devoted to educational issues. A review of *IAE* shows that only a few articles related to faculty development as teachers were published in the past few years (e.g., Callahan et al., 2016; Bagranoff, 2019). The TLC section publishes a newsletter, runs a midyear conference and offers education-oriented sessions at AAA annual meetings. Even with these efforts, very few of the activities would be considered directly related to classroom development and teaching competence.

The AICPA and AAA (2012) published a report (commonly known as the Pathways Report) and also cosponsored education-oriented task forces (e.g., Lawson et al., 2014), all of which are focused more on what accounting faculty members should teach and not how faculty members can be effective teachers. The AAA is involved with other faculty-oriented programs, such as the Accounting PhD Rookie Recruiting and Research Camp and the New Faculty Consortium, both of which are primarily focused on getting junior faculty members off to a good start with their research programs, with minimal, if any, attention paid to faculty teaching competence.

A review of the EAA's Mission shows that 'teaching skills' is mentioned once in the organization's three-paragraph mission, with the remainder of the mission focused on research. This emphasis on research is reflected in the program for the 2019 EAA Congress, where only 22 of the 947 papers on the conference program (2.3%) were classified as Education. The EAA organizes a Doctoral Colloquium in Accounting prior to its Annual Congress to provide doctoral students with the opportunity to present and discuss their research. The Colloquium includes other career-oriented sessions for doctoral students, but the program focuses on research. The EAA publishes the *European Accounting Review* and *Accounting in Europe* journals, neither of which focuses on education.

Given that the reward structure in most university accounting departments emphasizes research output, our conclusion is that accounting faculty members receive little training as teachers in the research-focused doctoral programs. In addition, the two major accounting academic professional associations offer relatively little assistance with teacher training throughout faculty members' careers. Instead, the emphasis of faculty training and career development from accounting doctoral programs and professional education associations is on research, which may be of questionable value to most undergraduate accounting students. Universities likely offer orientation programs for new faculty members and training on, for example, using technology, but it is assumed that faculty members are competent teachers until there is evidence to the contrary. De-emphasizing accounting faculty members' formal training to be teachers risks reduced effectiveness in the classroom, including the teaching of soft skill topics such as ethics.

Most accounting faculty members have undergraduate degrees in accounting and many are professionally certified with relevant work experience. This background makes teaching technical accounting material somewhat more natural; it is what we know and do best. There is also significant support for teaching technical accounting material, including textbooks, solutions manuals, test banks, PowerPoint slides and online course management software. Exhibit areas at any AAA or EAA meeting will reinforce that there is no shortage of support for teaching technical accounting material. A question we raise in this chapter is whether there is support for teaching ethics to accounting students?

Apostolou, Dull and Schleifer (2013) provide a framework that accounting faculty members can use to incorporate ethics in their courses. Elements of the framework include:

1) Articulating learning objectives
2) Identifying the nature of ethics content
3) Determining modes of delivery
4) Conducting learning assessment

Accounting faculty members have used games and role-playing (Taplin, Singh, Kerr & Lee, 2018), but Apostolou et al. (2013) note that cases are the most common pedagogical tool used to teach ethics to accounting students. Their article provides a list of ethics cases published in accounting education journals, along with information on ethics coverage in specific accounting courses and general approaches used by accounting faculty members to teach ethics. The Apostolou et al. (2013) article is an excellent source of information for accounting faculty members seeking guidance on incorporating ethics coverage in their courses.

Since Apostolou et al. (2013) included ethics cases published through 2013, we examined the three major accounting education journals *IAE, the Journal of Accounting Education* (JAE) and *Accounting Education* (AE) for the past five years to get some indication of the continuing interest in ethics education. *IAE* published a number of fraud cases, which may incorporate ethical issues, but only three cases published since 2014 included ethics in the title: one on students and staff auditors, one on tax planning and one on asset impairment. This is rather surprising, because *IAE* has published a large number of cases in recent years. The *JAE* published only four cases since 2014 having ethics in the title, although it did publish a special issue on ethics. *AE*'s mission is to publish research papers, and we did not find any specific ethics case published in this journal over the past five years.

Although developing accounting students' soft skills, including ethics, has been emphasized for more than four decades, faculty members receive relatively little training or support to achieve this learning objective. As discussed earlier, we found little evidence that accounting faculty members receive formal training to teach in general and no evidence that faculty are trained to teach soft skills, including ethics. This does not mean that accounting faculty members cannot effectively teach ethics, but it does mean that faculty members may be self-taught in this area. Whereas there is some institutional/professional support for teaching ethics, it is very minimal and random compared with the support available to teach technical accounting topics. Accounting faculty members are often told to cover ethics, and many attempt to address the topic without much guidance on what to cover or how to cover it. This deficiency in training, guidance and support for teaching ethics should be of concern to students, accounting education programs and the profession.

3. Student Ethical Training

Ethics is a complex competency for which university education can play only a limited role, primarily because parental or family influences largely determine students' ethical awareness and behaviors before they enter college.[1] For example, university professors know that students cheat and, despite our best efforts, the risk of cheating will never be reduced to zero. Cheating on homework, exams, papers, and so forth may actually start well before students enter college. McCabe (2001) found that a significant percentage of middle school students cheat and this cheating behavior is thought to continue through high school and college. Krohe (2012) reported that 85% of high school students cheat in some manner and that 125 Harvard students were found, in one specific situation, to have shared answers on exams. Ghostwriting is the practice of providing solution manuals, test-taking assistance or essays on assigned topics, which students then submit as their own work (Fisher, McLeod, Savage & Simkin, 2016). From an international perspective, *The New York Times* reported in 2011 that an entire industry has developed in China to take SAT exams, write admissions essays and falsify resumes for the purpose of helping students gain admission to prestigious universities in the United States of America, the United Kingdom and Australia.

Accounting faculty and administrators should question how ethics can be taught in an environment where we know cheating is occurring and where cheating may be more common than we want to admit. Ethics education may not have much effect on cheating behavior, as noted by Lowery and Beadles (2009), who found that ethics education had an immediate effect on cheating behavior but only a minimal long-term effect. For example, a survey of 1,000 students from 27 campuses found a majority thought corporate scandals were wrong and that executives should be held personally accountable yet also admitted to cheating on an exam (Weisul & Merritt, 2002). If ethics education does not significantly impact the risk, nature or frequency of cheating, how can we expect the same education to make accounting graduates more ethical professionals? This is not to say that ethics should not be taught as part of a university education. It does indicate, however, that faculty and administrators should temper their expectations about what ethics education can accomplish.

Regardless of what ethicists argue, many students have formed their core ethical compass at an early age, and covering this topic in a college accounting class may have little or no effect on their current or future behavior. In 2002, the Aspen Institute surveyed 2,000 Master of Business Administration (MBA) students and found their beliefs were altered during an ethics class; by the end of the class they cared less about customer needs and product quality and more about shareholder value – a far cry from the intent of the classes (Vickers, 2004). Andrew McAfee, speaking at an Association to Advance Collegiate Schools of Business (AACSB) Deans' Conference (Bisoux, 2015), surprised attendees by stating that business schools spend too much time teaching topics such as leadership, ethics and corporate strategy. McAfee clarified that it was not that he thought leadership and ethics were unimportant but that there was only so much business schools could achieve in these areas.

> The thought that we can instill a strong ethical sense that cannot be easily overwhelmed in students who are already in their mid-20s is naïve. The number of hours we spend on leadership and ethics with students seems disproportionate to the impact we can have on students.
>
> (Bisoux, 2015)

4. Faculty Ethical Behavior

One assumption in accounting ethics education is that faculty members act ethically when fulfilling their own professional responsibilities. Similar to auditors needing to be independent in fact and appearance, accounting faculty members must be ethical in both fact and appearance to enhance the credibility of accounting ethics education.

Accounting educators' professional responsibilities could be categorized according to research, teaching and relationships with colleagues. Examples of ethical behavior in research would include, but not be limited to, accurately collecting and reporting data or results from an empirical study and ensuring that all authors contributed to articles (i.e., no gift authorships). Behaving ethically when fulfilling teaching responsibilities would include such behaviors as being current and prepared for classes, meeting classes as scheduled and assigning grades that are fair and not biased by personal feelings toward students. Being civil to colleagues and contributing to department, school and university activities are part of fulfilling an accounting faculty member's responsibility in an ethical manner. Accounting administrators should be expected to be fair and consistent in their treatment of colleagues and must avoid engaging in any discriminatory, intimidating or retaliatory behavior.

Motivation, opportunity and rationalization are components of what is known as the fraud triangle. Accounting faculty members have some motivation to behave in a potentially unethical manner because outcomes such as tenure, promotion, raises and teaching schedules depend on research productivity or the number of articles published. Faculty members collect, analyze and report data from empirical studies, which provide the opportunity to manipulate data to achieve a positive or publishable result. A faculty member's rationalization for behaving unethically in research activities may never be known, but needing tenure for job security and family reasons might be one way for an unethical researcher to justify his or her behavior. In addition, faculty members might rationalize 'gift' authorships by thinking that they are merely helping a colleague who is facing a tenure or promotion decision. The recipient of the gift authorship might use the 'everyone does it' excuse to rationalize his or her unethical behavior.

We cannot state that unethical behavior among accounting faculty members and administrators is common, but we must acknowledge the risk that unethical behavior might occur and the reality that it does occur. One noteworthy example is when the AAA retracted all articles published by a former accounting professor because he fabricated data reported in research articles published in top AAA journals. More recently, the AAA retracted an article published in *IAE*.

In the combined academic careers of the authors (75 plus years of teaching, research and service in higher education at nine different universities, 28 years of serving as journal editors and 23 years as department chairs), we are personally aware of former colleagues being 'gifted' publications so that they could receive tenure and be promoted. We are also personally aware of accounting faculty members who miss or are unprepared for classes on a regular basis, who are not current in their fields, who treat students unfairly or who have exhibited retaliatory behavior against subordinate colleagues such as assigning undesirable teaching schedules or denying raises, promotion and tenure.

The AACSB is the major accrediting body for business schools and accounting programs worldwide. Getting and maintaining AACSB accreditation depends, in part, on faculty qualifications within a business school or accounting program. Research productivity is an important criterion for determining faculty qualifications under AACSB standards. AACSB accreditation is partly a compliance exercise where faculty qualifications are assessed against a standard to make decisions regarding accreditation. As with any compliance exercise (e.g., tax law), there is some risk that accounting faculty and administrators will push the ethical 'envelope' to meet standards and either obtain or maintain accreditation. The risk therefore exists that some accounting faculty members or administrators will be motivated to behave in a questionable manner to meet AACSB accreditation standards with the rationalization that they are helping the school, accounting program or stakeholders, including students.

Certainly, academia is not immune to the many 'unethical' behaviors found in other organizations, and we should not dismiss the possibility and reality of accounting faculty and administrators behaving unethically. Perhaps what makes academia unique or different from professional accounting firms or business organizations is that we have less formal control mechanisms to deter or detect unethical behavior and the consequences of unethical behavior may be less severe for academicians than for accounting practitioners. For example, a licensed accountant who behaves unethically when fulfilling his or her professional responsibilities risks being fired, losing his or her license to practice or possibly going to jail (McKenna, 2019). Accounting faculty members are not licensed to teach, and, with tenure, losing one's position would only occur in the most extreme cases of unethical behavior.

Neither the AAA nor the EAA has an enforceable code of conduct for their members, so unethical behavior would not result in losing membership in these organizations. The AAA had a Professionalism and Ethics Committee whose charge included promoting professionalism and ethical conduct in the practice of accounting education, but that committee has not existed for the past several years. This reinforces our position that accounting faculty members and administrators largely, although not entirely, police themselves when it comes to ethical behavior.

5. Recommendations

Formal training to teach, and actually being and appearing to be ethical, are two factors affecting accounting faculty members' qualifications to teach ethics. Our recommendations are developed from these two issues. Because faculty members are not specifically trained to teach ethics, our recommendations relate to the general faculty development of teaching, with the assumption that more training in teaching will make accounting educators better able to teach ethics. Because formal training to teach should begin in accounting doctoral programs, we focus on several things that can be done at this faculty career stage to improve teaching effectiveness. We acknowledge that whether accounting students can actually 'learn' ethics in a college classroom raises the possibility that no matter how well faculty members are trained, their efforts may not succeed.

Albrecht and Sack (2000) note that faculty development is an individual responsibility, but they recommend that programs and schools provide a more supportive environment to assist doctoral students and faculty develop as researchers and teachers. Accounting doctoral programs can provide a more supportive environment for students to develop as teachers without compromising time and attention given to developing research skills. One suggestion is for accounting doctoral programs to have bi-weekly or monthly lunchtime seminars devoted to teaching. These would be informal sessions where students and faculty can discuss general teaching issues (e.g., Bain, 2004) or teaching articles specific to accounting education (e.g., Wygal & Stout, 2015; Wygal, Stout & Cunningham, 2017; Wygal, Watty & Stout, 2014). Universities generally have separate colleges of education, and education faculty involved with training future teachers could be invited to these lunchtime seminars. These informal seminars would help doctoral students work on their development as teachers and students would be exposed to different ideas and perspectives on effective teaching.

Accounting doctoral students are mentored throughout their early development as researchers. Faculty members teaching accounting doctoral seminars serve as research mentors to students, whereas dissertation committees serve a mentorship role for students' first major research projects. No similar mentorship relationship generally exists for accounting doctoral students to develop as teachers. Faculty coordinators might be assigned for courses taught by doctoral students and students can always seek advice on teaching from the faculty, but formal or ongoing mentoring relationships for teaching are generally not part of an accounting doctoral student's education.

Teaching mentors for accounting doctoral students must be chosen carefully, and it should not be assumed that faculty who are research mentors should also mentor students on teaching. It may be that senior accounting faculty members who are no longer actively involved with research have a wealth of experience and are among the best teachers in a department. Assigning these faculty members as teaching mentors would involve them in the accounting doctoral program and allow students to learn from those with the most classroom experience.

An article by Schnader, Westermann, Downey and Thibodeau (2016) describes a mentorship program used by one accounting doctoral program to help train students as educators. The two-semester program involves the doctoral program director serving as the teaching mentor for doctoral students. Whereas the mentoring program described in the article is a step in the right direction, our recommendation would be to select mentors based on their experience and expertise as teachers and not because they administer doctoral programs.

Accounting doctoral students may be introduced to the importance of teaching ethics, and they should be made aware of resources available to teach ethics. Some ethical issues – for example, tax avoidance – might be subject-specific, but students need to be informed that teaching ethics is a necessary part of teaching accounting. Because cases are commonly used to teach ethics, accounting doctoral students should be exposed to the incorporation of cases in their teaching. This training might include sitting in case discussions led by experienced accounting faculty members.

As we previously mentioned, the AAA and EAA do relatively little to help accounting doctoral students and junior faculty members develop as teachers. After agreeing with the accounting profession that teaching ethics is important, these professional associations have provided almost no guidance or support for meeting this educational objective. Supporting some of the ideas presented here would be an excellent first step by these organizations.

Finally, as noted at the beginning of this section, we believe it is important that accounting faculty members and administrators act ethically when fulfilling their professional responsibilities and that they appear ethical to students, colleagues and other accounting education program stakeholders. There will always be bad actors in any organization, and instances of unethical behavior by faculty members and administrators show that accounting education is no exception. Policies and mechanisms must be put in place to encourage ethical behavior by accounting educators, and faculty should respond when other accounting faculty members or administrators act unethically.

Professional accountants, lawyers and physicians are all licensed to practice, and becoming and remaining licensed require complying with a professional code of ethics. Practitioners violating the profession's code of ethics risk censure and loss of their license to practice. Accounting educators who teach ethics to students are not similarly bound by a code of ethics, as neither the AAA nor EAA has an enforceable code. Bordeman and Westerman (2019) describe a classroom exercise where accounting students research the profession's code of conduct to determine whether a hypothetical practitioner's behavior violates the code. Whereas this can be a valuable exercise, we need to recognize that accounting faculty members who choose to use this exercise in their classes are not themselves bound by a professional code of conduct. Students would not realize this, but accounting educators should be concerned about the inconsistency of examining a code of ethics for practitioners when we are not bound by a similar code.

We recommend that the AAA and EAA establish a code of ethics for accounting educators. The code would cover ethical issues related to research, teaching and relationships with colleagues, and all AAA and EAA members would be required to agree to comply. Failure to comply with the code would risk censure or loss of membership, with these actions being published on the AAA and EAA websites. The code would clarify what ethical behavior for accounting educators means and require compliance by members. This action would enhance the credibility of accounting ethics education and place our profession on a level comparable to the practice side of our discipline.

6. Conclusion

We believe that the accounting profession has not clearly identified or defined those soft skills that most accounting graduates might need to be successful in the profession. Instead, we have a long list of skills that even the most qualified leaders of our discipline may lack; yet these same leaders ask those of us in higher education to develop the sought-after skills/attributes. Specific to this chapter, ethics education for accounting students has been of limited effectiveness, in part, because there is no clear educational objective for what we are trying to accomplish. Individual faculty members are therefore forced to decide what ethics education for accounting students means and to then select materials to accomplish their chosen objective.

In this chapter, we have questioned the qualifications of accounting faculty to help develop ethical awareness and behavior in college-age students during our limited class time and whether accounting faculty members have the capacity to accomplish this task. Given the amount of technical accounting material we have to teach (which is ever expanding) along with technology skills and data analytic requirements, it is not reasonable to assume we have sufficient time to address critical soft skills such as ethics in the curriculum. The lack of preparation for teaching in general and for teaching an abstract concept such as ethics makes the task even more difficult for accounting educators.

We do not offer complete answers to the questions we raise but simply suggest some possible first steps in addressing the issues noted. Perhaps, at some point the professional organizations involved in accounting education will attempt to address our concerns and provide much-needed guidance and support for developing students' soft skills, including ethics.

Note

1. See Rebele and St. Pierre (2019) for an extended discussion on the teaching of soft skills, including critical thinking, communications and ethics.

References

Accounting Education Change Commission (AECC). (1990). Objectives of Education for Accountants: Position Statement Number One. *Issues in Accounting Education, 5*(2), 307–312.

Albrecht, W. S., & Sack, R. J. (2000). *Accounting Education: Charting the Course Through a Perilous Future.* Sarasota, FL: American Accounting Association.

American Institute of Certified Public Accountants (AICPA). (2018). *The AICPA Pre-Certification Core Competency Framework.* Retrieved October 12th, 2020, from www.aicpa.org/interestareas/accountingeducation/resources/corecompetency.html

American Institute of Certified Public Accountants (AICPA), & American Accounting Association (AAA). (2012). *Charting a National Strategy for the Next Generation of Accountants.* Retrieved October 12th, 2020, from http://commons.aaahq.org/files/0b14318188/Pathways_Commission_Final_Report_Complete.pdf

Apostolou, B. A., Dull, R. B., & Schleifer, L. L. F. (2013). A Framework for the Pedagogy of Accounting Ethics. *Accounting Education: An International Journal, 22*(1), 1–17.

Arthur Andersen, Arthur Young, Coopers & Lybrand, Deloitte Haskins & Sells, Ernst & Whinney, Peat Marwick Main & Co., & Touche Ross. (1989). *Perspectives on Education: Capabilities for Success in the Accounting Profession* [White Paper]. New York, USA.

Bagranoff, N. A. (2019). Summaries of the Teaching Domain Statements of the 2018 Cook Prize Winners. *Issues in Accounting Education, 34*(2), 1–9.

Bain, K. (2004). *What the Best College Teachers Do.* Cambridge, MA: Harvard University Press.

Bisoux, T. (2015). B-Schools: Stop Teaching Ethics? *BizEd.* Retrieved October 12th, 2020, from https://bized.aacsb.edu/articles/2015/02/bschools-stop-teaching-ethics

Bordeman, A., & Westermann, K. D. (2019). The Professional Ethics Exam and Acts Discreditable: An Introductory Assignment. *Issues in Accounting Education, 34*(4), 39–53.

Callahan, C. M., Spiceland, C. P., Spiceland, J. D., & Hairston, S. (2016). Pilot Course: A Teaching Practicum Course as an Integral Component of an Accounting Doctoral Program. *Issues in Accounting Education, 31*(2), 191–210.

Dunn, K. A., Hooks, K. L., & Kohlbeck, M. J. (2016). Preparing Future Accounting Faculty Members to Teach. *Issues in Accounting Education, 31*(2), 155–170.

Fisher, E., McLeod, A. J., Savage, A., & Simkin, M. G. (2016). Ghostwriters in the Cloud. *Journal of Accounting Education, 34*, 59–71.

Indiana University (IU). (2020). *Qualifications.* Retrieved July 10th, 2020, from https://kelley.iu.edu/programs/phd/admissions/index.cshtml

Korn, M. (2013). *Does an 'A' in Ethics Have Any Value?* Retrieved May 25th, 2020, from www.wsj.com/articles/SB10001424127887324761004578286102004694378

Krohe, J. (2012). *Cheating Is the American Way.* Retrieved May 25th, 2020, from www.illinoistimes.com/springfield/cheating-is-the-american-way/Content?oid=11454229

Lawson, R. A., Blocher, E. J., Brewer, P. C., Cokins, G., Sorensen, J. E., Stout, D. E., & Wouters, M. J. F. (2014). Focusing Accounting Curricula on Students' Long-Run Careers; Recommendations for an Integrated Competency-Based Framework for Accounting Education. *Issues in Accounting Education, 29*(2), 295–317.

Lowery, C., & Beadles, N. (2009). Assessing the Impact of Business Ethics Instruction: A Review of the Empirical Evidence. *Journal of the Academy of Business Education, 9*, 31–48.

Mastracchio, N. (2005). *Teaching CPAS About Serving the Public Interest.* Retrieved May 25th, 2020, from http://archives.cpajournal.com/2005/105/perspectives/p6.htm

McCabe, D. (2001). Cheating: Why Students Do It and How We Can Them Stop. *American Educator, 25*(4), 38–43.

McKenna, F. (2019). The KPMG Cheating Scandal Was Much More Widespread Than Originally Thought. *MarketWatch*. Retrieved October 12th, 2020, from www.marketwatch.com/story/the-kpmg-cheating-scandal-was-much-more-widespread-than-originally-thought-2019-06-18

McNair, F., & Milam, E. (1993). Ethics in Accounting Education: What Is Really Being Done? *Journal of Business Ethics, 12*(10), 797–809.

Rebele, J., & St. Pierre, K. (2019). A Commentary on Learning Objectives for Accounting Education Programs: The Importance of Soft Skills and Technical Knowledge. *Journal of Accounting Education, 48*, 71–79.

Schnader, A. L., Westermann, K. D., Downey, D. H., & Thibodeau, J. C. (2016). Training Teacher-Scholars: A Mentorship Program. *Issues in Accounting Education, 31*(2), 171–190.

Taplin, R., Singh, A., Kerr, R., & Lee, A. (2018). The Use of Short Role-Plays for an Ethics Intervention in University Auditing Courses. *Accounting Education, 27*(4), 383–402.

University of Connecticut (UCONN). (2020). *Ph.D. in Business.* Retrieved July 10th, 2020, from https://warrington.ufl.edu/phd-in-business-administration-accounting/

University of Florida Warrington College of Business (UF). (2020). *Program Overview*. Retrieved July 10th, 2020, from https://warrington.ufl.edu/phd-in-business-administration-accounting/

Vickers, M. (2004). Striving for Ethical MBAs. *Trendwatcher*. Retrieved October 12, 2020, from www.i4cp.com/trendwatchers/2004/05/28/striving-for-ethical-mbas

Weisul, K., & Merritt, J. (2002). You Mean Cheating Is Wrong? *Business Week, 8*.

Wygal, D. E., & Stout, D. E. (2015). Shining a Light on Effective Teaching Best Practices: Survey Findings From Award-Winning Accounting Educators. *Issues in Accounting Education, 30*(3), 173–205.

Wygal, D. E., Stout, D. E., & Cunningham, B. M. (2017). Shining Additional Light on Effective Teaching Practices in Accounting: Self-Reflective Insights From Cook Prize Winners. *Issues in Accounting Education, 32*(3), 17–31.

Wygal, D. E., Watty, K., & Stout, D. E. (2014). Drivers of Teaching Effectiveness: Views From Accounting Educator Exemplars in Australia. *Accounting Education, 23*(4), 322–342.

3   Audit Education
Toward Virtue and Duty

Bruce Wayne Stuart, Iris Caroline Stuart &
Lars Jacob Tynes Pedersen

1. Introduction

Accounting standards, auditing standards and regulatory institutions seek to hold public accountants to principles, rules and normative patterns of decision-making. Decision-making by public accountants in a given accounting situation is to serve stakeholders and the public interest. Such service is best achieved through the accountant's adherence to the principles of the profession, by following the appropriate rules and by the exercise of judgment. Ideally, this judgment will be shaped by the knowledge of technical prescriptions and encompass practical insight into the salient features of a given situation. This judgment should also employ a complex intellectual and moral analysis that reveals sensitivity to moral issues and a capacity to resolve ethical dilemmas. The accountant ought to exercise a dual competency marked by technical proficiency and ethical sensibility.

In this context, auditing as one among several accounting specialties is a professional practice that calls for its own educational process and curricular goals. The first auditing course is the critical setting for introducing students to audit practice, particularly to the requirements of the audit itself. The classroom should be the arena in which students have an extensive encounter with the ethical expectations of audit practice and where they might acquire the virtues necessary for later achieving the goals of the practice. This chapter presents a framework for teaching the auditing course with a special focus on students' learning of the ethical obligations of auditing and developing practical judgment which integrates technical expertise and ethical sensibility. It specifies the conditions that promote such learning and how to achieve it in practice. The contribution made by the chapter to the literature on auditing education is to provide a teaching framework that focuses on learning professional principles and acquiring personal virtues that facilitate professional service to business stakeholders and the public.

The auditing course is the student's first systematic exposure to the professional responsibilities of public accounting; thus, it constitutes a first step toward membership in the profession. Given this function of the auditing course, this chapter will argue that technical and ethical requirements for audit practice mandate learning not only an ethics of professional duty but also an ethics of personal virtue. The principles, rules and patterns of professional judgment that are mandated by legislation, prescribed by professional codes of conduct and supervised by regulatory institutions set the parameters of professional duty for auditors. These standards are the foundation of an ethics of professional duty, and these same standards are the basis for an ethics of virtue. This is because compliance with the norms of audit practice, in letter and spirit (an ethics of duty), depends on the individual accountant's quality of character. The auditor must possess the distinctive qualities of character and exhibit the capacity to demonstrate specific intellectual and moral traits, virtues', while executing the practical tasks of reviewing financial statements and assessing internal controls for business entities. In a word, such compliance emerges from an ethics of personal virtue.

The structure of the chapter is as follows. First, we review existing literature that treats the teaching of auditing ethics. Thereby, we situate our chapter in the discourse on the ethical duties and virtues of the auditor. Second, we outline a theoretical framework that emphasizes the dual ethical approach to teaching auditing ethics. The core of this effort concentrates a virtue ethics perspective toward the preparation for entering a principles-based, rules-oriented profession. In particular, we focus on the moral development – the character formation – of auditors, including the tasks of inculcating auditor virtues and enhancing their practical judgment. Third, we present our teaching framework for cultivating virtues and honing the skills of practical judgment, discussing six elements of the learning situation that are salient for these tasks. Fourth, we illustrate our framework, treating several duties of public auditing and examining examples of auditor virtues. In these sections, we demonstrate how practical judgments are made regarding specific stakeholders. Finally, we summarize and conclude.

2. Literature Review

From the late 1980s, there has been much discussion about teaching business and accounting ethics in universities and business schools. The literature that we highlight deals with whether ethics can be taught in the classroom, the educational goals of specific courses and curricula, debates over who should give instruction and the various methods of assessing faculty performance and student learning. One aspect of these debates considers the impact of ethics training on professional practice – especially on whether coursework enhances the ability to recognize ethical issues and resolve ethical dilemmas in business settings. There has been widespread discussion of Kohlberg's (1981) research on moral development and the use of Rest's (1994) four-part model of ethical decision-making (Thorne, 1998). There are numerous empirical studies of student responses to ethics education; many of these studies employ the concepts and vocabulary of Rest's (1994) model – ethical sensitivity, judgment, motivation and behavior – as their authors develop hypotheses and analyze findings.

Some literature presents frameworks for teaching ethics, outlining curriculum proposals, educational goals, teaching strategies and vehicles of assessment (Cheffers & Pakaluk, 2005; Mintz, 1995, 2006). These articles consider business ethics courses and specialized courses in accounting ethics, with attention given to professionalism and the ethical dimension of public accounting (Jennings, 2004; Levy & Mitschow, 2008; Williams, 2010). Many scholars suggest teaching techniques and classroom activities designed to increase knowledge about ethics and foster ethical behavior (Armstrong, Ketz & Owsen, 2003; Low, Davey & Hooper, 2008 Mintz, 2006). The literature links the specialized courses in business, accounting and professional ethics to traditions of moral philosophy as these are taught in the curricula of academic philosophy. Such efforts have prompted a lively debate on whether the concepts, terminology and argumentation of moral philosophy are actually helpful for accounting practice. At the same time, a number of accounting scholars assert that business, accounting and professional ethics can be construed as aspects of 'applied ethics', and it makes little sense to ignore the rich history of philosophical inquiry whenever ethical aspects of these fields are examined (Dolfsma, 2006; Gaffikin, 2007).

In addition to this review of the journal articles that examine both the technical and the ethical dimensions of accounting practice, the authors deeply appreciate the lengthy text by Cheffers and Pakaluk (2005). A major portion of this book presents a complex analysis of the major accounting scandal involving the American International Group (AIG). This aspect of the text merits a careful reading for its details of accounting practice and its sharp critique of unethical accounting decision-making.

The present chapter finds the book valuable in another way. Consistent with our own agenda, the book directs its readers to concentrate on accountants' exercising of virtuous behavior in their professional activities. The authors repeatedly exhort public accountants to exercise due diligence to apply their technical expertise to the complexities of reviewing contemporary business finance and producing truthful accounting information on the rapid-fire (and often bewildering) transactions of large-scale corporations. Furthermore, Cheffers and Pakaluk (2005) emphasize the significance of accounting excellence and the professional requirement to resist the many temptations of narrow self-interest. They advocate the professional requirement to effectively serve a wide variety of stakeholders and the public good. Optimistic in their hopes for the profession's ability to serve the business community and serve the public, the authors link this hopefulness to the individual accountant's capacity to embody the traits and habits of moral character and self-consciously to exercise acquired virtues as responsible professionals (Cheffers & Pakaluk, 2005). In a word, Cheffers and Pakaluk (2005) advocate a virtue-based approach to accounting ethics. They discuss accounting education to highlight this virtue ethics orientation as a vital component of the accountant's specialized contribution to public good and as crucial for the preparation and enhancement of the skills and virtues necessary to serve business and society. Such an education focuses on training for the development of technical skills and character formation that support ethical discernment and sound principles-based decision-making (Cheffers & Pakaluk, 2005).

Cheffers and Pakaluk (2005) inductively (sketching historical comments from the founders of the American accounting profession) and deductively (from analysis of accounting standards and codified guidelines) emphasize the fundamental principles of the profession. The book argues that accounting standards, the rules of practice and decision-making procedures ought to be subordinated to principles (rules should serve principles) as the standards to guide accountants' decision-making. The authors presuppose (and advocate) accountants' passion for technical proficiency and the centrality of a personal drive for excellence in ethical discernment. Given this intellectual and moral commitment to the truth-telling function of accounting, they express the goal and high priority that accountants seek the practical realization of their intellectual and moral virtues in the performance of professional tasks.

We, as accountants and ethics scholars, share these values and professional commitments. The argument of this study reflects our concern that accounting education should facilitate the development of technical skills and moral character. In this way, the professional goal of public service can be realized by knowledgeable and ethical accountants (whom we label as 'The Virtuous Accountants'). Cheffers and Pakaluk (2005) make this point as well, in an assertive fashion.

What is more, these authors emphasize that accountants should learn specific intellectual and moral virtues – that is, acquire through education and mentored experience traits of character and skills to support honorable behavior. For example, these virtues should include 'courage', 'moderation' and 'justice', as well as 'prudential judgment', also called 'conscience' (Cheffers & Pakaluk, 2005). They argue that these virtues are crucial because the traits enable the accountant to resist narrow self-interest and to act rationally and speak truthfully. For accountants, this means that properly trained practitioners can formulate and verify

> an accurate representation of the results of operations and financial position of a company, as found in the financial statements of that company. An accountant is something like a financial truth-teller,

where part of the job of telling the truth is grasping well the financial reality which is being represented and finding the best terms for representing it.

(Cheffers & Pakaluk, 2005, p. 94)

Note that this claim that an accountant should acquire these specific virtues to be realized in professional activity assumes the acquisition of the virtues through an education that encompasses both intellectual and moral components (training for what this study calls 'technical proficiency' and 'ethical sensibility'). In this perspective, the accountant's character will be shaped by formal education and supervised experiences so that future practitioners can cope with the special demands of the profession for which they prepare. Cheffers and Pakaluk (2005) assume that this training will enable the accountant to flourish personally and effectively serve the needs of stakeholders and the public.

Cheffers and Pakaluk (2005) conclude their treatment of accountants' distinctive work and accountants' character formation with its significant virtues by calling attention to the specialized role that accountants acquire through training and their entrance into a profession:

The virtues of an accountant qua accountant are those traits, which are so ingrained that they have the aspect of second nature to the practitioner, which make an accountant a good professional and enable him or her to carry out attest or truth-telling work well (in the broadest and original sense of that term).

(Cheffers & Pakaluk, 2005, p. 95)

In keeping with this literature that argues the necessity of technical training and character formation in the educational process to prepare for professional life, the present study pays special attention to the concepts, vocabulary and questions regarding moral development, as well as the ideas of character and virtue as they emerge in the tradition of virtue ethics. This tradition of ethical reflection is an ancient form of moral philosophy that once again has inspired contemporary philosophical debate among moral philosophers, a debate of relevance to accounting ethics discourse (Melé, 2005; Mintz, 1995, 1996). Even as we consider the relevance of virtue ethics categories of thought for our teaching and scholarship, we deem it crucial to emphasize that standards and institutions guide professional accounting. We claim that professionals are duty-bound to adhere to principles and act in accordance with the rules that are prescribed by their profession. This chapter will demonstrate this commitment to professional duty and the understanding that decision-making in accounting encompasses both technical and ethical obligations. It will make use of a virtue ethics approach to moral development, character formation and the enhancement of practical judgment. Its treatment presupposes that accounting and auditing standards – principles, rules and auditor decisions – that reflect sound character, specific virtues and practical judgment are critical to the process of realizing moral virtues in professional activity.

We affirm the virtue ethics ideal of excellence in public activity and the significance of communal support for ethics-driven and principled action on the part of professionals. Given these commitments, this chapter construes auditing education as a process relating 'an ethics of duty' and 'an ethics of virtue' (Doucet & Doucet, 2004). This chapter contributes to the literature on auditing education by providing a teaching framework for promoting ethical sensibility through a combined orientation of attention to professional principles and personal virtues.

3. Theoretical Framework: A Virtue Ethics Perspective on a Rule-Oriented Profession

3.1. An Ethics of Duty: The Traditional Language of Auditor Responsibility

The traditional language of auditing classes has emphasized the auditor's obligation to conform to auditing standards – in the language of Doucet and Doucet (2004) – an 'ethics of duty'. Technical requirements of the audit, methods of gathering evidence to determine whether accounting standards have been met and treatment of the professional codes of conduct are foundational principles and catalogues of rules. These are presented as the auditor's duties and as the expectations of the profession. In addition, and of equal import, the auditing class focuses attention on presentations and exercises designed to enhance specific aspects of the auditor's judgment.

In ethical terms, this traditional approach to the auditing course as the setting for learning professional duties can be described in the following manner. The practice of accounting, particularly the profession of public accounting, has 'regulative ideals', guiding norms and constraining conditions. These patterns of expectation promulgated within the profession set the parameters for the particular roles of the professional accountant and establish guidelines for the types of behavior that most properly determine how the accountant will achieve the goals of the profession and satisfy the ideal of public service. These regulative ideals are the principles, rules and prescriptions for decision-making established by accounting institutions and by governmental legislation as the standards for public accounting. These prescriptions for professional life are presented through codes of professional conduct, through law and through the regulations of the stock exchange commissions in each country. An auditing course will demonstrate that these codes, statutes and regulations (and the conversations among regulators and audit professionals concerning extensions of the principles and applications of the rules) constitute the foundational rule for auditors and are the basis of the technical and ethical obligations for members of the profession.

This approach assumes that public accounting is a principles-based and rule-oriented practice. Since 1990, the many articles on accounting ethics presuppose this traditional characterization of the public accountant's professional role as grounded in accounting and auditing standards and public service. Consequently, the professional training through the auditing course should give high priority for students to affirm an ethics of duty, so that they commit themselves to work within the limits set by the regulative ideals, the standards, of the profession they will enter. The auditing course will familiarize students with these key principles and supporting rules and initiate the practical process for conducting the audit in conformity with these standards. The classroom experience will offer examples of auditing rules and should involve the students in exercises to apply the rules. These exercises should help the students to work through the appropriate procedures as financial statements are reviewed and mechanisms of internal control assessed. These examples and exercises will demonstrate the technical dimensions of public accounting, the knowledge-based aspects of professional duties that lie ahead for students, pointing out the basic specialized responsibilities of public accounting.

3.2. The Language of Virtue: The Auditor's Character

Auditing practice demands more than just technical knowledge and intellectual skill. Proficiency in conducting an audit presupposes more than the knowledge of principles and rules, more than 'book learning', rote memorization of professional codes and accounting standards or familiarity with classroom examples/exercises. In the language of an ethics of virtue, auditors must exercise a practical judgment that expresses intellectual and moral virtues – a complex of character traits. This view presupposes that the professional judgment that comes into play in the conduct of an audit should demonstrate ethical sensibility as well as technical competence. The auditing course plays a key role in the educative process to develop such judgment. In addition to teaching that auditors have a duty to conform to the standards of the profession, the auditing course provides the intellectual foundation and the practical experience for developing an ethics of virtue consistent with the ethics of duty. This is because both technical knowledge and ethical discernment are vital and necessary to facilitate adherence to accounting principles and technical compliance to rules.

In this context, the auditing course should pay special attention to the ethical dimension of auditing, especially in terms of the character of the auditor. Focus should be given to the distinctive virtues or character traits that come into play in decision-making (the elements of decision-making include recognizing ethical issues, resolving dilemmas and motivating and sustaining ethical behavior) as the auditor seeks to achieve the goals of the profession. These emphases presuppose that the professional duties of the auditor and the proper performance of his or her role cannot be achieved simply by following the rules of the profession or by somehow encoding the standards neatly into real-life practice.

The significant virtues treated in an auditing course will include both intellectual and moral traits, as well as the capabilities for rendering judgment that constitute the resources for reviewing internal controls and financial statements and for issuing audit opinions. Accordingly, the course should sketch the process of an audit not only as a technical task of gathering evidence to ensure the accuracy of financial statements or to measure the quality of internal controls but also as 'a field of virtue'. By this, we mean the specific domain in which the auditor seeks to meet with ethical thought and action the demands of the world (in this case, the prescribed professional duties). To address these audit demands, the virtuous auditor directs his or her intellectual and moral virtues (aiming them) toward excellence by embodying the virtues in the auditing processes and the specialized texts of the profession – the creative productions (pre-audit planning papers, work papers and the final audit opinion). These processes and texts are thus construed as the internal goods necessary for achieving the goals of audit practice (Stuart, Stuart & Pedersen, 2011).

3.3. Practical Judgment: The Capacity to Act Virtuously and to Manage Stakeholders

The capacity to direct virtues toward excellent performance within a given audit situation is described (in virtue ethics terms) as the function of 'practical wisdom' (or practical judgment). The auditing course should treat this concept in some detail. Practical judgment (in Greek, 'phronesis') is an intellectual capacity to assess salient features of situations, make judgments about specific human behaviors and relationships and consider how to exercise a particular virtue (or virtues) in a given situation (e.g., Aristotle, 1985; MacIntyre, 1984). Practical judgment in its ethical dimension is the moral capacity to carry out or realize an intention to act virtuously – first, to be motivated and then to act in an appropriately ethical manner. This moral capacity is a comprehensive ability that integrates technical knowledge, awareness of the significant features of a given situation, realistic insight into the nature of human behavior and the ability to bring appropriate virtues to bear in doing the right thing for the situation.

We have thus far argued that practical judgment is a virtue of primary significance for auditors and that auditing education should promote such judgment among auditing students. We defined practical judgment as the intellectual capacity to assess salient features of situations, to make judgments about particular human behaviors and relationships and to consider how to exercise a particular virtue (or virtues) in a given situation.

In a concrete and practical sense, this relates closely to the process of identifying and prioritizing (or managing) stakeholders (Mitchell, Agle & Wood, 1997); Freeman (1984). In the auditing context, stakeholders are those individuals or groups influenced by the decisions and activities of the auditor. A key challenge, then, for the auditor is to be able

1) to identify those stakeholders
2) to identify what is at stake for them
3) to make judgments about the implications of the decisions the auditor is to make.

Making decisions in view of stakeholder concerns is a central part of the auditor's professional responsibility, and this requires the ability for practical judgment. Ethical decision-making is difficult precisely because ethical problems do not come pre-labeled as such, and it is not necessarily evident who the individuals or groups are who should be taken into account or to see how they may be influenced positively or negatively by the auditor's decision. Given recent accounting scandals and changes in regulation, the auditor must be reminded that he or she must give primacy to the interests of shareholders and other legitimate external stakeholders (e.g., regulatory bodies) in priority over management's interests. The ability for awareness and discernment related to such questions constitutes a large part of the ethical dimension of auditing.

Accordingly, the auditor must identify the involved parties and their interests, as well as acknowledge the technical and ethical responsibilities to attend to these parties and their interests. A related challenge for the auditor that requires considerable practical judgment is to detect instances of attempted fraud. Sensitivity to cues of such misbehavior is a central aspect of the auditor's judgment, and judgments about these matters will be based, in part, on the knowledge and the interests of the stakeholders involved in the situation. For instance, fraud has been explained as the interaction of three causal influences:

1) incentive, i.e. motivation or pressure to commit fraud
2) opportunity, i.e. conditions that allow committing fraud
3) attitude, i.e. what allows the individual to rationalize fraud.
(Wilks & Zimbelman, 2004)

This explanation of the conditions of fraud implies that the auditor should critically scrutinize the interests of the stakeholders, consider the incentives their interests may give each stakeholder and anticipate potential opportunities to act opportunistically to obtain benefits. They must consider any behavioral cues that might indicate a willingness to commit fraud. This treatment of practical judgment in relation to the assessment of stakeholders (who are affected by an accounting circumstance or a particular audit decision) fits well into a traditional Aristotelian virtue ethics understanding of practical judgment. In this tradition, practical judgment involves both assessing individuals and their (possible) motivations for particular actions and discerning with realism the salient features of the situation in which these people might act. Unethical behavior arises within the interaction between people who are willing to transgress norms on the one hand and the practical social conditions that allow a transgression to occur on the other hand. The auditor's practical judgment involves scrutinizing these dimensions of business practice and making quality assessments of risks and transgressions.

3.4. Two Languages of Auditor Obligation in the Auditing Course

The special province of the auditing course is to ensure that the intellectual and moral traits and the complex trait of practical judgment (which embodies both intellectual and moral aspects) are developed (acquired or enhanced), so that in future practice the special obligations of the profession can be fulfilled. This presupposes a professional practice shaped by principles and rules (with a corresponding ethics of duty) and designed to foster the distinctive character traits of the virtuous auditor. Such an auditor will demonstrate a capacity for practical judgment that integrates a grasp of technical knowledge and moral sensibility appropriate for auditing situations (thus demonstrating an ethics of virtue). To meet these expectations, the auditing course will employ two 'languages' of auditor obligation. One language will express the technical vocabulary, concepts and decision rules of accounting standards. The second language will reflect the history of moral inquiry; in particular, it will express the concepts and vocabulary of virtue ethics in its treatment of character formation, the inculcation of virtues and the fostering of practical judgment.

These two languages of auditor obligation – the ethics of rules and the ethics of virtues – should be used throughout the auditing course to form the basis for teaching strategies designed to facilitate development of the auditor's dual competency of technical proficiency and ethical sensibility. Most importantly, both languages ought to support the auditing student's moral motivation and behavior whenever he or she conducts audits and serves the public in future professional practice.

4. Learning From a Virtue Ethics Perspective

4.1. Assumptions of Learning: Virtue Ethics in the Classroom

A virtue ethics perspective in its Aristotelian variation makes specific assumptions about learning and the development of intellectual and ethical competence (e.g., Aristotle, 1985). Let us consider some of these key assumptions in order to move toward a practical, virtue ethics approach to auditing education. First, learning is 'teleological', that is, it is goal-oriented, aimed toward one or more objectives held by the individual. In virtue ethics, we may distinguish between intermediate goals, such as learning to become a proficient archer or an auditor, and more comprehensive goals, such as the cultivation of a wide range of virtues that contribute to personal happiness and/or the well-being of humanity. Second, learning is experiential, that is, the individual learns through the practical experience of deliberation, making choices, taking actions and subjecting these decisions to thoughtful reflection (Dunne, 1999). Through such experience, the individual reinforces activities and strategies that prove successful from a teleological point of view and rejects those that do not. In the ethical domain, the responses from others serve as valuable inputs for the individual in the process of discerning between appropriate and inappropriate modes of action.

In the practical or intellectual domain, individuals learn experientially in a direct sense, that is, by the trial and error of one's own activity and by observing the proficient execution of the tasks that will be addressed in professional practice. This combination of one's own action and the observation of others points to the third feature of learning according to virtue ethics, namely that the learning of virtues is integrally linked to observing and identifying with role models. By observing the actions of intellectually or morally virtuous persons as they practice their crafts (or perform professional duties), the individual may emulate these experts in his or her experiences: In this way, he or she is privileged to discern a virtuous manner of acting and subsequently – through conscientious repetition and regularized imitation – to form one's own habit of virtuous action. Finally, learning is 'social', meaning that individuals learn in communities. Learning from role models is one example of this, but more generally, individuals learn together, with each other, through dialogue and mentoring, rather than as isolated individuals (e.g., Lave & Wenger, 1991; Saugstad, 2002). This social engagement is particularly important for moral development. We develop our moral virtues in interaction with others – by observing their actions and their responses to our activity, by engaging in dialogue (about right and wrong, virtue and vice, salient features of ethical dilemmas, etc.) and by thoughtful reflection on how best to serve the needs of others (and what is best for our own well-being).

4.2. Cultivating Virtue: Elements of the Learning Situation in Teaching Auditing Ethics

As we aim to translate the virtue ethics assumptions about learning to a practical framework for learning, we consider the following elements of the learning situation. These together comprise the different

Table 3.1 Elements of Learning and Their Role in the Learning Situation

	Element of the learning situation	Role in the learning situation
1	Intended outcome	Aim of learning
2	Student	Subject in learning
3	Teacher	Source of learning
4	Learning material	Source of learning
5	Practical experiences	Process of learning
6	Learning community	Process of learning

characteristics of learning outlined earlier. Table 3.1 summarizes these elements and their role in the learning situation. First, the learning situation has an 'intended outcome', that is, an objective. For instance, a student of auditing may aim to become proficient at recognizing subtle forms of fraudulent financial reporting, or, indeed, his or her teacher may have that objective on behalf of the student. This constitutes the 'aim' of learning. Second, and very importantly, the learning process involves a 'subject', the student as an individual in learning. According to the virtue ethics perspective, the student is more than a mere receptor of knowledge. Rather, he or she actively engages in a dialogical process with the teacher, the other students and the learning material, thereby taking part in shaping what is learned. The student, thus, is the 'subject' of learning. Third, the 'teacher' plays an important part in the learning process, not only by setting the learning objectives, selecting the relevant material and communicating it to students, but also by being a role model for students. Fourth, the 'course resources' – whether it is books, articles, cases, videos, exercises, role play or the like – play a prominent role in the learning process. We may say that the teacher and the resources together constitute the source of learning. Fifth, the 'practical experiences' of the student are of primordial importance in the learning process. Whether these experiences are primarily individual or social, intellectual or practical, value-laden or value-neutral, they are pedagogical choices that have important implications for the learning process. This focus on experiential learning is linked to the sixth and final element of the learning situation, namely the 'learning community' (Lave & Wenger, 1991). The degree to which the student learns with others is an important feature of learning and is naturally linked to the other elements listed earlier. We may say that, together, the practical experiences of the student and the composition and characteristics of the learning community constitute 'the process of learning' (see Table 3.1 for a summary of the six elements).

5. A Practical Approach to Teaching Auditing Ethics: Duties and Virtues

Following Doucet and Doucet (2004), the teaching strategies of the auditing course presuppose an ethics perspective that emphasizes both duty and virtue (as well as the commitment to the dual competency of technical proficiency and ethical sensibility). Those authors reviewed several professional codes of conduct to highlight these codes' use of the two languages of duty and virtues – 'Code of Professional Conduct' by the American Institute of Certified Public Accountants (AICPA, 1997) and two Canadian codes: the 'Code of Ethics and Rules of Professional Conduct' by the Certified General Accountants Association of Canada (CGAAC, 1994) and the 'Rules of Professional Conduct' by the Institute of Chartered Accountants of Ontario (ICAO, 1995). Their article identifies several principles delineated in the aspirational aspects of these codes, demonstrating that these principles express the critical duties of the public accountant. For example, some of these duties prescribe normative patterns of action for accountants: a duty to public interest, to inform the public, a requirement to discharge this duty with competence and a duty of confidentiality to clients. From the AICPA (1997) Code, the article elaborates on the professional duties to maintain objectivity, to be independent both in fact and in appearance and to exercise due care and diligence, and from the CGAAC (1994) Code, 'integrity and honesty'. In addition to these behavior-oriented duties, Doucet and Doucet (2004) list several character virtues, emphasizing self-discipline and integrity (the ability to discern right from wrong), competence (in both technical judgment and moral sensibility) and courage.

By treating principles and virtues in this twofold fashion approach to professional duty, Doucet and Doucet (2004) effectively emphasize that professionalism encompasses role identity ('who to be', character virtues) and role behavior ('what to do', duties on the job). The professional codes blend and mix the languages of duty and virtue and specific rules for conducting audits emerge from the accounting and auditing standards that prescribe duties (actions on the job). These standards presuppose specific virtues that make possible the compliance with professional principles (even as rules may conflict, dilemmas arise and judgments are called for under conditions of uncertainty).

Within this context, teaching strategies to encourage ethical awareness and behavior that supplement the technical training for gathering evidence to assess accounting procedures and review mechanisms of internal control for a client should employ these two languages of duty and virtue (as expressed in the professional codes). The auditing curriculum will include practical means (lectures, guest speakers, dialogue and reading) for impressing upon students that their professional duties include learning the technical requirements (the rules and procedures) mandated by accounting and auditing standards. They will also learn to commit themselves to adhere to these principles and act in accordance with the rules (i.e., to adopt the standards as their professional ethical obligation). The student becomes aware of the ethics of duty. In addition to this process of becoming acquainted with the technical dimensions of accounting and in service to the goal of becoming a fully prepared professional, the classroom cases, discussions and decision-making exercises are the means through which the distinctive character virtues of the public accountant are fostered and the intellectual/moral skills of audit judgment are developed. The student should learn to discern ethical problems, resolve dilemmas and persistently act with right behavior, with honor and appropriate virtue. With this comprehensive approach, the student becomes acquainted with (indeed, imbued with) an ethics of duty and an ethics of virtue.

Doucet and Doucet (2004) elaborate on the close ties of an ethics of duty and an ethics of virtue, arguing that virtuous accountancy mandates both the aspects of a knowledge-driven sense of duty and the qualities of character that enable the professional to comply with the principles, rules and decision-making procedures of a specialized profession. In their presentation, the authors list and comment on a set of accounting/auditor virtues. Their presentation places these scholars within the community of discourse into which the Cheffers and Pakaluk (2005) book and several of the journal articles already mentioned have also been drawn (Libby & Thorne, 2004, 2007; Melé, 2005; Mintz, 1995, 1996, 2006).

Each of these scholarly treatments presupposes the specialized tasks of the accounting profession. All of them emphasize the responsibilities of public service for which virtuous behavior is crucial to the fulfillment of public expectations. We appreciate the discussion in the scholarly literature and support every effort to identify the relevant virtues and distinctive tasks of accounting practice. In a word, we also place ourselves within this community of discourse, a conversation that not only emphasizes the twofold obligation of accountants to be technically proficient and ethically sensible but also focuses on the special moral tradition of virtue ethics as a key component of influence on accounting education. In our own accounting ethics courses, we have discussed at length accountants' and auditors' virtues, the character traits and learned skills that guide their practice (in addition, one of us devotes much attention in her auditing and fraud courses to this topic). Accordingly, we might well have contributed our own list of virtues within the current study. However, we will take a slightly different track. Rather than present a lengthy list of virtues and elaborate on them, the chapter will follow the pattern of presentation of Doucet and Doucet (2004). Their study concentrated on identifying several distinctive virtues of public accounting in the published principles of the profession, specifically those traits highlighted in several codes of professional conduct promulgated in Canada and the United States of America. To be sure, Doucet and Doucet (2004) do include a lengthy list of duties and virtues relevant to accounting. These, among others, include self-discipline, expertise (both technical and ethical forms), capacity to maintain independence and objectivity (to be impartial, intellectually honest and free of conflicts of interest) and conscientiousness (right actions and consideration of the moral rules and requirements of the particular community in which one lives and functions) (Doucet & Doucet, 2004).

The listing, however, plays a secondary role in the article. The core of their argument has to do with how particular virtues (indeed, the whole set of the virtues they treat) can be construed both as professional duties (as external expectations, the norms, that are codified in codes of conduct and published principles) and as intellectual and moral traits that are critical components of the accountant's character. These duties are to be performed and the intellectual and moral traits expressed/realized as the skills and virtues that mark the conscientious behavior of the accountant actions performed in accordance with the norms of the profession.

Reviewing three codes of conduct, the AICPA Code, the ICAO Code and the CGA Code, Doucet and Doucet (2004) present a digest of traits which they label as those of the 'conscientious accountant'. This well-trained and publicly oriented professional thinks and behaves in a conscientious fashion: he or she performs accounting tasks by working within the expectations of professional life – manifesting expertise, courage and integrity. Shaped by the distinctive demands of a specialized community, accountants do their duty by being competent both in technical decision-making and in making ethical choices, by unswerving commitment to honorable actions and by persistently demonstrating the intent to do the right thing and to resist pressures to seek personal advantage at the expense of others (Doucet & Doucet, 2004). This treatment, with its review of particular sections of these three professional codes, anticipates the teaching strategies employed by us in our own lectures and classroom discussions. In the classroom setting, we define or characterize the accountant/auditor virtues by direct reference to pertinent sections of the professional codes. Elaboration and commentary clarify these codified expressions, and class discussion includes case studies and student–teacher dialogue regarding accounting situations in which specific virtues come into play. Like the article by Doucet and Doucet (2004), our classroom interaction treats the codes of professional conduct and the virtues they highlight as the standards for accounting practice; that is, as the norms and guidelines for individuals and firms and whenever financial transactions are examined, accountants produce financial statements and auditors review them. To illustrate this approach to professional duty and accountant virtue, we discuss auditor independence and integrity in the following section and show how these concepts can be illuminated through consideration of four short case studies.

5.1. Auditor Independence

Doucet and Doucet (2004) referred to Canadian and USA standards and codes of conduct as they discussed the relationships between the principles of the accounting profession (auditing, in particular) and the character traits (virtues) vital for the practice of accounting and audit decision-making. In a similar way, in our auditing and accounting ethics courses, we explore this relationship in lecture and discussion with our students. As teachers who prepare students to work in a variety of international settings, we use international standards to describe and elaborate on particular principles. We emphasize specific educational processes that convey distinct virtues to the students – auditor independence, objectivity and professional integrity. Our classroom presentations emphasize that the professional standards are realized because of the character traits (virtues) learned by accounting professionals. These virtues are learned through formal education, classwork practice in problem-solving and ethics decision-making, and on the job professional experience. This process makes possible the accountant/auditor's adherence to principles and enhances the capacity to employ judgment to follow principles-based rules and procedures. In the following paragraphs, we develop a treatment especially pertinent to audit education.

First, let us consider the principle of auditor independence and the rules associated with this principle as important professional duties to be affirmed by auditing students. The independence requirement is critical to the auditing profession. This mandates a primary professional responsibility of the auditor. The professional code expresses this in several ways.

International Independence Standards included in Section 400 of the International Code of Ethics for Professional Accountants requires the auditor to be independent in mind and in appearance. This principle is described in detail in Section 400.5 of the code of ethics. The code requires firms to comply with the fundamental principles and be independent when performing audit engagements. It is in the public interest that professional accountants in public practice be independent when performing audit engagements. Auditor independence is intended to ensure that stakeholders can trust the opinions issued by auditors and that the financial information given in the financial statements will be valuable to outsiders and the public because it is reliable.

In the classroom, the lectures and the discussions can treat the principle of auditor independence and the rules associated with such independence. The teacher might lecture about the importance of independence for outsiders, emphasizing that the interests of the auditor must be separate from those of the client. In this context, the lecturer might elaborate on several relationships that will impair auditor independence. Referencing the international principles and several specific rules, the lecturer-discussion leader should clarify the concept – define and elaborate on its components. The lectures might include examples of auditor decision-making and highlight specific audit tasks where the issue of independence is demonstrated to be especially significant. The lecturer might call attention to the complexities faced by audit firms that perform non-audit client services, even as these firms make complex audit decisions for that same client. Descriptions of other types of pressure and forms of conflicts of interest can be treated in classroom discussions.

Given that the international regulations interpret the principle of independence through elaborations of specific rules, the teacher-mentor might select a couple of these rules and point out how they apply to specific aspects of the auditor–client relationship or specific choices that are made in the process of conducting an audit. In these ways, the teacher can illuminate the rationale for adhering to the principle of independence and show the importance of following specific rules for the sake of maintaining stakeholders' trust in the audit. Knowledge and ethical sensibility gained through these presentations may even become a means of self-protection for the auditor himself, because this sensibility encompasses technical and ethical awareness as buttresses against business-related pressures or even institutional pressures originating in the audit firm.

For example, two serious relationships that impair independence occur (1) when the auditor has a financial interest in the client or (2) receives or pays contingent fees or commissions to the client. In the second situation, independence is impaired if the auditor has any direct financial interest in the client or a material indirect financial interest in the client. A direct financial interest includes stock ownership or a loan to or from a client. This means that the auditor (plus his or her spouse and dependent children) cannot own even one share of stock of the client business. In addition, an indirect financial interest in the client might occur if the auditor has a financial interest in a company associated with the audit client. To impair independence, the indirect financial interest must be material. In a third example, independence is also impaired if the auditor provides a service or a product to the client for a contingent fee or a commission or receives from the client a contingent fee or commission.

Students can read about the independence principle and find the rules in publications of the standards, described in an auditing textbook or in handouts distributed to the students. In the professional codes, the independence principle and rules are very brief (less than one-page total), but the interpretations are very long (more than 100 pages, with much more detail than can easily be grasped). Because of this, reading in and of itself may not be helpful to students. Their efforts can be supplemented with case studies and discussions by the teachers (with their extensive knowledge of the rules). In the following, we outline some cases that should be helpful.

Note that in the following cases all the written questions assume the student will refer to the standards, the Codes of Conduct, for the statements about the principle of auditor independence and the interpretation of the principles offered by the rules. The students will allude to this material as they identify the salient features of the accounting situation and grapple with the elements of the technical and ethical dilemmas that constitute their classroom challenge. They will determine which definitions, interpretations or rules are appropriate to the situation. If classroom discussion is used, reference to these materials will be a central feature of the students' explanations, arguments and justifications that they share among their peers.

Case One Ernst & Young Violations of Independence Rules

The US Securities and Exchange Commission (SEC) charged Ernst & Young with ethics code violations for engaging in lucrative business deals with an audit client. Ernst & Young had entered into a marketing arrangement with PeopleSoft to sell and install People-Soft software. Under the agreement, Ernst & Young agreed to pay royalties to PeopleSoft of 15–30% for each software sale, with a minimum guaranteed payment of $300.000. During the time of this agreement, Ernst & Young served as the auditor for PeopleSoft. In the audit firm's summary of the SEC decision, the spokesperson emphasized the SEC position that an auditor can't be in business to jointly generate revenues with an audit client without impairing independence (Schroeder & Paltrow, 2002). Ernst & Young vigorously contested the charges saying that its work for PeopleSoft was appropriate and permissible under the profession's rules and the company did harm its client, its shareholders, or the investing public. In addition, the Ernst & Young spokesperson asserted that the SEC did not find any error in the audits or in any of its client's financial statements that may have resulted from these audits.

Questions

1) Evaluate the statement made by Ernst & Young that they did nothing wrong because no one was harmed. Is this an appropriate defense against a claim of lack of independence?
2) Develop an argument supporting the SEC's statement; that is, explain why the joint production of revenue by auditor and client is an impairment of independence. Why might outsiders be concerned about such a relationship?

Case Two PricewaterhouseCoopers Independence Rule Violations

The SEC settled an independence case with PricewaterhouseCoopers (PwC) in July 2002. The case found that from 1996 to 2001, PwC engaged in contingent fee arrangements with 14 public companies. In each instance, the client hired the audit firm's investment bankers to perform financial advisory services for a fee that was based on the success of the services. PwC agreed to pay the SEC $5 million and to provide independence training to all PwC professionals.

Questions

1) Does this arrangement impair independence?
2) Explain why outsiders might find this arrangement to be a problem.
3) If the partners in charge of the audits were not themselves directly involved in the consulting services, would this be sufficient to ensure that independence is not impaired? Discuss (Consider 'independence in appearance').

5.2. The Auditor Virtue of Integrity

Within the auditing course, special attention should be given to the distinctive auditor virtue of integrity. Section 111 of the Code of Professional Conduct published by the AICPA requires the auditor to perform all professional responsibilities with the highest sense of integrity. In this blending of ethics languages, the virtue of auditor integrity is also the professional duty of public accounting. Section 111 requires the professional accountant to comply with the principle of integrity, which requires an accountant to be straightforward and honest in all professional and business relationships. This pattern of thought and behavior is a regulatory ideal for the professional. It constitutes the norm for decision-making, for the interaction of auditor and client, review of financial statements and issuance of audit opinions.

In virtue ethics language as employed by Doucet and Doucet (2004), auditor integrity is a complex moral virtue. In their treatment, the virtue includes the moral agent's being (1) 'objective' – open-minded in considering evidence and relevant information, as well as fair-minded – impartial with regard to the interests of various stakeholders; (2) the auditor is also supposed to be 'independent'; (3) the public accountant must act with 'due care' – that is, be technically knowledgeable about accounting standards and auditing methods of gathering and assessing evidence – due care encompasses the demand for auditor persistence in disciplined and diligent effort in the performance of official duties; (4) the auditor will have the intent to do the right and just thing without regard to 'personal gain an advantage'. These four expectations presuppose the capacity to subordinate one's own interests and ambitions in order to serve a client and, most importantly, to serve public interest. They constitute a duty 'to do the right thing for the right reason', resist pressures and the temptations of self-interest and, in complex situations, to follow the spirit of the virtue of integrity and not merely the rules as stipulated in the codes (Doucet & Doucet, 2004).

The principle of auditor integrity and the aspects of character that constitute it as a distinctive virtue are crucial for the auditing profession. The foregoing discussion suggests the complexity of integrity as a concept of virtue and a practical duty. Moreover, an adequate treatment of integrity as a moral virtue and a professional duty necessitates a discussion of the idea of practical judgment (see Section Practical Judgment: The Capacity to Act Virtuously and to Manage Stakeholders). This is because acting with integrity presupposes the intellectual capacity to discern right from wrong in a given circumstance. The auditor must both know the principles and the rules of the profession and have an adequate grasp of how normal human beings might behave in business circumstances. These are necessary preconditions for doing the right thing in an accounting or auditing situation, for acting virtuously as an auditor.

Given the complex task of teaching students to affirm professional duties, exercise practical judgment and demonstrate appropriate virtues in complicated situations, how might the auditing instructor deal with this principle in the classroom? One cannot simply tell students to read about the principle and advise them to act with integrity. The auditing course should go beyond reading and lecture to engage students in practical exercises. Experience-oriented techniques should be employed to give students opportunity to discern right from wrong in auditing situations, to acknowledge the types of stakeholder pressure that can impair independence and to encounter conflicts of interest that challenge decision-making objectivity. Real-world cases and supervised discussions of regulators' decisions may well afford such learning. In virtue ethics language, these techniques allow for mentored, interactive teaching moments through which virtues can be acquired, ethical habits formed and the distinctive character of the virtuous auditor developed. The following cases are designed to achieve such goals.

Case Three Internal Control at the United Parcel Service (UPS)

Michelle LaRue recently visited the UPS office in Washington, DC, to mail a package to her sister in Norway. The UPS employee opened the box that was addressed for mailing, looked at the packages inside, re-taped the box and then accepted the box for mailing. LaRue asked her what she was looking for. The UPS clerk replied that she did not know but her supervisor had told her to open and search all boxes before they were accepted.

Questions

1) Considering the employee's response to the question about what she was looking for, is anything wrong with this internal control procedure? Explain your answer.

---

2) Assume that the control required the employee to initial the mailing invoice after performing the control. The auditor has reviewed a sample of invoices and found no deviations. All forms included the UPS clerk's initials. What would the auditor assume about the control?
3) How would the auditor consider the principle of integrity in making this decision?
4) Consider the integrity rule that is part of the international code of conduct requiring the auditor to be straightforward and honest in all professional and business relationships. If the auditor followed this rule, what would be his or her decision about the internal control described in the case?

Case Four Johnson Chemicals

Jeff Clairmont, the controller for Johnson Chemicals, has just received a notice from the Environmental Protection Agency (EPA) regarding the cleanup of the Mendota Heights Toxic Disposal Site. The cleanup is scheduled to begin next year and to last for five years. Estimated costs of the cleanup are $958 billion. Johnson Chemicals will be charged a share of the cleanup to represent their dumping activity over the past fifty years. This is estimated to be $748 million and it may go much higher. Jeff knows the accounting standards require the company to record a provision for loss if the expense associated with the clean-up is likely and the amount is known. If only one condition is present, the disclosure may be appropriate. The chief financial officer, Jennifer Ordahl, suggests ignoring the potential liability until the actual charges are received in a bill from the EPA. At most, Jennifer suggests using footnote disclosure to indicate the potential liability.

Questions

1) Is anything wrong with this proposal to delay the recording of the liability? Explain your answer. Why does the audit client want to delay recording the liability? Why might the auditor disagree?
2) Consider the integrity requiring the auditor to be straightforward and honest in all professional and business relationships. What decision will Clairmont make to comply with this requirement?

As these tasks have been discussed (presenting the concepts of auditor independence and auditor integrity, sketching the strategies for developing the virtue within students and persuading them to affirm the principle as their professional duty, whereas supporting their exercise of a knowledge-based and ethics-discerning judgment), this section of the study has illustrated the main idea of Doucet and Doucet (2004). That study had claimed that the two languages of duty and virtue come into play in the auditing training program. We also affirm this position by treating the codified material on the principle and the rules of auditor independence in relation to the virtue of integrity (along with the subsidiary virtues of objectivity, professional competence and due care, confidentiality and professional behavior). All these virtues, in fact, have a place in the three codes examined by Doucet and Doucet (2004). With this close correspondence of codified expectations and this specific group of acquired virtues, we can – with those scholars – assert that accountants do indeed make decisions within a framework of an ethics of duty and an ethics of virtue.

The present study argues as well that the intellectual virtue of practical judgment should be addressed in the auditing classroom. Most importantly, we have shown that our approach to classroom presentations and discussion and the employment of other teaching strategies support the pedagogical goal of fostering the auditor's dual competency of technical proficiency and ethical sensibility. Finally, we have highlighted a particular tradition of moral philosophy in relation to accounting practice, the tradition of virtue ethics. In virtue ethics language, the auditing course should provide a practically oriented educational effort to form virtuous habits in auditing students through supervised decision-making, dialogue and reflection, within an experiential, interactive and mentored learning environment.

6. Conclusion

As we have seen, the particular strategies seek not only to teach about ethics but also to facilitate the students' adoption of the principles of public accounting – in their technical and ethical dimensions – as their professional responsibilities. In accordance with a virtue ethics approach to learning, the students engage in practical exercises, within a learning community – under the supervision of an exemplary mentor – in order to have successful experiences of complying with principles and following rules. They are also able to acquire virtues through habit formation, subsequently realizing these distinctive traits whenever their skills of practical judgment enable discernment of right from wrong and direct the appropriate virtues into activity that fits complex accounting or auditing situations.

The present study highlighted the principle of auditor independence, illustrated key features of the virtue of auditor integrity (and its close associations with the distinctive auditor virtues of independence, objectivity and due care) and asserted the necessity of practical judgment for discernment of right and wrong. In expressing these views, the study affirms the insight of Doucet and Doucet (2004) that the languages of an ethics of duty and an ethics of virtue are integral to understanding and affirming the ethical obligations of public accounting. Calling attention to a variety of teaching techniques, the chapter argues that technical skills, the intellectual and the moral virtues and practical judgment are crucial for compliance to professional duty. It further asserts that these crucial virtues can be acquired through a rich and varied classroom experience. Such learning can be gained through a combination of individualized study and cooperative learning, by reading and listening to lectures and through dialogical methods that call for knowledge of accounting and auditing standards and the exercise of practical judgment. These efforts should make use of the supervision of mentors and reflective engagement with peers. This mix of teaching strategies has as its main goal the successful realization of specific virtues in decision-making and the dutiful compliance with accounting and auditing standards. Thus, the classroom strategies anticipate a future of professional activity. The auditing course will set students on the path of both knowing their technical and moral obligations and motivating them to act as virtuous auditors – to serve the public and their clients by acting ethically.

This chapter's suggested framework for an auditing course, with its treatment of the basic elements of the learning situation and specific teaching strategies, emerges from a generation of scholarly discussions about virtue ethics and professional duty. This treatment supports an educational enterprise designed to introduce students to a principle-oriented, rule-guided professional practice. By learning the principles, examining the rules of public accounting and benefiting from an educational environment that fosters character virtues and emphasizes the exercise of practical judgment, auditing students will be well equipped for their task of professional service to stakeholders and the public.

References

American Institute of Certified Public Accountants (AICPA). (1997). *Code of Professional Conduct*. New York, NY: AICPA.

Aristotle. (1985). *Nicomachean Ethics* (Trans. T. Irwin). Indianapolis, IN: Hackett Publishing Company.

Armstrong, M. B., Ketz, J. E., & Owsen, D. (2003). Ethics Education in Accounting: Moving Toward Motivation and Ethical Behavior. *Journal of Accounting Education, 21*(1), 1–16.

Certified General Accountants Association of Canada (CGAAC). (1994). *Code of Ethics and Rules of Professional Conduct*. Burnaby: CGAAC.

Cheffers, M. L., & Pakaluk, M. (2005). *A New Approach to Understanding Accounting Ethics: Principles, Professionalism, Pride*. Manchaug: Allen David Press.

Dolfsma, W. (2006). Accounting as Applied Ethics: Teaching a Discipline. *Journal of Business Ethics, 63*(3), 209–215.

Doucet, M., & Doucet, T. A. (2004). Ethics of Virtue and Ethics of Duty: Defining the Norms of the Profession. In C. Jeffrey (Ed.), *Research on Professional Responsibility and Ethics in Accounting, 9* (pp. 147–168). Bingley: Emerald Group Publishing.

Dunne, J. (1999). Virtue, Phronesis and Learning. In D. Carr & J. Steutel (Eds.), *Virtue Ethics and Moral Education* (pp. 51–65). London: Routledge.

Freeman, R. E. (1984). *Strategic Management: A Stakeholder Approach*. Boston, MA: Pitman.

Gaffikin, M. (2007). *Accounting Theory and Practice: The Ethical Dimension*. Retrieved May 25th, 2020, from https://ro.uow.edu.au/cgi/viewcontent.cgi?article=1001&context=accfinwp

Institute of Chartered Accountants of Ontario (ICAO). (1995). *Rules of Professional Conduct*. Ontario: ICAO.

Jennings, M. (2004). Incorporating Ethical and Professionalism into Accounting Ethics and Research. *Issues in Accounting Education, 19*(1), 7–26.

Kohlberg, L. (1981). *The Philosophy of Moral Development: Moral Stages and the Idea of Justice (Vol.1): Essays on Moral Development*. San Francisco: Harper & Row.

Lave, J., & Wenger, E. (1991). *Situated Learning: Legitimate Peripheral Participation*. Cambridge: University of Cambridge Press.

Levy, D., & Mitschow, M. (2008). Accounting Ethics Education: Where Do We Go From Here? In C. Jeffrey (Ed.), *Research on Professional Responsibility and Ethics in Accounting, 13* (pp. 135–154). Bingley: Emerald Group Publishing.

Libby, T., & Thorne, L. (2004). The Identification and Categorization of Auditors' Virtue. *Business Ethics Quarterly, 14*(3), 479–498.

Libby, T., & Thorne, L. (2007). The Development of a Measure of Auditors' Virtue. *Journal of Business Ethics, 71*(1), 89–99.

Low, M., Davey, H., & Hooper, K. (2008). Accounting, Scandals, Ethical Dilemmas and Educational Challenges. *Critical Perspectives on Accounting, 19*(2), 222–254.

MacIntyre, A. (1984). *After Virtue: A Study in Moral Theory* (2nd ed.). Notre Dame: Notre Dame University Press.

Melé, D. (2005). Ethical Education in Accounting: Integrating Rules, Values, and Virtues. *Journal of Business Ethics, 57*(1), 97–109.

Mintz, S. (1995). Virtue Ethics and Accounting Education. *Issues in Accounting Education, 10*(2), 247–267.

Mintz, S. (1996). The Role of Virtue in Accounting Education. *Accounting education, 1*, 67–91.

Mintz, S. (2006). Accounting Ethics Education: Integrating Reflective Learning and Virtue Ethics. *Journal of Accounting Education, 24*(2/3), 97–117.

Mitchell, R. K., Agle, B. R., & Wood, D. J. (1997). Toward a Theory of Stakeholder Identification and Salience: Defining the Principle of Who and What Really Counts. *Academy of Management Review, 22*(4), 853–886.

Rest, J. R. (1994). Background: Theory and Research. In J. R. Rest & D. F. Narvaéz (Eds.), *Moral Development in the Professions: Psychology and Applied Ethics* (pp. 1–26). Hillsdale: Lawrence Erlbaum Associates.

Saugstad, T. (2002). Educational Theory and Practice in an Aristotelian Perspective. *Scandinavian Journal of Educational Research, 46*(4), 373–390.

Schroeder, M., & Paltrow, S. J. (2002). *SEC Says Ernst & Young Violated Independence Rules in Past Audit.* Retrieved November 6th, 2020, from www.wsj.com/articles/SB1021926901265500280

Stuart, B., Stuart, I., & Pedersen, L. J. T. (2011). *Accounting Discourse: Technical Proficiency and Ethical Sensibility.* Unpublished Manuscript, Norwegian School of Economics, NHH, Bergen, NOR.

Thorne, L. (1998). The Role of Virtue in Auditors' Ethical Decision-Making: An Integration of Cognitive-Developmental and Virtue-Ethics Perspectives. *Research in Accounting Ethics, 4,* 291–308.

Wilks, T. J., & Zimbelman, M. F. (2004). Decomposition of Fraud-Risk Assessments and Auditors' Sensitivity to Fraud Cues. *Contemporary Accounting Research, 21*(3), 719–745.

Williams, P. (2010). The Focus of Professional Ethics: Ethical Professionals or Ethical Profession? In C. Jeffrey (Ed.), *Research on Professional Responsibility and Ethics in Accounting, 14* (pp. 15–35). Bingley: Emerald Group Publishing.

4   Accounting Ethics in the Undergraduate Curriculum and the Impact of Professional Accreditation

Christopher J. Cowton

1. Introduction

The discussion on how to increase accounting ethics education is not new. Some of the debates about requiring ethics coverage, developing class materials and ensuring that faculty are capable of teaching it have going on for decades (Loeb & Rockness, 1992). Unfortunately, there has been "insufficient action and progress to date", despite several initiatives (Boyce, 2014, p. 535).

There are many topics contained in it, but the literature on accounting ethics education can be positioned in at least two complementary ways. On the one hand, it can be viewed as a significant strand within the literature on accounting ethics, with a quarter of the journal articles reviewed by Bampton and Cowton (2013) falling within education. From this perspective, ethics education offers the prospect of more ethical accounting practice. On the other hand, accounting ethics education can be positioned within the context of accounting education more generally. Framed in this way, it can be viewed as part of an attempt to provide a more rounded accounting education that eschews an over-emphasis on techniques – with a view to improved graduate skills upon entering employment.

The realization of such positive prospects for ethical accounting practice depends on many factors, including how ethics is positioned in the curriculum (e.g., level; standalone versus integrated), what is covered (content) and how it is taught and assessed. There are thus many variables to be understood and much sharing of good practice to be done if accounting ethics education is to be effective. Some signs of progress are apparent (this book and its contents being one), but if full potential is to be achieved there still remains the logically prior challenge of finding space in the curriculum for accounting ethics. Despite long-standing concerns about the narrowness of the education that accounting students receive, it seems that techniques still tend to dominate. One way of summing this up might be to say that, whereas the supply of accounting ethics education material and insights has improved encouragingly, there still seem to be significant barriers, resistance or reluctance on the demand side. Ethics does not get the time and space in the curriculum that proponents would advocate.

This chapter is concerned with the inclusion of ethics as a core component of undergraduate accounting programs, by which I mean not only that it is compulsory for students to study it but that it has significant time devoted to it. I will not determine what 'significant' might be; I simply take it that this will tend to be considerably more than is usually the case now and that its realization would tend to encounter noticeable resistance from at least some quarters. Indeed, the appearance of resistance might be a good sign that the time proposed to be devoted to ethics really amounted to being significant.

The chapter is thus not concerned with what should or can be covered when accounting ethics is taught (cf. Armstrong, 1993; Sims, 2000) or how it is taught, although some comments are made on this toward the end. Nor will I debate whether ethics coverage should be provided as a standalone component, integrated into other elements of the program, or both (Armstrong, 1993; cf. Dunfee & Robertson, 1988) – although I should state that my preference is for the latter. I will also not consider how accounting education is assessed, although this undoubtedly drives learning. Furthermore, I will simply take it as given that accounting ethics education is, in general, a 'good thing'; in other words, my primary concerns is not with why accounting ethics should be taught in undergraduate programs – although I will consider, in a subsequent section, arguments as to why it should not be, drawing heavily on Bampton and Maclagan (2005).

Instead, in the light of a perception that ethics coverage is currently insufficient, I will consider how the incorporation of ethics can be encouraged and achieved. Whereas several barriers are identified, I am particularly interested in the way in which programs are influenced by the demands that the accounting profession is said to place upon them. Accreditation of university courses by professional accountancy bodies is a defining feature of accountancy education in many countries and this has often been blamed for constraining undergraduate programs to such an extent that an overly 'technical' focus tends to result, with limited opportunity to develop ethics or other 'soft' skills. However, I will argue that this reason – or excuse, perhaps – highlights the possibility that professional bodies could act as powerful influencers in favor of ethics coverage in the curriculum; and, further, I suggest that there is reason to suppose that it is in their interests to do so. I make many of the points with undergraduate accounting education in the United Kingdom in mind, but, based on the extant literature, I believe that the core of the argument is very likely to apply in many other countries too.

The remainder of the chapter develops and elaborates the argument in three main sections. The next section reviews contentions that the undergraduate accounting curriculum is typically too narrow, with accreditation widely blamed for this state of affairs. The section also provides some background information on accounting education in the United Kingdom. The following section then reviews the main reasons for not incorporating ethics in the curriculum, including the 'excuse' that it is not possible in practice because of the constraints of accreditation and all the technical knowledge that must be covered. The third main section explores the possibility that it is, in fact, possible to provide coverage of ethics within an accredited program, although it is admitted that the scope is likely to be limited. The final main section then finds in accreditation the possible solution to the problem that it is said to cause. The conclusion section summarizes the key points.

2. The Narrowness of Accounting Education

Accounting education takes place in many different ways across the world, but in general there are two elements, which can take the form of different stages. The first might be described as the 'pre-professional' (Flood, 2014) or 'academic' component, where students typically study for a degree. For the purposes of my argument, the second might be termed the 'professional' training stage, at which aspiring accountants take examinations required by professional bodies. The first component typically takes place within a higher education context.

The pattern for accounting education and training varies enormously from one jurisdiction to another (Wilson, 2011), including the distinction between academic and professional elements. The distinction is probably more pronounced in the United Kingdom, where the two elements have remained "resolutely separate" (King & Davidson, 2009, p. 261), albeit with partial integration through a system of accreditation and exemptions. The United Kingdom is also probably unusual in the variety of routes to professional qualification. Whereas in some countries an accounting degree is the only route into the profession, in the United Kingdom some people take a full set of professional examinations without studying for a degree, a large proportion of graduates seeking to enter the profession have first studied some other subject at university (King & Davidson, 2009) and only a minority of graduate entrants have taken an accounting degree. For example, in 2018 less than 30% of students of the Institute of Chartered Accountants in England and Wales (ICAEW), at the time of registration as students, were graduates who held a 'relevant degree' in accounting (Financial Reporting Council, 2019). Indeed, the relationship between university accounting education and professional bodies – particularly between English universities and the prestigious ICAEW (Annisette & Kirkham, 2007) – is somewhat unusual and probably not as straightforward as in many other countries. However, many students who hope to enter the profession in due course do register on accounting degrees in the United Kingdom and the issues that affect the provision of ethics in the undergraduate curriculum in the United Kingdom appear to be similar to those in the United States of America and elsewhere.

Historically, because of its vocational nature and assumptions about what it involves, accounting has had a struggle for academic respectability or legitimacy as a degree subject (King & Davidson, 2009; Zeff, 1989). However, as an undergraduate degree program, even one focused on, or majoring in, a specific professional subject, it would be expected to offer an element of breadth, reflecting the liberal tradition of the modern, post-Newman university.

Unfortunately, however, the interface between academic education and professional training in accounting "has been a contentious issue over many decades" (Evans, 2014, p. 633). As Apostolou and Gammie (2014, p. 667) comment:

> Accounting educators have been highly critical of the influence that accreditation has on the content and assessment of modules in undergraduate accounting programs, highlighting the constraints of academic freedom in terms of curriculum content . . . and patterns of assessment.

Undergraduate curricula are typically aligned with the professional curriculum so that passing the university assessments can substitute for, or provide exemption from, a proportion of subsequent professional examinations. This is attractive to many students who have "instrumental expectations" (Hopper, 2013, p. 132), but it leads to an education that is widely regarded as unduly narrow. Hopper (2013, p. 128, emphasis added) expands on this: "Much accounting education overly inculcates technical skills and rote, rule-based learning; neglects theory (especially other than positive economics and agency theory), *ethics and morality* and is overly concentrated on the interests of private capital". It is not unusual to see ethics cited as an element in the desired broadening or liberalization of the accounting curriculum (Boyce, 2014).

Perhaps surprisingly, given the criticisms of an approach that seems to prioritize vocationalism over liberal education, undergraduate accounting programs have also been criticized for failing to provide an education that is appropriate to the needs of the profession and its future entrants. Flood (2014, p. 84) comments that "the failure to prioritize the development of the wide variety of skills required to survive in the dynamic professional work environment" has been widely remarked upon. Concern has been expressed that graduates do not possess the 'soft' skills, such as teamworking and communication skills, that employers seek (Albrecht & Sack, 2000; Apostolou & Gammie, 2014; Hassall, Joyce, Arquero Montano & Donoso Anes, 2003; Paisey & Paisey, 2004; Scribner, 1990; cf.

St. Pierre & Rebele, 2014). The general criticism is that, in focusing too much on the teaching and assessment of numerical techniques, the undergraduate accounting curriculum typically neglects to develop skills that are deemed essential to successful functioning in the workplace and a flourishing career. Various reasons are given for this state of affairs, such as faculty preferences and the lack of curriculum innovation, but accreditation is frequently an important element of the narrative. The demands of accreditation are believed to lead to an over-emphasis on technical aspects of the curriculum and tend to reduce opportunities for discussion and critical appraisal, made all the more challenging as the accounting profession, like many others, faces a 'knowledge explosion' (Paisey & Paisey, 2004), resulting in an even more overcrowded curriculum (Paisey & Paisey, 2007).

However, degrees offering professional exemptions are attractive to students – even in the United Kingdom, where the possession of an accounting degree is not necessary for subsequent professional qualification. Faculty feel compelled to offer 'what the market demands', particularly in the modern 'financialized' university (Parker, 2012, 2013). In such a context, the direction of pressure on the curriculum is reinforced by the growth of recruitment of international students who, if English is not their first language (or if they come from a different educational tradition), tend to prefer the more structured form and technical numerical content of assessment methods that are designed to satisfy professional requirements (Hopper, 2013).

In these criticisms of current accounting education, then, accreditation looms large. It is viewed, and objected to, as an oppressive constraint on the curriculum. Weetman (1979, p. 138) comments, in dramatic terms: "Degrees should not be sold into bondage to professional accounting training". Yet many critics have suggested that this is in effect what happens.

King and Davidson (2009) state that almost all United Kingdom institutions offering accountancy degrees participate in accreditation arrangements, a situation confirmed by Ellington and Williams (2017), who collected information from the websites of the professional accounting bodies. In follow-up interviews with academics, Ellington and Williams (2017) discovered that not all universities offered the same exemptions, because some professional bodies were considered to be of limited relevance to the type of student a university tended to recruit. However, most programs were well aligned with at least one professional body (usually more), so that students could maximize, or get close to maximizing, exemptions from professional examinations. Furthermore, interviews conducted with 18 accounting academics from a cross-section of 12 UK universities confirmed that

> accreditation is seen as essential for student recruitment to degree programmes and that it leads to degree programmes imitating professional

syllabi and examinations, resulting in technical content and didactic methods, which in turns crowds out broader educational activity . . . the consensus view is that accreditation constrains degree programmes leading to a missed opportunity to provide a wider liberal education.

(Ellington & Williams, 2017, p. 501)

In such a context, it is unsurprising that the teaching of ethics does not have a strong tradition and that it struggles to gain a foothold in the curriculum. As in the case of other apparently desirable 'soft' skills, the design of programs, predicated on the perceived desires of students for exemptions from professional examinations, means that accreditation is a problem for ethics. However, as the next section explains before returning to look at the issue of accreditation in a different way, there are also some other, very particular headwinds that accounting ethics faces.

3. Against Ethics

A very useful overview of the reasons typically proffered against the incorporation of ethics into the accounting degree curriculum is provided by Bampton and Maclagan (2005), who then proceed to set out reasons to refute the arguments of the 'skeptics'. Originating their paper in the research reported in Bampton and Cowton (2002a, 2002b) and drawing on more general business ethics sources where appropriate (e.g., McDonald & Donleavy, 1995), they pull together in a systematic manner the various arguments. They outline four objections – relating to relevance, necessity, effectiveness and responsibility – and then proceed to provide a response to each, which I will briefly summarize.

The first objection is that teaching ethics to accounting students is irrelevant because accountants do not face ethical issues, accounting being an objective process.

Bampton and Maclagan's (2005, p. 293) principal response is that this "reflects a naïve view of business and accounting practice" and flies in the face of many criticisms of accounting and auditing over the years – criticisms which, I might add, the profession has seen fit to respond to in various ways, even if there might still be more to do.

The second objection is that ethics is relevant, but teaching it is not necessary, because legal (and presumably other regulatory) frameworks, codes of ethics and the prior influence of family, church and other institutions in society are sufficient.

In response, Bampton and Maclagan (2005) comment that codes of ethics (and presumably legal and regulatory frameworks) are insufficient. Whether other influences – influences that might be expected to motivate and guide the application of laws and codes – can take up the slack is doubtful. Some observers might have a more pessimistic view of the general moral state of the community, but the key issue would appear to be that professional judgment is often required in the application of codes of ethics and other resources. "Such dilemmas cannot be resolved purely by reference to personal values any more than they can by adherence to codified principles" (Bampton & Maclagan, 2005, p. 294).

The third objection is that teaching ethics is ineffective; it will not change people's fixed views or disreputable behavior if they are so minded.

Bampton and Maclagan's (2005) response first notes that this objection makes an assumption about the aim of ethics education, which has in fact been subject to some debate and is characterized by a variety of goals. Indeed, Apostolou, Dull and Schleifer (2013) provide evidence on different objectives of ethics teaching, which is rarely, if ever, concerned with making students 'more ethical' in a direct way. For example, as Bampton and Maclagan (2005) comment, some would see a more appropriate aim as being to help 'well intentioned' people recognize and deal with moral issues and dilemmas arising at work – thus enabling them to exercise their professional judgment. Thus, the assessment of the effectiveness of an ethics course depends, at least in part, on what the aim is.

The fourth and final objection is that teaching ethics to accounting students is not a responsibility of universities or their staff anyway. This objection is often built on an assumption of unwarranted moralization.

According to Bampton and Maclagan (2005), such a viewpoint fails to appreciate the difference between inculcating particular moral values, which is likely to be considered inappropriate in most modern institutions, and training in systematic thinking and reasoning about ethics in the context of accounting. In principle, the latter permits students to bring their own moral values to the table and enhances the likelihood that they will be able to work them through in a professional context. Bampton and Maclagan (2005) view this as an important competence. It could also be noted that the opinion that teaching ethics to accounting students is not a responsibility of universities or their staff sits uneasily with many conceptions of what universities are for. It would certainly require an extended argument to say that they should not be permitted to do it. A comparison with a view that medical or healthcare ethics should not feature in the education of doctors is salutary.

Bampton and Maclagan (2005) not only outline and refute four 'objections' to, or arguments against, the incorporation of ethics into the accounting curriculum, but they also identify a further issue: that, for practical reasons, it is not possible to include ethics in the curriculum (Bampton & Maclagan, 2005). People who espouse this position are not – apparently – against the teaching of ethics in principle; it is simply a matter of facing up to the constraints encountered by accounting educators. Bampton and Maclagan (2005) call this the 'feasibility' issue. It is usually expressed as having insufficient time or space in the curriculum, which will be explored in greater depth in the next section.

4. Time and Space

Like other professions, accounting has experienced an explosion in its knowledge base, putting the academic curriculum under pressure (Paisey & Paisey, 2004, 2007). In her survey of the teaching of ethics in management accounting in the British Isles, Bampton found that lack of space in the curriculum was by far the most cited reason for not including ethics (Bampton & Cowton, 2002a). Similarly, Mintz (1990) found that demands on time in the curriculum was the most common reason for not covering ethics. According to Bampton and Maclagan (2005, p. 297), subjects claimed that "there were not enough teaching hours to include ethics, a problem exacerbated by the professional bodies' accreditation demands", which resonates strongly with the widespread belief, discussed earlier, that accreditation priorities severely narrow the accounting curriculum.

Bampton and Maclagan (2005) comment that such an explanation is often put forward by people who claim to be sympathetic to the teaching of ethics. However, this might at times be viewed as little more than an excuse. Bampton and Maclagan (2005, p. 293) suspect that it might be a cover for a more negative opinion or reluctance, which they signal by saying "if taken at face value" when referring to the feasibility issue. Be that as it may, Bampton and Maclagan (2005) accuse those who put forward such a view as failing to take ethics teaching seriously, effectively depicting it as a "luxury" (p. 297) that 'unfortunately' cannot be afforded when it comes to making room in the curriculum.

It should be acknowledged, however, that there are other desirable things to cover and those who object to the current narrowness of the accreditation-constrained accounting curriculum have identified plenty of candidates, as discussed earlier. This is not something that Bampton and Maclagan (2005, p. 297) explicitly consider, but presumably they believe that ethics trumps alternatives, and they do make the point: "If ethics is concerned with what is important in life, then why is it not treated as important in the curriculum?" Various answers to that rhetorical question might simply repeat the objections discussed in the previous section and be responded to accordingly, but one might also clarify or develop Bampton and Maclagan's (2005) point by observing that ethics is important not only in life in general but also in *professional* life. There are specific codes of ethics for accountants and the application of ethics is not necessarily straightforward, with professional judgment often required. This is a point I will come back to later.

Of course, some might continue to assert that, although it might be desirable, or a 'nice-to-have', there *really* is not enough time and space to cover ethics. Bampton and Maclagan's (2005) second counterargument to the question of feasibility is relevant here. It is less concerned with what *should* be the case (the view that ethics is important) than with what *can* be the case. In this regard, Bampton and Maclagan (2005) note that a significant minority of respondents to the first named author's survey did manage to include ethics in their teaching of management accounting, thus providing evidence that it is possible.

It should be admitted, however, that such coverage was generally not extensive. Indeed, according to Bampton and Cowton (2002a, p. 55), about half the claimed ethics coverage was 'implicit only'. This might be regarded as consistent with Fleming's (1996, p. 281) assertion that "where universities do cover ethics for accountants they do so in a peremptory manner". However, it does mean that some other respondents claimed to find opportunities for the explicit consideration of ethics. Again, however, this does not mean that coverage was extensive. Perhaps it was still a peripheral theme, maybe pursued in discussions and not contained in the formal syllabus and assessment exercises.

Nevertheless, the evidence does suggest that faculty can at least raise the question of ethics in an accredited module, which management accounting is very likely to have been. After all, it would be surprising, given the varied ways in which university faculty approach teaching ostensibly the same syllabus, if what happens in the classroom were so tightly prescribed that absolutely no opportunities to consider ethical facets of the topic at hand could be taken. Such ethics coverage has the advantage of 'integration', namely being directly related to the technical accounting content, although its scope might be limited not only by time available but also by whether students have received some specific teaching aimed at providing them with ethical skills and understanding. This would seem to be necessary for a reasonably thorough coverage of accounting ethics.

Bampton's research was concerned only with management accounting, but there might be room for a module devoted to accounting ethics or, at least, a module containing a significant component of ethics, even in accredited programs. It seems that exemptions do not necessarily take up the whole of the curriculum, even when maximized, and not all universities do actually maximize the exemptions offered anyway (Ellington & Williams, 2017). Indeed, there is evidence in the literature that some have successfully pursued the substantive teaching of accounting ethics (Apostolou et al., 2013; e.g., Armstrong, 1993; Dellaportas, 2006). They will have had to meet familiar challenges, such as developing their skills and discovering or creating appropriate teaching resources, but they must also have overcome the hurdle of finding time in the timetable. However, it has to be acknowledged that any spare space in the curriculum is quite likely to be devoted to optional modules; and, although an accounting ethics optional module would be desirable, including for developing a track record for the teaching of the subject, the prime concern of this chapter is with compulsory coverage.

In conclusion, there are grounds for arguing that it is possible to teach ethics even within programs that are accredited and provide a high number of professional exemptions. There is room for some agency. However, this is not to say that accreditation is not a serious constraint on the curriculum, so even where there is coverage of ethics, the amount is almost certain to be considerably less than ideal. Furthermore, ethics is in competition with other demands upon what space in the timetable is available. As Bampton and Maclagan (2005) say, when it comes to incorporating ethics into the curriculum, it may be a problem of motivation as much as anything and faculty might be motivated to use any significant discretion in the curriculum in other ways. If the problem is motivation, the solution to the problem might, perhaps surprisingly, lie in accreditation's ability to influence motivation, given that universities seem highly motivated to secure accreditation from professional bodies. I turn to the idea of hitching ethics to the accreditation agenda in the next section.

5. For Accreditation

For many commentators, the current impact of professional accreditation on the content of undergraduate accounting programs is malign, leading to a narrowing of students' education in a manner that is not only inconsistent with the liberal tradition of the university but also less than ideal for future employment and careers. The failure to incorporate ethics into the curriculum would appear to be one of the deleterious consequences of this situation – even where there might otherwise be positive attitudes toward ethics if feasibility is the issue.

Although the previous section suggested that there might be some scope for more ethics in the curriculum than is usually the case, thus far the tone of the chapter has tended to echo the negative tenor of commentary on the influence of accreditation on ethics education. However, if it is accepted that accreditation is a major barrier (if not the only one) to the inclusion of ethics in the curriculum, in this section I aim to flip the analysis, seeking to show that the problem contains the seeds of its solution. In effect, I wish to contend *for* accreditation – of the right sort.

The argument of the chapter can be summarized as follows:

- There is insufficient coverage of ethics in the undergraduate accounting curriculum.
- Accreditation is the dominant influence on the content of the undergraduate accounting curriculum.
- Therefore, to ensure its significant inclusion in the curriculum, ethics should feature appropriately in the requirements of accrediting bodies.

At one level, it might be possible to insert any desirable feature – such as teamwork or communication skills – that is currently squeezed out of the curriculum in the place of ethics in the aforementioned statements.

However, an exception can be made for ethics. In some ways this is allied to Bampton and Maclagan's (2005) 'importance' argument, which I glossed with a comment on *professional* ethics – but it goes deeper than this, by considering the nature of professions.

What makes an occupational group a profession is subject to considerable debate, but the literature (e.g., Abbott, 1988; Larson, 1977) tends to agree on the importance of the following characteristics (see Cowton (2009, 2019) for further details):

- There is a widely agreed and extensive specialist skill and knowledge base, the latter often of a relatively theoretical or abstract kind.
- Acquiring those skills and knowledge involves a long period of training, with formal certification of competence (usually involving written examinations) and, in some cases, some form of license to practice.
- The work entails the use of discretion and judgment, not just the application of rules (however complex) to routine circumstances.
- The occupational group enjoys a significant degree of independence and self-regulation, with control over the knowledge base, the setting of entry standards and criteria for membership and responsibility for the disciplining of members.
- There are often high levels of personal and financial reward.
- There is an expectation that the occupational group operates in the public interest, particularly by acting ethically – usually supported by an explicit ethical code.

There is a debate about the extent to which some professional groups live up to this characterization, but the crucial point is that this is what they are meant to be like. It would be very hard for any occupational group that enjoys, and seeks to protect, the benefits of professional status to object to being judged against the expectations expressed in the list of characteristics. That list has implications for the argument of this chapter.

First, ethics is an essential characteristic of a profession, so it should be reflected in the accounting curriculum. There seems to be no obvious reason to hold ethics back until the professional training stage and for professional bodies to accredit programs that do not take ethics seriously gives students a misleading impression of what accounting is, or should be, about as a professionally organized endeavor.

Second, in the list, ethics appears along with technical professional knowledge, whereas the other elements that many critics would like to see featuring in a less technically focused curriculum do not. This does not mean that those other elements should not be incorporated in the curriculum, but ethics has priority status.

This argument could have been made at any point since accredited degrees offering professional exemptions began to appear. However, whereas there has been mounting pressure on the technical content of the accounting curriculum (Paisey & Paisey, 2004), the accounting profession itself has also been paying increased attention to ethics in the past 20–30 years. (So much for the first objection identified by Bampton and Maclagan (2005) that there are no ethical issues in accounting!) There is no need to rehearse the reasons for this here, but there are two points that I would like to make. First, this reinforces the case for ethics to be included in accreditation. Neglecting to do so does nothing to enhance the credibility of the profession's attempts to repair its reputation. Second, the profession's activities around ethics have generated material that could be usefully studied by students on accounting programs. Codes of ethics are the most prominent examples of such material. Indeed, Apostolou et al. (2013) note that, where ethics is taught, it is common to include reference to a code of ethics.

However, just as some people are skeptical about professions (and accounting, for that matter!), so some commentators are skeptical about codes of ethics, whether professional or business codes. Perhaps they expect too much; a code might be necessary, but it is not sufficient (Webley & Werner, 2008). Perhaps they also misunderstand the nature of a code. The second objection to ethics addressed by Bampton and Maclagan (2005) was that teaching is unnecessary, partly because accountants have codes of ethics. This seems to imply that accountants can simply turn to their code, in the guise of a rulebook, and straightforwardly apply what they find there to their situation. However, the process of identifying, defining and resolving ethical dilemmas is much more complex than that, requiring professional judgment in a wide range of circumstances, which is why the American Institute of Certified Public Accountants' Code of Professional Conduct (AICPA, 1988) has become increasingly principles-oriented, as the International Ethics Standards Board for Accountants' Code of Ethics for Professional Accountants (IESBA, 2018) has always been. As well as providing plenty of material for students to learn, these codes, used constructively, offer a great deal of scope for thought and discussion. Such classroom activity does not preclude the possibility of critiquing the codes, however. Indeed, critique informed by a good understanding of what a code contains and how it can be used is likely to be of a much higher quality and of more value to the future reflective member of the profession than more general criticism or cynicism.

This is not to say that codes are the only things that should feature when accounting ethics is taught. As I said in the introduction, I do not want to examine in any detail the teaching of accounting ethics. The reference to codes of ethics merely shows that there is something to work with when professional bodies take ethics seriously in the accreditation of accounting programs.

Were this approach to be undertaken, professional accreditation would no longer be the enemy of ethics in the undergraduate accounting curriculum; it would be its champion. Once appropriately operational-ized, the feasibility issue would necessarily disappear. Time and space in the curriculum would simply have to be found. Traditional objections would fade away or be overruled, faculty developed and resources put in place. Accounting ethics would have arrived at last.

6. Conclusion

The desirability of incorporating ethics into the undergraduate curriculum has been recognized by at least some faculty for many years, but progress appears to have been limited. There are several objections to the inclusion of ethics, all of which can be met with reasonable counter-arguments, but there are also practical matters that impinge on the feasibility of dedicating a significant proportion of the curriculum to ethics. One of the key barriers is widely believed to be accreditation. Accreditation not only brings professional examination exemptions, much valued by students, but it also promotes an overwhelming focus on technical knowledge. This leads to a narrow curriculum in which time and space for ethics, along with other 'soft' skills, are largely squeezed out. Some room for ethics can be found, but it is likely to be limited and highly dependent on the efforts of enthusiastic faculty. If ethics is ever going to become well established in the curriculum on a widespread basis, it is going to require a considerable impetus to make it happen. Whereas accreditation is currently widely seen as a problem, its powerful influence means that it is also capable of providing the solution. The requirement of a significant presence for ethics in the curriculum for programs to gain accreditation would be consistent with professional bodies' status claims and the enhanced ethics agenda that they have been pursuing in recent years. It is time for such a development to occur.

I have written this chapter with undergraduate accounting education in the United Kingdom primarily in mind. I recognize that several features of accounting education in the United Kingdom are far from typical internationally, including the fact that people can embark upon professional qualification via multiple routes: without a degree, with a degree in accounting or with a degree in some other subject. This means that there is a very clear distinction between the higher education-based academic study of accounting and training for the examinations of professional bodies; yet even in the United Kingdom, accreditation is still felt by many to constrain severely the incorporation of ethics and other non-technical material into accounting degree programs. Therefore, the argument pro-pounded in this chapter is very likely to apply in many other countries, where there is often a tighter coupling between academic education and professional pre-qualification training. The bottom line is that, if there exists in a particular country an accounting profession that has, or could have, a significant influence over the content of the undergraduate accounting curriculum, it should use that influence and take responsibility for ensuring that ethics is adequately covered.

Finally, an assumption of this chapter is that professional bodies do not currently impose significant demands on undergraduate accounting programs to include ethics in the curriculum. Both the literature that bemoans the lack of ethics content in accounting education and that which laments the excessive focus on technical content imply that this is the case. Further work might subject this assumption to systematic verification and note any virtuous anomalies. However, perhaps a broader focus with a more transformative mission would be more valuable: namely, to investigate what particular professional bodies say about their ethical responsibilities and commitments and, especially, how that is reflected in the syllabus and assessment practices for their qualification (with improvement where appropriate); and then to work through how that could and should be aligned with the accreditation requirements for elements of their qualification for which they grant exemptions to accounting graduates. If professional accounting bodies wish to take, and be seen to take, ethics seriously, this would be a worthwhile program of work for them. It is time for them to exercise their undoubted influence over the undergraduate accounting curriculum to promote the coverage of ethics in line with their professional mission and responsibilities. If they fail to do so, I expect that we will be having the same worthy, but largely unproductive, discussions about how to give ethics its due place in the curriculum, for many years to come.

Acknowledgments

I would like to acknowledge the contribution of previous collaboration and conversations with Roberta Bampton, Julie Drake, Abdulaziz Mosbah, Wilma Teviotdale and Alison Zimmer. All opinions and errors are my own.

References

Abbott, A. (1988). *The System of Professions*. Chicago, IL: Chicago University Press.

AICPA (American Institute of Certified Public Accountants). (1988). *Code of Professional Conduct*. New York: AICPA.

Albrecht, W. S., & Sack, R. J. (2000). *Accounting Education: Charting the Course Through a Perilous Future* (Accounting Education Series, Vol. 16). Sarasota, FL: American Accounting Association.

Annisette, M., & Kirkham, L. M. (2007). The Advantages of Separateness Explaining the Unusual Profession-University Link in English Chartered Accountancy. *Critical Perspectives on Accounting*, 18(1), 1–30.

Apostolou, B., Dull, R. B., & Schleifer, L. L. F. (2013). A Framework for the Pedagogy of Accounting Ethics. *Accounting Education*, 22(1), 1–17.

Apostolou, B., & Gammie, E. (2014). The Role of Accreditation in Accounting Education and Training. In R. M. S. Wilson (Ed.), *The Routledge Companion to Accounting Education* (pp. 652–672). Abingdon: Routledge.

Armstrong, M. B. (1993). Ethics and Professionalism in Accounting Education: A Sample Course. *Journal of Accounting Education*, 11(1), 77–92.

Bampton, R., & Cowton, C. J. (2002a). The Teaching of Ethics in Management Accounting: Progress and Prospects. *Business Ethics: A European Review*, 11(1), 52–61.

Bampton, R., & Cowton, C. J. (2002b). Pioneering in Ethics Teaching: The Case of Management Accounting in Universities in the British Isles. *Teaching Business Ethics*, 6(3), 279–295.

Bampton, R., & Cowton, C. J. (2013). Taking Stock of Accounting Ethics Scholarship: A Review of the Journal Literature. *Journal of Business Ethics*, 114(3), 549–563.

Bampton, R., & Maclagan, P. (2005). Why Teach Ethics to Accounting Students? A Response to the Sceptics. *Business Ethics: A European Review*, 14(3), 290–300.

Boyce, G. (2014). Ethics and Accounting Education. In R. M. S. Wilson (Ed.), *The Routledge Companion to Accounting Education* (pp. 533–557). Abingdon: Routledge.

Cowton, C. J. (2009). Accounting and the Ethics Challenge: Re-Membering the Professional Body. *Accounting and Business Research*, 39(3), 177–189.

Cowton, C. J. (2019). Professional Responsibility and the Banks. In C. Cowton, J. Dempsey, & T. Sorell (Eds.), *Business Ethics After the Global Financial Crisis: Lessons From the Crash* (pp. 106–126). New York: Routledge.

Dellaportas, S. (2006). Making a Difference With a Discrete Course on Accounting Ethics. *Journal of Business Ethics*, 65(4), 391–404.

Dunfee, T. W., & Robertson, D. C. (1988). Integrating Ethics Into the Business School Curriculum. *Journal of Business Ethics*, 7(11), 847–859.

Ellington, P., & Williams, A. (2017). Accounting Academics' Perceptions of the Effect of Accreditation on UK Accounting Degrees. *Accounting Education*, 26(5/6), 501–521.

Evans, E. (2014). The Interface Between Academic Education and Professional Training in Accounting. In R. M. S. Wilson (Ed.), *The Routledge Companion to Accounting Education* (pp. 632–651). Abingdon: Routledge.

Financial Reporting Council. (2019). *Key Facts and Trends in the Accountancy Profession October 2019*. Retrieved June 2nd, 2020, from www.frc.org.uk/getattachment/109373d4-abc2-424f-84d0-b80c2cec861a/Key-Facts-and-Trends-2019.pdf

Fleming, A. I. M. (1996). Ethics and Accounting Education in the UK – A Professional Approach? *Accounting Education*, 5(3), 207–217.

Flood, B. (2014). The Case for Change in Accounting Education. In R. M. S. Wilson (Ed.), *The Routledge Companion to Accounting Education* (pp. 81–101). Abingdon: Routledge.

Hassall, T., Joyce, J., Arquero Montano, J. L., & Donoso Anes, J. A. (2003). The Vocational Skills Gap for Management Accountants: The Stakeholders' Perspectives. *Innovations in Education and Teaching International*, 40(1), 78–88.

Hopper, T. (2013). Making Accounting Degrees Fit for a University. *Critical Perspectives on Accounting*, 24(2), 127–135.

IESBA (International Ethics Standards Board for Accountants). (2018). *International Code of Ethics for Professional Accountants*. Retrieved July 20th, 2020, from www.ethicsboard.org/iesba-code

King, R., & Davidson, I. (2009). University Accounting Programs and Professional Accountancy Training: Can UK Pragmatism Inform the Australian Debate? *Australian Accounting Review, 19*(3), 261–273.

Larson, M. S. (1977). *The Rise of Professionalism: A Sociological Analysis*. Berkeley, CA: University of California Press.

Loeb, S. E., & Rockness, J. (1992). Accounting Ethics and Education: A Response. *Journal of Business Ethics, 11*(7), 485–490.

McDonald, G. M., & Donleavy, G. D. (1995). Objections to The Teaching of Business Ethics. *Journal of Business Ethics, 14*(10), 829–835.

Mintz, S. M. (1990). Ethics in the Management Accounting Curriculum. *Management Accounting, 71*(12), 51–54.

Paisey, C., & Paisey, N. J. (2004). Professional Education and Skills: Liberalising Higher Education for the Professions in the United Kingdom. *Research in Post-Compulsory Education, 9*(2), 161–182.

Paisey, C., & Paisey, N. J. (2007). Balancing the Vocational and Academic Dimensions of Accounting Education: The Case for a Core Curriculum. *Journal of Vocational Education and Training, 59*(1), 89–105.

Parker, L. D. (2012). From Privatised to Hybrid Corporatised Higher Education: A Global Financial Management Discourse. *Financial Accountability & Management, 28*(3), 247–268.

Parker, L. D. (2013). Contemporary University Strategising: The Financial Imperative. *Financial Accounting & Management, 29*(1), 1–25.

Scribner, E. (1990). A Glimpse into an Accounting Department in the Year 2000. *Issues in Accounting Education, 5*(1), 143–145.

Sims, R. L. (2000). Teaching Business Ethics: A Case Study of an Ethics Across the Curriculum Policy. *Teaching Business Ethics, 4*(4), 437–443.

St. Pierre, E. K., & Rebele, J. E. (2014). An Agenda for Improving Accounting Education. In R. M. S. Wilson (Ed.), *The Routledge Companion to Accounting Education* (pp. 102–121). Abingdon: Routledge.

Webley, S., & Werner, A. (2008). Corporate Codes of Ethics: Necessary But Not Sufficient. *Business Ethics: A European Review, 17*(4), 405–415.

Weetman, P. (1979). Accounting Degrees: A Conflict of Objectives. *Accountancy, 137*(8), 137–138.

Wilson, R. M. S. (2011). Alignment in Accounting Education and Training. *Accounting Education, 20*(1), 3–16.

Zeff, S. A. (1989). Does Accounting Belong in The University Curriculum? *Issues in Accounting Education, 4*(1), 203–210.

5 Corporate Sustainability and Social Responsibility in the Accounting Profession

Educational Tools to Advance Accounting Ethics Education

Michael Kraten & Martin T. Stuebs, Jr.

1. Introduction

This chapter facilitates the integration of corporate sustainability (CS) and corporate social responsibility (CSR) topics into accounting ethics education. First, it connects foundational ethical concepts and theories to related CS and CSR concepts and tools. Then it applies the CS and CSR measurement tools to a case analysis, supplemented by brief historical references to other historical events.

Currently, the global impact of the novel Coronavirus Disease 2019 (COVID-19) is increasing the importance of companies' Environmental, Social and Governance (ESG) practices for stakeholders (Broughton & Sardon, 2020; McCabe, 2020). Indeed, investors are increasingly including desired improvements in companies' ESG practices to their standard lists of demands (Driebusch, 2020). As a result, CS and CSR reporting in the financial markets have emerged as an important mainstream practice (Boiral, Heras-Saizarbitoria & Brotherton, 2019).

Most accounting ethics curricula, however, narrowly focus on ethical reporting issues that involve financial accounting information and financial resource management. Little attention is given to the ethical issues that involve the measurement, management and reporting of data regarding the stewardship and management of nonfinancial, social and environmental resources. The current situation raises two important questions:

- At an individual level, how should the field of accounting ethics education expand to encompass contemporary topics, such as sustainability and corporate social responsibility and how should it improve the ethical development of accounting professionals?
- At an organizational level, what role should account functions play in enabling organizations, industries and the global economy to transform business practices to adapt to the evolving ethical demands of society?

The principle of stewardship relies on a fundamental ethic that assigns significant moral value to the responsible planning for (and management of) a wide variety of non-financial resources. In other words, stewardship does not solely focus on the generation of financial resources.

Indeed, corporate managers maintain stewardship responsibilities for their organizations' business resources. Likewise, all individuals (including, of course, all business personnel) have stewardship responsibilities for our environment's natural resources. Accountants vitally manage and steward informational resources, thereby supporting the activities of managers:

• Who serve in an administrative role by ensuring the efficient use of various nonfinancial, social and environmental assets.
• Who serve in an accountability role by addressing the effective and responsible use of those resources.

The relationship between the stewardship of resources by organizations and by individuals is presented in Figure 5.1. The purpose of Figure 5.1 is to establish the importance of:

• Broadening the scope of the accounting professional beyond its current focus on financial reporting information.
• Recognizing that the information generated by accounting professionals is necessary to lay the foundation for the successful stewardship of business and environmental resources and systems.

Ineffective stewardship functions, such as the mismanagement of resources, impose significant costs on organizations. Many unethical professionals, such as Enron Chief Financial Officer Andrew Fastow or

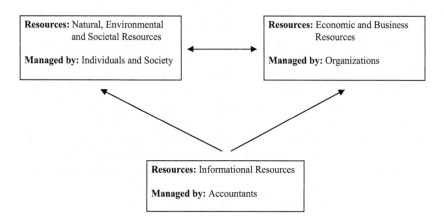

Figure 5.1 Management and Stewardship of Resources

Amaranth Advisors trader Brian Hunter, continue to take excessive risks whereas mismanaging business resources. Other stewardship disasters, such as the Exxon Valdez oil spill or BP's Deepwater Horizon oil spill, involve managers who continue to take excessive risks mismanaging environmental resources.[1] Both types of disaster, although, involve the mismanagement of informational resources, that is, the domain that is managed and stewarded by accountants. The significant costs that are produced by the mismanagement of business, environmental and informational resources highlight:

- The general importance of incorporating CS and CSR concepts into business education curricula.
- The specific importance of incorporating these concepts into accounting ethics education.

As a result, CS and CSR are now important issues in business and management (Sasse-Werhahn, Bachmann & Habisch, 2020); they are also legitimate areas of study and research in academia (Hahn, Figge, Aragón-Correa & Sharma, 2017). Because of the growing relevance of CS and CSR issues, many are now advocating for the integration of relevant topics into business school curricula (Montiel, Gallo & Antolin-Lopez, 2020; Painter-Morland, Sabet, Molthan-Hill, Goworek & de Leeuw, 2016). Nevertheless, although CS and CSR concepts can be integrated into accounting courses such as financial accounting and auditing (e.g., Kraten, Ryack, Sheikh & Simione, 2019), they may represent more natural 'fits' for integration into accounting ethics education courses. This chapter contributes to these efforts by exploring how CS and CSR topics can fit into and thus improve accounting ethics education.

First, at a conceptual level, we connect foundational moral development concepts (e.g., Kohlberg, 1969) and moral reasoning theories to related CS and CSR concepts, tools and frameworks. These connections assist accounting students by demonstrating that the same ethical principles and concepts that apply to accounting professionals at an individual level correspond to CS and CSR concepts at an organizational level.

Ethics is the study and pursuit of *eudaimonia*, or the well-lived, flourishing life. Certainly, all individuals should seek to develop professional and personal lives that are sustainable; by exploring how the underlying moral principles of accounting professionals are equivalent to related CS and CSR concepts, educators can convey the insight that the same general principles that contribute to an individual's sustainable professional flourishing will also contribute to an organization's sustainable business flourishing. Throughout this chapter, we refer to this insight as individual-organizational equivalence (IOE).

Second, at a practical level, we apply several common CS and CSR measurement tools to a case analysis, supplemented by the historical examples of Enron, Amaranth, Exxon and BP. Such exercises provide students with insight regarding the management of informational resources by challenging them to practice the application of CS and CSR. With such learning activities, educators can achieve an important goal of all curricula: to teach students to contribute to a sustainable, well-lived society, thereby achieving both individual and societal *eudaimonia*.

The remainder of this chapter is organized in the following manner. The next section connects the common moral development concepts and moral reasoning theories of accounting ethics education to corresponding CS and CSR concepts. It is a conceptual section that provides an understanding of and a basis for, the practical application of CS and CSR techniques. The following section presents four management accounting tools: a Triple Bottom Line analysis, a Sustainability Cube Analysis, a Balanced Scorecard Analysis and an Integrated Reporting Framework (IRF) analysis.[2] Next, these tools are applied to a pedagogical case entitled 'Save the Blue Frog!' (Kraten, 2015; case content presented at the 'Save the Blue Frog!' website).[3] Finally, a summary section concludes the chapter.

2. Connecting Ethical and Moral Concepts

2.1. Connecting Moral Development Concepts to Resource Management Development

Traditional approaches to accounting ethics education focus on improving students' moral judgment, reasoning and decision-making skills (Melé, 2005). This traditional approach is rooted in Kohlberg's (1969) theory of moral development; it identifies three primary levels of moral reasoning development:

- Pre-conventional moral reasoning, guided by economic, self-interested values
- Conventional moral reasoning, guided by values of compliance with social norms and legal standards
- Post-conventional moral reasoning, guided by natural laws, professional ideals and moral principles such as social justice.

The left-hand column of Table 5.1 presents these three primary levels.

The link between ethical concepts (such as wisdom and moral reasoning development) and CS and CSR topics has received considerable attention (Intezari, 2015; Marker, 2013; Roos, 2017; Xiang, 2016). Recently, Sasse-Werhan et al. (2020) link wisdom and moral reasoning development to the management of interdependent tensions and complexities regarding the economic, social and environmental resource demands that are placed on businesses (Gladwin, Kennelly & Krause, 1995; Schneider & Meins, 2012).

Table 5.1 Levels of Moral and Sustainable Resource Development

A Professional's Sustainable Moral Development	A Business' Sustainable Resource Management Development
Pre-conventional moral reasoning guided by economic, self-interested values	Economic resources
Conventional moral reasoning guided by values of compliance with social norms and standards	Social resources
Post-conventional moral reasoning guided by natural laws, professional ideals and moral principles	Environmental resources

The development of wisdom and of the decision-making skills that are required to manage an organization's economic, social and environmental resources correspond to Kohlberg's (1969) development of moral reasoning skills at pre-conventional, conventional and post-conventional levels. These connections are presented in the right-hand column of Table 5.1. The field of sustainability encompasses economic, sociocultural and environmental considerations (Ketola, 2015); these categories of resources correspond to the values that guide pre-conventional, conventional and post-conventional moral reasoning. Wisdom and moral reasoning development activities guide the development of CS and CSR resource management abilities (Hahn, Preuss, Pinkse & Figge, 2014).

A major implication of Kohlberg's (1969) moral development theory is that moral reasoning develops over time as individuals gain experience and extend their education (Rest, 1980). Thus, a resultant professional development objective for individuals is the advancement of moral development toward post-conventional levels. Similarly, a CS and CSR development objective for organizations is to advance its resource management development function from the management of economic resources toward the expected and desired management of social and environmental resources. This objective is illustrated in Figure 5.2 by connecting Kohlberg's (1969) levels of moral development to Carroll's (1991) pyramid of corporate social responsibility. As illustrated in Figure 5.2, the IOE is portrayed by individual moral reasoning and organizational resource management responsibilities that advance, develop and evolve in an upward manner.

We also illustrate the concept of evolving and expanding moral reasoning development and resource management responsibilities in Figure 5.3.

Ethics and CS and CSR concepts can become mutually and beneficially reinforcing in nature. The ethics and moral development of individuals with sustainable careers and sustainable lives can provide an ethical underpinning for sustainable businesses and a sustainable economy (Becker, 2015). By exploring these connections, students can understand

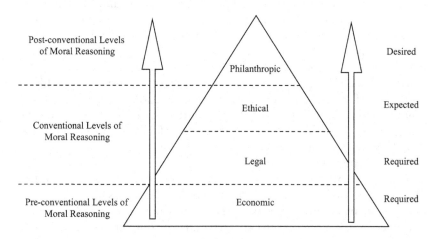

Figure 5.2 Connecting Kohlberg's (1969) Levels of Moral Development to Carroll's (1991) Pyramid of Corporate Social Responsibility

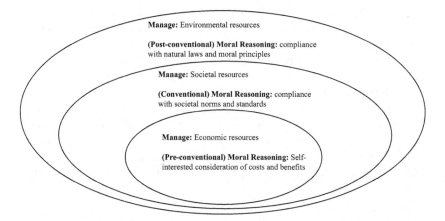

Figure 5.3 Expanding Moral Reasoning and Resource Management Responsibility Considerations

the importance of moral development in building a society of flourishing individuals and organizations.

2.2. Connecting Moral Reasoning Theories and Approaches to Practical Analytical Tools

How can analytical tools guide the moral reasoning of accounting professionals and the resource management of businesses? How can students learn to apply these tools as they continue their education in college and then throughout their careers? At the individual level, moral reasoning theories can guide judgments. Teleological (or consequentialist) theories guide moral reasoning by focusing on a decision's consequences or outcomes, that is, its comparative costs and benefits. For example, utilitarianism is a consequentialist theory by which actions are judged morally good if their outcomes result in the "greatest amount of good for the greatest amount of people affected" (Crane & Matten, 2007, p. 100). Stakeholder theory is another moral reasoning theory that considers the consequences of a decision by identifying a decision's outcomes for various stakeholders.

Instead of focusing on the outcomes of decisions, deontological (or non-consequentialist) theories apply moral rules or societal norms to evaluate the 'goodness' of an action regardless of its consequences (Campbell, 2005). Kant's categorical imperative (Paton, 1948) is a type of non-consequentialism in which a decision is moral if (and only if) it and the reasons for it can exist as a universal law that is applicable to all (Godar, O'Connor & Taylor, 2005). The focus is on the 'goodness' of the decision and the behavior itself; conversely, the focus is not on its consequences.

Rather than considering the characteristics or outcomes of an 'action', virtue ethics (Mintz, 1995, 1996a, 1996b) focuses on the virtues or characteristics that are required by a 'good' actor to choose 'good' decisions and actions (Solomon, 1992; Crane & Matten, 2007; Cheffers & Pakaluk, 2011). These virtues are defined as normative qualities that reflect an individual's ability to think and act in an ethical manner (Libby & Thorne, 2004; MacIntyre, 2013). They draw attention to the type of individual that one should *be* to achieve the actions that one should do. The middle column of Table 5.2 identifies these moral reasoning theories and tools.

The left-hand column of Table 5.2 categorizes moral reasoning theories by their areas of focus. Whereas utilitarianism and stakeholder theory draw attention to outcomes, deontology considers an action's characteristics and virtue ethics focuses on the required characteristics and virtues of the actor. Figure 5.4 illustrates that the virtues of the actor influence actions and behavioral processes, which in turn result in behavioral outcomes.

Table 5.2 Informational Tools for Sustainable Moral Reasoning and Resource Management

Area of Focus	Sustainable Moral Reasoning Tools	Sustainable Resource Management Tools
Outcomes	Utilitarianism	Triple Bottom Line
Outcomes	Stakeholder Impacts	The Sustainability Cube
Process (Action)	Deontology	(Sustainability) Balanced Scorecard
Character of the Actor (Virtues, Capitals)	Virtue Ethics	Integrated Reporting Framework

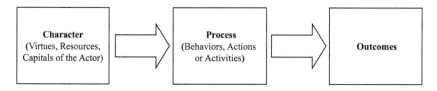

Figure 5.4 Elements in the Resource Utilization Process

The question of optimally managing the inherent tensions among resources, processes and outcomes is a key challenge in CS and CSR practices (Bansal, 2005; Brinkmann, 2001; Epstein, Buhovac & Yuthas, 2015; Gladwin et al., 1995; Hahn, Pinkse, Preuss & Figge, 2015; Maon, Lindgreen & Swaen, 2008; Van der Byl & Slawinski, 2015). The IOE posits that moral reasoning theories for 'individuals' provide a suitable foundation for developing 'organizational' strategies, methods and analytical tools (Sasse-Werhahn et al., 2020). Just as consequentialist, non-consequentialist and virtue ethics theories focus on the respective outcomes, actions and virtues of the actor at the 'individual' moral reasoning level, analytical tools in CS and CSR forums focus on different areas of Figure 5.4's resource utilization process at the 'organizational' level.

3. Practical Tools for Applying Ethical Concepts

The right-hand side of Table 5.2 identifies four reporting and analysis tools:

1) Triple Bottom Line analysis
2) The Sustainability Cube
3) The Balanced Scorecard
4) The IRF[4]

By connecting moral reasoning theories to corresponding CS and CSR analytical tools, Table 5.2 reinforces the IOE.

3.1. The Triple Bottom Line

The concept of the Triple Bottom Line, as first defined by business author, management advisor and entrepreneur Elkington (2018), refers to the management philosophy that a single financial 'bottom line' does not adequately express the comprehensive health of an organization and the impacts that it generates on (and for) its stakeholders. A responsible organization must thus design a pair of additional 'bottom lines' that express its internal condition and its stakeholder impacts:

• A social 'bottom line'
• An environmental 'bottom line'

According to the Global Reporting Initiative (GRI),

> GRI has pioneered sustainability reporting since the late 1990s, transforming it from a niche practice into one now adopted by a growing majority of organizations. The GRI reporting framework is the most trusted and widely used in the world . . . of the world's largest 250 corporations, 92% report on their sustainability performance and 74% of these use GRI's Standards to do so.
>
> (GRI, 2020)

The GRI standards are organized into one foundational universal category and three applied categories. These three categories encompass Economic Standards, Environmental Standards and Social Standards, reflecting the three perspectives of the Triple Bottom Line.

The Exxon Valdez case is a historical example that provides a pedagogical opportunity to explore how the Triple Bottom Line, in general, and how the GRI standards, in particular, can serve to broaden accounting analyses beyond simple economic considerations. If the GRI standards had been in existence at the time of the Valdez disaster and if they had been employed by Exxon, metrics in the Social Standards category may have flagged deficiencies and the risk of employee error. For example, metrics measuring the management of social resources in the areas of training and education (GRI 404), security practices (GRI 410) and local communities (GRI 413) could have heralded important warning signs. Furthermore, environmental measures such as environmental compliance metrics (GRI 307) and economic measures such as indirect economic impacts (GRI 203) may have enabled Exxon to identify how its corporate activities were impacting the local Alaskan shoreline ecosystems. Subsequent investigations revealed that under-investment in employee training programs and risk management activities directly impacted the extent of the environmental damage that the oil spill imposed on the Alaskan geography and its residents.

3.2. The Sustainability Cube

The Sustainability Cube analysis analyzes the effects of outcomes (i.e., a Triple Bottom Line analysis), on stakeholders (i.e., a geographic community analysis) and on time itself (i.e., a time horizon analysis). It thus builds on the Triple Bottom Line analysis by adding supplemental information about the dimensions of space and time. Each of these three dimensions contains three different levels of analysis, resulting in a 3 × 3 × 3 Sustainability Cube:

- The first Triple Bottom Line dimension analyses economic, social and environmental results and outcomes.

- The geographic community dimension identifies and analyzes the stakeholders who are affected by these results and outcomes at the local, national and global levels of community. These levels can be scaled up or down to fit the company and the situation; for example, neighborhood, city and regional levels could be used for more localized matters.
- The time horizon dimension considers changes over time. It encompasses short-term, medium-term and long-term levels.

The Sustainability Cube can be used to map issues, risks, challenges, strengths and potential solutions by using colors such as red, yellow and green to identify each area's severity level. It is not necessary to 'fill in' all 27 boxes of the $3 \times 3 \times 3$ cube. Nevertheless, the clustering of certain factors in certain sections of the cube can help managers 'map out' different approaches to managing resources.

3.3. The Balanced Scorecard

Whereas the Triple Bottom Line and the sustainability cube draw attention to outcomes, the Balanced Scorecard supplements this data by directing attention to the underlying processes and activities that lead to those outcomes. Kaplan and Norton (1992, 1993, 1996) first developed the concept of the Balanced Scorecard. Whereas each scorecard is tailored to a specific setting, the traditional scorecard generally encompasses financial and non-financial performance measures in four categories: learning and growth activities, internal business process activities, customer satisfaction activities and financial performance outcomes.

Strategic connections between these four categories can help managers manage organizational resources in a sustainable manner. For example, an employee workforce that learns and grows will operate internal business processes more effectively. Effective internal operations will increase customer satisfaction and sales. Growing sales will improve financial results and cash flows.

Recently, sustainable balanced scorecards (SBSCs) have been developed and used in many applications (Hansen & Schaltegger, 2016, 2018). Topor, Capusneanu and Tamas-Szora (2017), for instance, produced an SBSC for an aluminum company that featured four strategies (organizational, internal processes, customer and financial) and six activities (strategy development, strategy clarification, objective alignment, planning operations, monitoring and learning and testing and adjusting).

Thus, instead of narrowly focusing on financial performance outcomes, the SBSC can aid sustainability efforts by shifting attention toward the development of sustainable underlying strategies and processes. Consider, for instance, the BP Deepwater Horizon case. BP's decision to outsource significant components of its operations to independent sub-contractors reduced its operating costs and improved financial outcomes in the short-term; however, it also outsourced BP's control over the learning, growth and development activities of its workforce, thereby jeopardizing the ethical focus of its workforce and risking both the under-prioritization of environmental safety and the over-prioritization of short-term financial considerations. As a result, BP relied on independent contractors who were unable to perform the necessary internal business processes to prevent and control a catastrophic explosion. Customers and other stakeholders were repelled by the resulting oil spill and the long-term financial position of the organization was severely damaged.

3.4. The IRF

Whereas the Triple Bottom Line and Sustainability Cube focus on outcomes and whereas the Balanced Scorecard supplements this information by presenting data about processes, the IRF further supplements this information by presenting metrics about the resources or capitals that are required to perform all integrated business functions; it is thus colloquially known as 'the Six Capitals Model'. The IRF has grown in popularity with educators and practitioners; Kraten (2017) provides an annotated version of the IRF. It is reproduced verbatim in Figure 5.5 with the approval of the publisher.[5]

The 'tentacles' of capital that are invested into the resources of an organization (on the left-hand side), as well as outcomes of those investments that are produced by the organization (on the right-hand side), give the IRF an 'octopus-like' appearance. As a result, it is also colloquially known as the 'Octopus Model'.

The use of the IRF to develop and manage organizational resources and capitals is equivalent to the use of virtue ethics to develop and manage an individual's virtues. At the individual level, for instance, the virtue ethics approach generally involves three primary steps or questions (Cheffers & Pakaluk, 2011):

- Mission and distinctive work: what is the mission, purpose or distinctive work of an individual in a professional role (e.g., an accountant)?
- Virtue development: what virtues would make a 'good' individual in this professional role? In other words, what virtues would make for a good accountant, that is, an accountant who can perform his or her distinctive work well?
- Operation and activity: what would an individual in this professional accounting role do in a given situation, assuming that the individual possesses the appropriate developed virtues and that the individual is motivated to carry out his or her purpose by producing work distinctively well?

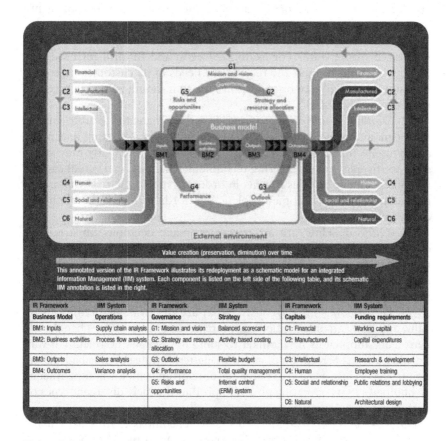

Figure 5.5 Integrated Reporting Framework

In a similar fashion, at an organizational level, organizations must prepare strategic plans, financial and capital resource investment plans and operational plans. Thus, the IRF is far more complex than the Triple Bottom Line, the Sustainability Cube and the Balanced Scorecard because it summarizes and reports the returns on the capital that must be invested in strategic, financial and operational resources.

Accordingly, the IRF measures a total of fifteen strategic, financial and operational factors, far more than the three or four factors that are addressed in each of the other three analyses. The following information describes each of these fifteen factors.

3.4.1. Strategic Governance Factors

The IRF contains five strategic governance factors; they are presented in the large central circle of Figure 5.5 (i.e., factors G1 to G5). These factors are designed to help the organization define its approach to implementing its strategy.

G1. *Mission and vision.* What is the entity attempting to do to reach its desired future state? For example, Exxon and BP drill for crude oil (i.e., its mission) to meet the fuel supply needs of its customer base (i.e., its vision). Generally, an organization's mission should be tied to meeting unmet societal needs.

G2. *Strategic resource allocation.* How does the entity plan to ensure that it maintains a reliable supply of resources? In allocating and managing intellectual capital resources, a global energy company may strategize to diversify its engineering technologies (i.e., its intellectual capital resources) among various patents in order to 'spread the risk' that a single technology may become obsolete, unaffordable or overly reliant on costly labor.

G3. *Outlook.* How are an entity's strategic decisions impacted by expectations regarding future trends? Expectations of increasing government regulation regarding climate change, for instance, may compel oil and gas companies to shift production from carbon-based to renewable products.

G4. *Performance measurement.* What are the strategic definitions of value and how can organizations measure them? For example, when British Petroleum adopted its BP moniker to stand for 'Beyond Petroleum' it was signaling that its perception of its own long-term strategic value had shifted significantly. Thus, its need to purchase, develop and employ non-petroleum technologies in its operating portfolio produced widely divergent types of performance measurements.

G5. *Risks and opportunities.* This factor encompasses the classic management analysis of Strengths, Weaknesses, Opportunities and Threats (SWOT). Its emphasis, however, is on enterprise risk management and on the ability of organizations to turn challenges into opportunities for success. The Brian Hunter case at Amaranth Advisors, for instance, illustrates this strategic factor. In permitting a single highly skilled market trader to leverage huge amounts of capital on intuitive bets about economic trends, the firm made a profoundly misguided strategic decision about the importance of exploiting risky trading opportunities to (hopefully) earn immense short-term profits. Apparently, although, Amaranth failed to invest in the risk oversight controls that were required to prevent Hunter's disastrous overreach.

3.4.2. Capital Resource Factors

The IRF also includes six financial investment factors that are illustrated by 'the Octopus' as 'tentacles' in Figure 5.5 (i.e., factors C1 to C6). These factors are utilized by organizations to manage and develop their investments in their resources in order to carry out their strategies.

C1. Investments in financial resources. An entity may dedicate expenditures to maintaining a banking relationship or to developing the administrative infrastructure that it needs to prepare for a public offering of equity. Enron, for instance, spent considerable sums to maintain its corporate image among investors in publicly traded equities.

C2. Investments in manufactured resources. These expenditures are invested in tangible assets, such as inventory, equipment, buildings and furniture.

C3. Investments in intellectual resources. In addition to expenditures in trademarked, patented and copyrighted material, this category also encompasses the costs of developing distinctive and unique policies and procedures. An energy company that hires a consultant to develop a carbon emissions trading system, for instance, may consider the 'deliverable' to be valuable intellectual capital even though it may not be eligible for a government patent.

C4. Investments in human resources. These are investments in a company's employees. Training costs are considered investments in human resources, even though they may be expensed in accordance with Generally Accepted Accounting Principles (GAAP) or International Financial Reporting Standards (IFRS).

C5. Investments in social and relationship resources. These are investments in systems for managing relationships with individuals who can affect the performance of organizations, even though they are not legally defined as employees. Expenditures for customer relationship programs and political lobbying activities, for instance, would be included in this category.

C6. Investments in natural environmental resources. In addition to investments in recycling programs and community service initiatives, this category also encompasses the costs of bringing the natural environment into the workplace. A firm that builds a glass walled atrium and skylights into its main building to bathe its employees in natural sunlight, for example, would classify the cost of the wall as a natural environmental investment. The cost of heating such a space in winter or cooling such a space in summer may also be classified in this manner.

3.4.3. Operational (Business Model) Factors

Finally, the IRF displays four operational or business model factors that are presented as four small circles in the mid-section of Figure 5.5 (i.e., factors BM1 to BM4). The objective of these factors is to illustrate how organizations manage resources by employing business operations and activities to convert inputs to outputs and how these processes enable the achievement of the organization's mission. The factors define outputs as the short-term products or services that are sold to customers; they define outcomes as the long-term results (that may be financial, social, or environmental in nature) of operating the business.

In this sense, the IRF comes full circle. This final step, the (hoped for and planned for) actual achievement of the mission and vision (BM4 – see ahead), should be consistent with the first step, the definition of the mission and vision (G1). The four operational factors also correspond to the resources, processes and outcome elements of the resource utilization process that are presented in Figure 5.4 and in Table 5.2.

BM1. *Inputs.* What resources must be situated in appropriate positions to begin the 'pipeline' of product or service development, followed by delivery to the customer? How can an entity ensure the quality and the availability of these resources? All resources necessary for production must be included in this analysis, including the adequate development of human resources at the individual level.

Consider, for instance, the poorly managed human resource function at Enron. It permitted the hiring and development of employees who did not conform to appropriate ethical behavioral norms. Likewise, consider the inebriated Exxon Valdez ship captain who failed to prevent a catastrophic collision; he represented a quality failure in human resource inputs.

BM2. *Business processes.* What operating activities are required to transform inputs into outputs? How does the entity 'shape' a finished product or service from its amalgamation of varied inputs? Consider, for example, the explosion of the Deepwater Horizon; it represented a quality failure in BP's risk response processes.

BM3. *Outputs.* What products or services are sold to customers? How do organizations remain responsive to the needs of end users when they are solely transacting with intermediary organizations? Upstream energy-producing entities, for example, must manage the risk of losing the support of their downstream customers and end users when they contract with midstream entities. For instance, when the struggling Enron sought the support of government regulators and the general public, it discovered that its shift of focus from energy distribution to energy trading and 'deal making' had inadvertently transformed it into a relatively remote (and thus unsympathetic) organization. Its unethical corporate behavior further reinforced this perception.

BM4. *Outcomes.* How do the short-term operations of an organization affect its long-term value for all internal and external stakeholders? The long-term implications of sustainability issues like climate change, environmental degradation, social unrest and wealth and income inequality, for instance, are impacted by the outputs of carbon-based energy firms. Here, too, the IRF can serve as a critical resource for understanding how organizations that operate at peak efficiency and profitability in the short-term may cause catastrophic outcomes for its external stakeholders in the long-term.

These CS and CSR tools can be employed by accounting students to learn how to gather, report and analyze CS and CSR information. The case 'Save the Blue Frog!' provides students with one such opportunity.

4. Practical Application of Sustainability Tools to a Case Analysis

4.1. 'Save the Blue Frog!' Case Summary

The full initial version of the 'Save the Blue Frog!' case is posted online (Kraten, 2015). However, students only require the following information to complete the Triple Bottom Line, Sustainability Cube, Balanced Scorecard and IRF analyses: a fictional global energy company, headquartered in the United States, secures a contract from the government of an emerging African nation to build a hydro-electric power plant over an undeveloped jungle waterfall. At first, the project's financial valuation is extremely high and its non-financial outcomes promise relatively inexpensive, reliable and clean electrical power for a population that desperately needs such a resource. However, before construction begins, a pair of disturbing revelations is reported by investigative journalists: (a) a local company representative paid a significant financial "gratuity" to a government official shortly before the official approved the construction contract and (b) an endangered species known as the Blue Frog is discovered on the construction site.

Students are grouped into teams, assigned roles (such as the Chief Executive Officer of the global energy company, the Audit Partner from the independent public accounting firm who is responsible for reporting on the company's financial statements and internal controls and an Environmental Activist who is sworn to protect all endangered species) and asked to jointly devise solutions that can both preserve the project and 'Save the Blue Frog!' in light of the revelations. Critical thinking and negotiation abilities are developed by the activity; valuation and enterprise risk management skills are developed too.

Each student team must:

- Develop a baseline financial and non-financial outcomes model.
- Evaluate the impact of each risk factor, propose potential solutions.
- Evaluate the impact of each proposed solution on the model.

However, a final stage must also be addressed before the teams can preserve the project and 'Save the Blue Frog!'. Namely, students must assess whether ethical considerations should compel the firm to pull back from the project, even though it may be able to devise a complex array of responses to the equally complex set of concerns. In other words, students must address the possibility that a project that is expected to generate a very high financial and non-financial Return on Investment (ROI) should yet be rejected for ethical reasons. This final challenge provides students with the opportunity to practice and apply their moral reasoning skills and to connect them to the management of CS and CSR resources.

In other words, the case provides an effective setting to address CS and CSR issues through the prism of moral reasoning. It encompasses considerations of economic, environmental and social outcomes (i.e., a Triple Bottom Line analysis). It presents a business dilemma involving many of the company's stakeholders and it assesses the Triple Bottom Line outcomes to these stakeholders at different geographic levels and across different time horizons (i.e., a Sustainability Cube analysis).

It also requires consideration of learning and growth, internal business, customer satisfaction and financial performance activities and processes (i.e., a Balanced Scorecard analysis). Finally, it requires students to weigh the strategic, financial and operational implications of their decisions (i.e., an IRF analysis). Indeed, the 'Save the Blue Frog!' case provides an opportunity for students to practice using tools to report sustainability information, thereby helping organizations to manage economic, social and environmental resources in a responsible and sustainable manner.

4.2. Triple Bottom Line Analysis

The following GRI standards are applicable to the 'Save The Blue Frog!' case. They reflect the case's emphasis on the regional economic growth that is expected to occur as a result of the construction of the hydro-electric power plant, the enrichment of the society through employment opportunities, the improvement in air quality as a result of the investment in renewable energy, the risk that government bribes may be extorted from the firm in the future and the potential extinction of an endangered species as a result of construction:

Economic Standards

> GRI 203: Indirect Economic Impacts
> GRI 205: Anti-Corruption

Environmental Standards

> GRI 302: Energy
> GRI 303: Water and Effluents
> GRI 304: Biodiversity
> GRI 305: Emissions
> GRI 306: Waste
> GRI 307: Environmental Compliance

Social Standards

> GRI 401: Employment
> GRI 413: Local Communities
> GRI 415: Public Policy
> GRI 419: Socioeconomic Compliance

By selecting a single relevant Key Performance Indicator from each Standard, students can construct a Triple Bottom Line table of a dozen outcome metrics (see Table 5.3). The reported information can help managers

Table 5.3 Triple Bottom Line Analysis

ECON 203: Indirect Economic Impacts	203–1a. Extent of development of significant infrastructure investments and services supported.
ECON 205: Anti-Corruption	205–3d. Public legal cases regarding corruption brought against the organization or its employees during the reporting period and the outcomes of such cases.
ENVI 302: Energy	302–1b. Total fuel consumption within the organization from renewable sources, in joules or multiples, and including fuel types used.
ENVI 303: Water and Effluents	303–2a (iii). Total number of water sources significantly affected by withdrawal and by type; biodiversity value (such as species diversity and endemism, and total number of protected species).
GRI 304: Biodiversity	304–4a. Total number of IUCN Red List species and national conservation list species with habitats in areas affected by the operations of the organization, by level of extinction risk: (i) critically endangered, (ii) endangered.
GRI 305: Emissions	305–5a. GHG emissions reduced as a direct result of reduction initiatives, in metric tons of CO_2 equivalent.
GRI 306: Waste	306–3a. Total weight of waste generated in metric tons, and a breakdown of this total by composition of the waste.
GRI 307: Environmental Compliance	307–1a (iii). Significant fines and non-monetary sanctions for non-compliance with environmental laws and/or regulations in terms of cases brought through dispute resolution mechanisms.
GRI 401: Employment	401–1a. Total number and rate of new employee hires during the reporting period, by age group, gender, and region.
GRI 413: Local Communities	413–2.2.2.4 The exposure of the local community to its operations due to higher than average use of shared resources or impact on shared resources, including land conversion and resettlement.
GRI 415: Public Policy	415–1a. Total monetary value of financial and in-kind political contributions made directly and indirectly by the organization by country and recipient/beneficiary.
GRI 419: Socioeconomic Compliance	419–1a (i) and (ii). Significant fines and non-monetary sanctions for non-compliance with laws and/or regulations in the social and economic area in terms of total monetary value of significant fines and total number of non-monetary sanctions.

make informed decisions about managing the tensions among economic, social and environmental resources and outcomes, as well as managing the tradeoffs between these resources and outcomes.

4.3. Sustainability Cube Analysis

The Triple Bottom Line represents one method for analyzing sustainability and social responsibility considerations on a triadic basis. As noted earlier, two other considerations are also suited for triadic categorizations.

In the 'Save the Blue Frog!' case, time horizons are relevant to the practice of ethical behavior because the business project opportunity may tempt the energy company with the ability to earn significant profits in the short term, but the threat of future demands for bribes from government officials may reinforce government corruption in the long term. And as a green energy project, the hydro-electric power project imposes significant construction costs on society in the short term, while promising the avoidance of a global climate change catastrophe for society in the long term.

Geographic regions are also often relevant because the destruction of the Blue Frog's habitat is a local concern, but the establishment of a precedent for valuing energy development over the rights of endangered species may affect many other regions around the planet.

Thus, a 3 × 3 × 3 framework can be utilized to classify and analyze three distinct sustainability considerations:

- *The Triple Bottom Line Considerations*: Economic, Social, Environmental
- *The Time Horizon Considerations*: Short Term, Moderate Term, Long Term
- *Geographic Considerations*: Local, Regional (or National), Global

In a truly three-dimensional visual medium, a literal 3 × 3 × 3 cube can be constructed for mapping risks, resources and other considerations. In a two-dimensional medium, this cube can be sliced into a trio of 3 × 3 squares as shown in Table 5.4.

In this example, implications regarding the bribery concern and the species extinction concern have been mapped across the three categories of the framework. The mapping process is helpful because organizations can learn to target resources toward areas of the cube that features clusters of concerns.

4.4. Balanced Scorecard Analysis

The Balanced Scorecard has provided a framework for business analysis since the early 1990s. Instead of a triad of analytical categories, although, it provides a quartet of considerations.

Table 5.4 Sustainability Cube Analysis

ECONOMIC	Local	Regional	Global
Short Term			
Moderate Term	Financial risk from demands to pay additional bribes	Legal risk from imposition of government fines regarding bribery	
Long Term			

SOCIAL	Local	Regional	Global
Short Term			
Moderate Term	Loss of local support if project cancellation generates public perception of abandonment		
Long Term		Reputational risk as a "bribe payer" may lead to lost business from regional governments	

ENVIRONMENTAL	Local	Regional	Global
Short Term			
Moderate Term		Increase in regional pollution if hydroelectric power is not utilized to replace coal power	
Long Term			Biodiversity risk from the loss of an amphibian species that attracts significant public sympathy

The Scorecard's Financial perspective is clearly analogous to the Financial element of the Triple Bottom Line. The Scorecard's Learning and Growth and Customers perspectives are likewise analogous to the Social element of the Triple Bottom Line. And the Scorecard's Internal Business Processes encompass the Environmental element of the Triple Bottom Line.

If the Balanced Scorecard and the Triple Bottom Line are similar in nature, why is it helpful to utilize both frameworks? As previously noted, although the two frameworks overlap, they are not identical. The Scorecard tends to emphasize internal efficiency and profitability, whereas the Triple Bottom Line places more emphasis on external stakeholder well-being.

Thus, a Balanced Scorecard may integrate certain standards from the Global Reporting Initiative with standards that are drawn from standard-setting organizations with a more internal focus. The COSO Enterprise Risk Management (ERM) framework, for instance, lists 20 key principles for developing risk management systems (COSO, 2017).[6] The following eight principles are particularly relevant to the 'Save the Blue Frog!' case:

#2. Establishment of Operating Structures
#4. Demonstrates Commitment to Core Values
#6. Analyzes Business Context
#8. Evaluates Alternative Strategies
#10. Identifies Risk
#13. Implements Risk Responses
#15. Assesses Substantial Change
#20. Reports on Risk, Culture and Performance

Thus, a Balanced Scorecard table can be constructed that integrates elements of the Triple Bottom Line analysis and a COSO analysis:

4.5. IRF Analysis

The International IRF was developed in the 2010s, in part, because of a perception that the various triad-based, quartet-based and other reporting models should be consolidated into a single condensed model. Nevertheless, as previously noted, the IRF itself is composed of three elements:

- A strategic component of five considerations
- An operational component of four considerations
- A financial component of six considerations

The resulting fifteen categories are thus designed to encompass all the considerations of a Triple Bottom Line analysis, a Sustainability Cube analysis, a Balanced Scorecard analysis and various other analyses. As a result, the considerations of Tables 5.3, 5.4 and 5.5 can be integrated into Table 5.6:

Table 5.5 (Sustainability) Balanced Scorecard Analysis

Balanced Scorecard	GRI	COSO
Financial	203: Indirect Economic Impacts 306: Waste	#8 Evaluates Alternative Strategies
Learning and Growth	205: Anti-corruption 401: Employment 419: Socioeconomic Compliance	#4 Demonstrates Commitment to Core Values #20 Reports on Risk, Culture, and Performance
Customers	304: Biodiversity 413: Local Communities 415: Public Policy	#6 Analyzes Business Context #15 Assesses Substantial Change
Internal Business Processes	302: Energy 303: Water and Effluents 305: Emissions 307: Environmental Compliance	#2 Establishment of Operating Structures #10 Identifies Risk #13 Implements Risk Responses

Table 5.6 Integrated Reporting Framework Analysis

Strategy: Mission and Vision	TBL GRI 415: Public Policy COSO #4: Demonstrates Commitment to Core Values
Strategy: Resource Allocation	TBL GRI 303: Water and Effluents
Strategy: Outlook	COSO #6: Analyzes Business Context COSO #8: Evaluates Alternative Strategies
Strategy: Performance	TBL GRI 413: Local Communities COSO #15: Assesses Substantial Change
Strategy: Risks and Opportunities	TBL GRI 205: Anti-corruption COSO #10: Identifies Risk
Operations: Inputs	TBL GRI 302: Energy
Operations: Business Activities	COSO #2: Establishment of Operating Structures
Operations: Outputs	Cube: Reputational risk as a bribe payer may lead to lost business from regional governments
Operations: Outcomes	TBL GRI 203: Indirect Economic Impacts
Financial: Financial Capital	Cube: Financial risk from demands to pay additional bribes Cube: Legal risk from imposition of government fines regarding bribery
Financial: Manufactured Capital	Cube: Increase in regional pollution if hydroelectric power is not utilized to replace coal power
Financial: Intellectual Capital	COSO #13: Implements Risk Responses
Financial: Human Capital	COSO #20: Reports on Risk, Culture, and Performance

(*Continued*)

Table 5.6 (Continued)

Financial: Social and Relationship Capital	TBL GRI 419: Socioeconomic Compliance Cube: Loss of local support if project cancellation generates public perception of abandonment
Financial: Environmental Capital	TBL GRI 304: Biodiversity TBL GRI 305: Emissions TBL GRI 306: Waste TBL GRI 307: Environmental Compliance Cube: Biodiversity risk from the loss of an amphibian species that attracts significant public sympathy

5. Summary and Conclusion

Although the integration of topics like CS and CSR into accounting ethics education can be a challenging activity, it also can provide tremendous opportunities for achieving learning goals. This chapter addresses the challenge and pursues the opportunity by focusing on two important questions:

1)   At an individual level, how can accounting ethics education expand to encompass modern topics like CS and CSR, thereby improving the ethical development of accounting professionals?
2)   At an organizational level, what role can accountants play in transforming business practices to adapt to the evolving ethical demands of society?

This chapter approached these questions by providing and applying several conceptual and practical tools. First, from a conceptual perspective, the chapter connected foundational moral development concepts (e.g., Kohlberg, 1969) and moral reasoning theories in accounting ethics education to related CS and CSR concepts and tools. Such connections can teach the principle of IOE to accounting students by demonstrating that the ethical principles and concepts that apply to accounting professionals at an individual level also correspond to CS and CSR concepts at an organizational level.

Second, from a practical perspective, the chapter applied several common CS and CSR measurement tools to a case analysis featuring the energy industry, adding supplemental references to historical examples from that industry sector. Such exercises provide students with valuable insights regarding the use of data resources to aid the management of CS and CSR resources, thereby contributing to the development of sustainable, well-lived individuals, organizations and societies (i.e., societal *eudaimonia*).

Ethics concepts and CS and CSR concepts may become mutually reinforcing in the classroom. The ethics and moral development of sustainable professionals can provide an ethical underpinning for sustainable businesses and a sustainable economy (Becker, 2015); exploring these connections can thus serve students by reinforcing the importance of moral development for building sustainable and flourishing individuals, organizations and societies. Indeed, it is beneficial to recognize and use similarities and connections between the development of ethical, socially responsible and sustainable accounting professionals at the individual level and that of socially responsible and sustainable businesses at the organizational level. The goal, in other words, is to achieve IOE in a manner that is beneficial at every level of our social structure.

Notes

1. The brief historical references that are included throughout this chapter can also serve as supplemental examples in the classroom. Enron, for instance, collapsed after engaging in risky business ventures whereas utilizing illegal accounting techniques to hide its transgressions. Amaranth failed to place appropriate trading controls over Brian Hunter, who incurred multibillion dollar losses that sunk his firm. The Valdez and the Deepwater Horizon spills, however, were different in that they imposed catastrophic damage on external environmental resources without posing existential threats to the firms that were at fault.
2. This chapter utilizes the acronym IRF when referring to the Integrated Reporting Framework of the International Integrated Reporting Council. Other acronyms have been utilized in the literature, including IR and < IR >.
3. For detailed information, please access https://savethebluefrog.com/
4. Table 5.2 indicates that the Triple Bottom Line and Sustainability Cube are primarily outcomes-focused analyses, that the Balanced Scorecard adds to these analyses by addressing internal business processes and that the Integrated Reporting Framework further adds to these analyses by addressing virtues and capitals. Thus, whereas reading Table 5.2, it should be noted that the last two analyses encompass outcomes and that the last analysis encompasses internal business processes.
5. We thank Mr. Richard Kravitz, Editor-In-Chief of the *CPA Journal* of the New York State Society of Certified Public Accountants, for providing permission to reproduce Figure 5.5 in this chapter.
6. The Committee of Sponsoring Organizations (COSO) of the Treadway Commission is the leading promulgator of standards and frameworks for systems of internal control and enterprise risk management in the United States of America. Its guidance is available for free in summary format at www.coso.org, and is available for purchase in detailed format from the American Institute of Certified Public Accountants (AICPA).

References

Bansal, P. (2005). Evolving Sustainably: A Longitudinal Study of Corporate Sustainable Development. *Strategic Management Journal, 26*(3), 197–218.

Becker, C. U. (2015). Social Approach: Virtue Ethics Enabling Sustainability Ethics for Business. In A. Sison (Ed.), *Handbook of Virtue Ethics in Business and Management* (pp. 1–12). Dordrecht: Springer.

Boiral, O., Heras-Saizarbitoria, I., & Brotherton, M. (2019). Assessing and Improving the Quality of Sustainability Reports: The Auditors' Perspective. *Journal of Business Ethics, 155,* 703–721.

Brinkmann, J. (2001). On Business Ethics and Moralism. *Business Ethics: A European Review, 10*(4), 311–319.

Broughton, K., & Sardon, M. (2020). *Coronavirus Pandemic Could Elevate ESG Factors.* Retrieved June 23rd, 2020, from www.wsj.com/articles/coronavirus-pandemic-could-elevate-esg-factors-11585167518

Campbell, T. (2005). Introduction: The Ethics of Auditing. In T. Campbell & K. Houghton (Eds.), *Ethics and Auditing* (pp. xxi–xxxii). Canberra: The Australian National University E Press. Retrieved June 23rd, 2020, from https://library. oapen.org/bitstream/id/2d04d4c9-1519-421c-91d6-a1e8357f4606/459097.pdf

Carroll, A. (1991). The Pyramid of Corporate Social Responsibility: Toward the Moral Management of Organizational Stakeholders. *Business Horizons, 34,* 39–48.

Cheffers, M., & Pakaluk, M. (2011). *Accounting Ethics – and the Near Collapse of the World's Financial System.* Sutton: Allen Davis Press.

Committee of Sponsoring Organizations of the Treadway Commission (COSO). (2017). *Enterprise Risk Management: Integrating with Strategy and Performance, Executive Summary.* Retrieved July 26th, 2020, from www.coso.org/ Documents/2017-COSO-ERM-Integrating-with-Strategy-and-Performance-Executive-Summary.pdf

Crane, A., & Matten, D. (2007). *Business Ethics: Managing Corporate Citizenship and Sustainability in the Age of Globalization* (2nd ed.). Oxford: Oxford University Press.

Driebusch, C. (2020). *The Next Wave in Shareholder Activism: Socially Responsible Investing.* Retrieved June 23rd, 2020, from www.wsj.com/articles/the-next-wave-in-shareholder-activism-socially-responsible-investing-11582892251

Elkington, J. (2018). *25 Years Ago I Coined the Phrase "Triple Bottom Line": Here's Why It's Time to Rethink It.* Retrieved June 23rd, 2020, from https:// hbr.org/2018/06/25-years-ago-i-coined-the-phrase-triple-bottom-line-heres-why-im-giving-up-on-it

Epstein, M. J., Buhovac, A. R. B., & Yuthas, K. (2015). Managing Social, Environmental and Financial Performance Simultaneously. *Long Range Planning, 48*(1), 35–45.

Gladwin, T. N., Kennelly, J. J., & Krause, T. (1995). Shifting Paradigms for Sustainable Development: Implications for Management Theory and Research. *Academy of Management Review, 20*(4), 874–907.

Global Reporting Initiative (GRI). (2020). *GRI and Sustainability Reporting.* Retrieved June 23rd, 2020, from www.globalreporting.org/information/sustain ability-reporting/Pages/gri-standards.aspx#:~:text=A%20record%20of%20 use%20and,GRI%20Standards%20continues%20to%20grow

Godar, S. H., O'Connor, P. J., & Taylor, V. A. (2005). Evaluating the Ethics of Inversion. *Journal of Business Ethics, 61,* 1–6.

Hahn, T., Figge, F., Aragón-Correa, J. A., & Sharma, S. (2017). Advancing Research on Corporate Sustainability: Off to Pastures New or Back to the Roots? *Business & Society, 56*(2), 155–185.

Hahn, T., Pinkse, J., Preuss, L., & Figge, F. (2015). Tensions in Corporate Sustainability: Towards an Integrative Framework. *Journal of Business Ethics, 127,* 297–316.

Hahn, T., Preuss, L., Pinkse, J., & Figge, F. (2014). Cognitive Frames in Corporate Sustainability: Managerial Sensemaking With Paradoxical and Business Case Frames. *Academy of Management Review, 39*(4), 463–487.

Hansen, E. G., & Schaltegger, S. (2016). The Sustainability Balanced Scorecard: A Systematic Review of Architectures. *Journal of Business Ethics, 133*, 193–221.

Hansen, E. G., & Schaltegger, S. (2018). Sustainability Balanced Scorecards and Their Architectures: Irrelevant or Misunderstood? *Journal of Business Ethics, 150*, 937–952.

Intezari, A. (2015). Integrating Wisdom and Sustainability: Dealing With Instability. *Business Strategy and the Environment, 24*(7), 617–627.

Kaplan, R. S., & Norton, D. P. (1992). *The Balanced Scorecard: Measures that Drive Performance.* Retrieved June 23rd, 2020, from https://hbr.org/1992/01/the-balanced-scorecard-measures-that-drive-performance-2

Kaplan, R. S., & Norton, D. P. (1993). *Putting the Balanced Scorecard to Work.* Retrieved June 23rd, 2020, from https://hbr.org/1993/09/putting-the-balanced-scorecard-to-work

Kaplan, R. S., & Norton, D. P. (1996). *The Balanced Scorecard: Translating Strategy Into Action.* Boston, MA: Harvard Business School Press.

Ketola, T. (2015). Genuine Sustainability as Virtuous Sustainable Development. In A. Sison (Ed.), *Handbook of Virtue Ethics in Business and Management* (pp. 1–4). Dordrecht: Springer.

Kohlberg, L. (1969). Stage and Sequence: The Cognitive Developmental Approach to Socialization. In D. A. Goslin (Ed.), *Handbook of Socialization Theory* (pp. 347–480). Chicago, IL: Rand McNally.

Kraten, M. (2015). Social Presence Theory and Experiential Learning Games. *Business Education Innovation Journal, 7*(2), 6–16.

Kraten, M. (2017). *Transforming Integrated Reporting into Integrated Information Management: A Proposal for Management Accountants.* Retrieved June 23rd, 2020, from www.cpajournal.com/2018/07/19/icymi-transforming-integrated-reporting-into-integrated-information-management/

Kraten, M., Ryack, K. N., Sheikh, A., & Simione, K. A. (2019). A Tale of Two Courses: Applying Sustainability Principles to the Intermediate Financial Accounting and Auditing Courses. *Business Education Innovation Journal, 11*(1), 82–98.

Libby, T., & Thorne, L. (2004). The Identification and Categorization of Auditors' Virtues. *Business Ethics Quarterly, 14*(3), 479–498.

MacIntyre, A. (2013). *After Virtue: A Study in Moral Theory.* London: Bloomsbury.

Maon, F., Lindgreen, A., &. Swaen, V. (2008). Thinking of the Organization as a System: The Role of Managerial Perceptions in Developing a Corporate Social Responsibility Strategic Agenda. *Systems Research and Behavioral Science, 25*(3), 413–426.

Marker, A. W. (2013). The Development of Practical Wisdom: Its Critical Role in Sustainable Performance. *Performance Improvement, 52*(4), 11–21.

McCabe, C. (2020). *ESG Investing Shines in Market Turmoil, With Help From Big Tech.* Retrieved July 8th, 2020, from www.wsj.com/articles/esg-investing-shines-in-market-turmoil-with-help-from-big-tech-11589275801

Melé, D. (2005). Ethical Education in Accounting: Integrating Rules, Values and Virtues. *Journal of Business Ethics, 57*(1), 97–109.

Mintz, S. M. (1995). Virtue Ethics and Accounting Education. *Issues in Accounting Education, 10*(2), 247–267.

Mintz, S. M. (1996a). Aristotelian Virtue and Business Ethics Education. *Journal of Business Ethics, 15*(8), 827–838.

Mintz, S. M. (1996b). The Role of Virtue in Accounting Education. *Accounting Education, 1*(1), 67–91.

Montiel, I., Gallo, P. J., & Antolin-Lopez, R. (2020). What on Earth Should Managers Learn About Corporate Sustainability? A Threshold Concept Approach. *Journal of Business Ethics, 162*, 857–880.

Painter-Morland, M., Sabet, E., Molthan-Hill, P., Goworek, H., & de Leeuw. S. (2016). Beyond the Curriculum: Integrating Sustainability Into Business Schools. *Journal of Business Ethics, 139*, 737–754.

Paton, H. J. (1948). *The Categorical Imperative: A Study in Kant's Moral Philosophy.* Chicago, IL: University of Chicago Press.

Rest, J. (1980). Moral Judgment Research and the Cognitive-Developmental Approach to Moral Education. *Personnel and Guidance Journal, 58*, 602–605.

Roos, J. (2017). Practical Wisdom: Making and Teaching the Governance Case for Sustainability. *Journal of Cleaner Production, 140*(1), 117–124.

Sasse-Werhahn, L. F., Bachmann, C., & Habisch, A. (2020). Managing Tensions in Corporate Sustainability Through a Practical Wisdom Lens. *Journal of Business Ethics, 163*, 53–66.

Schneider, A., & Meins, E. (2012). Two Dimensions of Corporate Sustainability Assessment: Towards a Comprehensive Framework. *Business Strategy & the Environment, 21*(4), 211–222.

Solomon, R. (1992). Corporate Roles, Personal Virtues: An Aristotelean Approach to Business Ethics. *Business Ethics Quarterly, 2*(3), 317–339.

Topor, D. I., Capusneanu, S., & Tamas-Szora, A. (2017). Efficient Green Control (EGC) Encouraging Environmental Investment and Profitability. *Journal of Environmental Protection and Ecology, 18*(1), 191–201.

Van der Byl, C. A., & Slawinski, N. (2015). Embracing Tensions in Corporate Sustainability: A Review of Research From Win-Wins and Trade-Offs to Paradoxes and Beyond. *Organization & Environment, 28*(1), 54–79.

Xiang, W. (2016). Ecophronesis: The Ecological Practical Wisdom for and From Ecological Practice. *Landscape and Urban Planning, 155*, 53–60.

6   The Case for Ethics Instruction in the Age of Analytics

Margaret N. Boldt & Robert L. Braun

1. Introduction

Technology is impacting accounting education in myriad and profound ways. We see the intrusion of the 'Age of Analytics' most clearly in the mandates to embrace technology agility in our accounting programs. The movement toward data analytics reflects a parallel trend in society. For many programs, the addition of data analytics courses and the integration of technology tools within courses could have the effect of marginalizing ethics education in our curricula. Data analytics is being added to accounting programs that have already been stretched by the proliferation and complexity of accounting and auditing standards. With the creation of courses and degree programs emphasizing big data comes difficult decisions about what to remove. As the Certified Public Accountant (CPA) credential and exam evolve toward data analytics, so too have academic programs. As a result, it may be increasingly difficult to make the case for retaining or adding ethics to the curriculum. Indeed, even before data analytics appeared on the radar, Blanthorne, Kovar and Fisher (2007, p. 374) found that accounting faculty ranked "The current demands of the accounting curriculum leave little or no time to teach ethics" as the second factor in a list of eight reasons why not to teach ethics.

Accounting programs flirted with the idea of a serious expansion of ethics education in the wake of scandals at the turn of the millennium. Interest waned in the years that followed, however. Such does not appear to be the case with the accounting academy's embrace of data analytics. As we commit ourselves and our accounting programs more fully to the pursuit of relevance in a business world dominated by artificial intelligence and bots, does ethics education become more or less important to our students and our profession? Perhaps just as importantly, what sort of ethics education will be relevant in this world? We explore these questions and present a framework for educators.

Although the trend to incorporate data analytics had built considerable momentum in recent years, events occurring during the first half of 2020 provided an extra boost of accelerant. In January, the American Institute of Certified Public Accountants (AICPA) and the National Association of State Boards of Accountancy (NASBA) introduced a draft proposal that would increase emphasis on technology by establishing it at the core of what they are calling the 'core plus discipline CPA licensure model' (Coffey, 2020a). In May, the AICPA Board of Directors voted overwhelmingly in favor of advancing the initiative (Coffey, 2020b). The measure of accountability that the CPA exam provides will add to that which the Association to Advance Collegiate Schools of Business (AACSB) initiated with its 2013 accounting standards and reemphasized with the 2018 version.

The developments in the CPA licensure model took place while a global pandemic changed everything. Accountants who might have thought they could never perform their job online were forced to do so by the public health crisis. For many accountants, the necessity of remote work required them to develop and create solutions that would eliminate the need for a human presence. It remains to be seen as to whether the accounting profession will return to its former state or will be forever changed following the novel Coronavirus Disease 2019 (COVID-19). For that matter, as we write this, we do not know whether there will be a 'post-COVID-19' or whether it will endure as a part of the business and social landscape. Whether through necessity in response to the pandemic or the steady drumbeat of progress, it seems certain that accounting must embrace technology solutions and the new role of data analytics to maintain relevance. The bell that called the accounting profession to fully join the 'Age of Analytics' in response to the public health crisis cannot be un-rung.

This chapter is divided into five sections. In the next section, we discuss the expanding role of data analytics in the accounting curriculum and the implications for ethics education. Then, we present the results of a survey that exposes serious deficiencies in the business as usual approach to accounting ethics instruction and perhaps even accounting instruction more generally. In the following section, we provide design principles for implementing ethics in either a dedicated course or integrated throughout the curriculum, or preferably, both. The final section provides some concluding remarks and an invitation to reflect on the role of accounting education in training relevant accountants for the 'Age of Analytics'.

2. The Expanding Role of Information and Data Analytics

Business intelligence is the combination of strategy, knowledge and technology to analyze information about the economic activity and opportunities that affect a business. Technology enables businesses to process vast quantities of data and complex events to recognize patterns leading to predictive analytics and strategic positioning. Although ideas that fit the current definition of business intelligence have been around for a long time, recent advancements in technology and the exponential rise in the volume of data stored online makes the power of today's business intelligence systems unrecognizable from earlier generations.

It seems likely that the duration of each generation is shortening on a similar scale. As such, the 2018 AACSB standards for accounting emphasize 'technology agility' (AACSB, 2018) over any particular concept or tool. The key to success for today's student is dependent on the willingness and ability to learn and adapt in tomorrow's workplace. Our current students would be in the middle of their careers in the year 2040. If we try to imagine the workplace of 2040 and how the residue of what they learned in our classrooms is helping them to live meaningful and productive lives, it can help us to better understand the choices that we make with our curricula. Consider how readily available information is today compared to just 10–15 years ago. Now consider the power of the exponential growth curve. At present, the device in our pocket holds more information about accounting than we can ever hope to teach. It seems unlikely that it will stay in our pocket, however, as we find ways to integrate technology and biology.

We are living at a time of 'big data' in which business views human beings as a collection of algorithms. The apparent goal of business is to leverage data to understand the algorithms that drive economic behavior. With the accumulation of data and ever more powerful algorithms, intelligence may be decoupling from consciousness. It could be true that non-conscious algorithms may know us better than we know ourselves (Harari, 2019). This leads to some really big questions:

- Are organisms really just algorithms and is life really just data processing?
- What do we value in our classrooms, intelligence, or consciousness?
- What will happen to society, business and daily life when non-conscious but highly intelligent algorithms know us better than we know ourselves?
- Do we live in a society? Or do we live in an economy?

Your answer to those questions leads to the key question for accounting educators: as we commit our programs more fully to data and analytics, does integrity and morality become more or less important?

We are living at a time when bots are programmed to perform complex tasks on large amounts of data collected in real time and artificial intelligence is used to predict trends and highlight potential problems. The value that human accountants provide no longer lies in the ability to calculate or generate reports. Indeed, the capabilities of the most proficient accountant pale in comparison to what even fairly simplistic technology solutions provide. The value of the accounting professional lies in the ability to apply and use information. We would put forth that in an age where data and information are collected and reported divorced from morality, it is more critical than ever that the accountants guiding and directing how it will be used have integrity.

3. Are Accounting Students Prepared for the 'Age of Analytics'?

3.1. Coronavirus – A Natural Experiment

Zimmerman (2020) made an appeal to academics to treat the transition to online classes mandated by the coronavirus pandemic as a natural experiment in online learning. As most universities and colleges in the United States of America transitioned to online learning for the remainder of the semester, there was an opportunity to assess whether online instruction was effective without the selection bias normally present in online learning studies. Of course, there would be other issues with such a study, including unprepared faculty and students with varying levels of technology resources and capabilities. As the transition was happening, our accounting program made plans to survey our students about their perceptions of the quality of instruction and learning in the traditional environment and the online environment.

As the Spring 2020 semester progressed, students cheating in the online environment and the measures faculty were and were not employing to prevent it, became a broadly discussed topic among faculty, students and the general public. News stories appeared in several major outlets (e.g., Kubena, 2020; Heilweil, 2020; Appiah, 2020). Of course, students did not invent cheating amid the coronavirus pandemic online learning environment. It seems safe to assume that some students, hopefully few in number, will try to cheat and faculty will try to prevent cheating, regardless of the instructional context. The spring 2020 transition to online instruction and assessment then presents a natural experiment of sorts on whether or not the integrity of accounting students would falter in an online environment lacking face-to-face monitoring. Specifically, the students and any personality or cultural factors affecting their propensity to cheat, were the same for both the traditional and online environments.

Choo and Tan (2008) applied the three fraud triangle factors (Cressey, 1973) of pressure, opportunity and rationalization to investigate students' propensity to cheat. Using vignettes where the three factors were present or absent, Choo and Tan (2008) surveyed United States of America business students at a California university. They find that each of the three factors and a three-way interaction of the three factors significantly affect the propensity to cheat. Recent research investigated the effect of the three fraud triangle factors along with self-efficacy and religiosity on academic fraud, or cheating, by surveying Indonesian accounting students (Melati, Wilopo & Hapsari, 2018). Melati et al. (2018) find a significant effect from both pressure and rationalization but conclude that there is not a significant effect from opportunity, self-efficacy, or religiosity.

Research on USA accounting students suggests that the vast majority (73.6%) of students believe that it is 'easier' to cheat on an exam in an online course than in a traditional classroom environment (King, Guyette, Jr. & Piotrowski, 2009). Further, King et al. (2009) find that the behaviors viewed as 'clearly inappropriate' by almost all the students (more than 90%) all had to do with prohibited collaboration with classmates. Interestingly, Kidwell and Kent (2008) find that unpermitted collaboration is one of the most frequent types of cheating. In their survey of Australian students, they also find that online students are less likely to cheat than students in traditional classes. They surmise that this difference may be due to the online students generally being more mature or, perhaps, that online students are not generally part of campus groups and do not usually know one another.

As with all-natural experiments, the researcher cannot control the 'treatment' experienced by subjects. In the case of our natural experiment, the subjects (students) experienced more than just a transition to online learning halfway through the semester. The pandemic caused some students to lose their job, take on additional family responsibilities, deal with illness themselves or with close family or friends, etc. The students also had different involvement levels with on-campus social networks prior to the transition. Some students commuted to campus for classes and returned home daily whereas others lived on campus, belonged to student organizations and were otherwise socially connected to classmates. Additionally, not all of the students had easy access to the technology required to fully participate in online courses. All of these factors may affect how students perceive the three fraud triangle factors of pressure, opportunity and rationalization with their online learning experience. Also, the University announced early into the transition that students would be permitted to change a course grade to Pass or withdraw completely from a course after final grades were posted. This policy may have lessened pressure for some students. Whereas it is impossible to separate out these confounding factors from the transition to online learning, the mandated transition to online learning still presents a unique opportunity to explore the fraud triangle factors and cheating where students had experienced both traditional and online learning environments with the same instructor and course.

3.2. Research Questions

The first set of research questions focuses on whether students believed cheating was more or less common in the online environment. To some faculty, this question may appear to have an obvious answer that cheating is more prevalent in the online environment. However, at least one study found that cheating was less common among online students (Kidwell & Kent, 2008). Also, Choo and Tan (2008) find a three-way interaction effect among pressure, opportunity and rationalization on the propensity to cheat. So, whereas the online environment may increase opportunity, pressure or rationalization may decrease with the result being no effect on cheating propensity. In our natural experiment, the university adopted a grade accommodation policy allowing students to change a grade of C or better to Pass as well as withdraw from a course completely for up to a week after final course grades had been posted. This policy may have reduced pressure for many students and, in turn, decreased the propensity to cheat. The first set of research questions are:

> Research Question 1A: do students believe cheating was any less or more common after the transition to online learning?
> Research Question 1B: do students believe the university grading accommodations made cheating any less or more likely?

The second set of research questions surrounds the role of the three fraud triangle factors of pressure, opportunity and rationalization. It is possible for the online learning environment to have a different effect on each of these factors. For example, students may believe the online learning environment may have provided a little more opportunity to cheat but much less pressure to cheat and no change in how hard or easy it is to rationalize cheating. In such a case, the net combined fraud triangle factors would actually decrease and lead to less cheating. The second set of research questions are:

> Research Question 2A: do students believe there was any less or more pressure to cheat after the transition to online learning?
> Research Question 2B: do students believe there was any more or less opportunity to cheat after the transition to online learning?
> Research Question 2C: do students believe it was any harder or easier to rationalize or justify cheating after the transition to online learning?
> Research Question 2D: do students' beliefs about pressure, opportunity and rationalization indicate a net change in this set of factors after the transition to online learning?

The natural experiment also provides an opportunity to explore the level of concern students have about the potential effects of cheating on grading fairness and the value of their degree. Of course, there may be no relationship between students' concern over these effects and cheating behavior. That is, a student may be very concerned about cheating devaluing their degree but still cheat. Conversely, a student may never consider cheating because of their own beliefs about academic integrity and be unconcerned about the effect of cheating on the fairness of grading. However, exploring students' concern levels about the effects of cheating may help educators frame the discussion of ethics and academic integrity.

3.3. Methodology

At the conclusion of the Spring 2020 semester, an online survey was sent to students enrolled in Accounting courses. The survey had a total of 11 questions asking the students to select a point on a five-point scale and two open-ended questions. The survey first asked about how common cheating was in the course before and after the transition to online instruction (two questions). Then, the survey had three sets of two questions that asked about the three fraud triangle factors before and after the transition. The survey also included three non-comparative questions:

1) to what extent the university grading accommodations for the Spring 2020 semester made cheating less or more likely
2) to what extent cheating concerned them related to fairness in grading
3) to what extent cheating concerned them related to the value of their degree

The survey concluded with two open-ended questions asking the students for any comments they may have regarding academic integrity in the online environment and what could be done better regarding academic integrity. The complete survey is in the Appendix.

After obtaining Institutional Review Board approval for the survey instrument, the survey was sent to students taking one or more of twelve accounting courses with enrollment almost exclusively comprised of students pursuing either a major or minor in accounting. The survey was sent to students' university email addresses during the interim period between the conclusion of the Spring 2020 semester and the beginning of the Summer 2020 courses. To maximize participation, two follow-up email reminders were sent with the final email reminder sent the day before Summer term courses started. 105 useable responses were received within 14 days of the first email survey being sent. One survey response left the question related to the effect of university grading accommodations (Q9) blank. The analysis of the effect of university grading accommodations is based on 104 responses.

3.4. Analysis and Results

Table 6.1 presents the results relevant to Research Question 1A and Research Question 1B. A t-test of the means for the paired responses on how common cheating was in the course before and after the transition to online learning (Q1 and Q2) was used to address Research Question 1A ($t = 7.367$, $p < .0001$). In addition, a difference score was calculated for each response by subtracting the score for how common they believed cheating was before the transition (Q1) from the score for how common they believed cheating was after the transition (Q2). Less than 1%

Table 6.1 Commonness of Cheating and the Effect of Grading Accommodations on Cheating

How common was cheating . . .	Before the transition to online instruction (Q1)		After the transition to online instruction (Q2)
Mean (n = 105)	1.305		2.219**
Standard Deviation	.590		1.263
After the transition to online learning, cheating was . . .	Less common (Q2 < Q1)	No more or less common (Q2 = Q1)	More common (Q2 > Q1)
Percentage	.95%	52.38%	46.67%
Number (n = 105)	1	55	49
Effect of university grading accommodations on the likelihood of cheating . . . (Q9)			
Mean (n = 104)	2.010++		
Standard Deviation	1.010		
University grading accommodations make cheating . . .	Less likely (Q9 < 3)	No more or less likely (Q9 = 3)	More likely (Q9 > 3)
Percentage	58.10%	36.54%	4.81%
Number (n = 104)	61	38	5

**Indicates that the mean is significantly higher than the other mean at the .0001 level.
++Indicates that the mean is significantly less than 3 at the .0001 level.

believed that cheating was less common after the transition whereas 46.67% believed cheating was more common after the transition.

To avoid biasing responses related to the effect of university grading accommodations on cheating (Q9), students could select a single point on a five-point scale with endpoints labeled as 1 – Far less likely and 5 – Far more likely. The mid-point of 3 thus represents the belief that university grading accommodations made cheating no more or less likely. A majority (58.10%) of responses were below 3 indicating that the university grading accommodations made cheating less likely. In addition, a t-test to determine if the mean response to this question (mean = 2.010) was less than 3 was done (t = 10.004, p < .0001). Taken together, these results imply that students believe cheating would be even more common in an online learning environment without the university grading accommodations.

Table 6.2 presents the results related to the three fraud triangle factors of pressure, opportunity and rationalization in Panels A, B and C, respectively. To address Research Question 2A, a t-test of the means for the paired responses related to how much pressure there was to engage in cheating before and after the transition to online learning (Q3 and Q4) was done (t = 3.87, p = .0002). Difference scores for pressure were also calculated by subtracting the response for before the transition (Q3) from the response for after the transition (Q4). The difference scores related to pressure show that 38.10% of students believed there was more pressure to engage in cheating after the transition to online learning whereas 12.38% of students believed there was less pressure. Given the results related to the effect of university grading accommodations (Research Question 1B), we might expect for students to experience even more pressure in an online learning environment with no grading accommodations.

To address Research Question 2B and Research Question 2C, t-tests were done for the paired responses on Q5 and Q6 related to opportunity (t = 9.66, p < .0001) and the paired responses on Q7 and Q8 related to the ease of rationalizing or justifying cheating (t = 8.22, p < .0001). Difference scores were also calculated for both opportunity (Q6 – Q5) and ease of rationalizing cheating (Q8 – Q7). A majority of students believe that the online learning environment had more opportunity for cheating (59.05%) and made it easier to rationalize or justify cheating (53.33%). Thus, we conclude that there was an increase in each of the three fraud triangle factors of pressure, opportunity and rationalization after the transition to online learning. That is, students believed there was more pressure to cheat, more opportunity to cheat and it was easier to justify cheating after the transition to the online learning environment.

Table 6.3 presents the results of the combined set of fraud triangle factors of pressure, opportunity and rationalization. To address Research Question 2D, we first calculated a combined score for the level of the three fraud triangle factors before the transition to online learning by adding the responses for Q3, Q5 and Q7 (mean = 4.743). Then, we

Table 6.2 Individual Fraud Triangle Factors Before and After the Transition to Online Learning

Panel A: Pressure

Pressure to cheat . . .	Before the transition to online instruction (Q3)		After the transition to online instruction (Q4)
Mean (n = 105)	1.733		2.257*
Standard Deviation	1.179		1.323
After the transition to online learning, there was . . .	Less pressure (Q4 < Q3)	No more or less pressure (Q4 = Q3)	More pressure (Q4 > Q3)
Percentage	12.38%	49.52%	38.10%
Number (n = 105)	13	52	40

Panel B: Opportunity

Opportunity to cheat . . .	Before the transition to online instruction (Q5)		After the transition to online instruction (Q6)
Mean (n = 105)	1.486		2.043**
Standard Deviation	0.722		1.429
After the transition to online learning, there was . . .	Less opportunity (Q6 < Q5)	No more or less opportunity (Q6 = Q5)	More opportunity (Q6 > Q5)
Percentage	0.95%	40.80%	59.05%
Number (n = 105)	1	42	62

Panel C: Rationalization

Hard/easy to rationalize cheating . . .	Before the transition to online instruction (Q7)		After the transition to online instruction (Q8)
Mean (n = 105)	1.524		2.667**
Standard Deviation	0.931		1.384
After the transition to online learning, cheating was	Harder to rationalize (Q8 < Q7)	No harder or easier to rationalize (Q8 = Q7)	Easier to rationalize (Q8 > Q7)
Percentage	3.81%	42.86%	53.33%
Number (n = 105)	4	45	56

*Indicates that the mean is significantly higher than the other mean at the .001 level.
**Indicates that the mean is significantly higher than the other mean at the .0001 level.

Table 6.3 Combined Set of Fraud Triangle Factors Before and After the Transition to Online Learning

The combined factors of pressure, opportunity and ease of rationalization to cheat . . .	Before the transition to online instruction (Q3 + Q5 + Q7)	After the transition to online instruction (Q4 + Q6 + Q8)
Mean (n = 105)	4.743	7.695**
Standard Deviation	1.956	3.487
After the transition to online learning, the level of combined factors were . . .	Lower (Q4 + Q6 + Q8) < (Q3 + Q5 + Q7)	The same (Q4 + Q6 +Q8) = (Q3 + Q5 + Q7)	Higher (Q4 + Q6 +Q8) > (Q3 + Q5 + Q7)
Percentage	1.90%	29.52%	68.57%
Number (n = 105)	2	31	72

**Indicates that the mean is significantly higher than the other mean at the .0001 level.

calculated a combined score for the level of the three fraud triangle factors after the transition to online learning by adding the responses for Q4, Q6 and Q8 (mean = 7.695). A t-test of the means for the paired combined scores was then done (t = 9.82, $p <. 0001$). Finally, a difference of the two combined scores was calculated by subtracting the combined score for before the transition from the combined score after the transition. A positive difference indicates a net increase in the set of three fraud triangle factors whereas a negative difference indicates a net decrease. Over 68% of students indicate a net increase in the set of fraud triangle factors after the transition to online learning. Thus, whereas there may be some variation in how students perceived a change in each of the three factors individually, an overwhelming portion of students perceived a net increase in the combined set of fraud triangle factors after the transition to online learning.

Table 6.4 presents the distributions of responses to the questions relating to students' level of concern over the effect of cheating on fairness in grading (Panel A) and the value of their degree (Panel B). The results from these questions show that many students are not concerned at all about the effect of cheating on fairness in grading (40.00%). Over half (54.29%) indicated they were either not at all concerned or had a low level of concern (score of 1 or 2) about the effect on fairness of grading. The distribution related to Q11 shows that many students either have no concern (33.33%) or a low level of concern (8.57%) about the effect of cheating on the value of their degree. Of course, the distributions in Table 6.4 also reveal that many students do have concerns about the effects of cheating on fairness in grading and the value of their degrees. However,

Table 6.4 Concern About the Effect of Cheating on Fairness in Grading and Value of Degree

Panel A: Effect of cheating on fairness in grading

Level of concern	Not at all 1	2	3	4	A great deal 5
Number	42	15	24	15	9
Percentage	40.00%	14.29%	22.86%	14.29%	8.57%
Cumulative Percentage	40.00%	54.29%	77.14%	91.43%	100.00%

Panel B: Effect of cheating on value of degree

Level of concern	Not at all 1	2	3	4	A great deal 5
Number	35	9	28	16	17
Percentage	33.33%	8.57%	26.67%	15.24%	16.19%
Cumulative Percentage	33.33%	41.90%	68.57%	83.81%	100.00%

given the large number of students who are unconcerned about these effects, an approach of appealing to students to refrain from cheating because honesty serves their own self-interest will likely be inadequate.

3.5. A Call for Change

Whereas the pandemic and the sudden transition to the online learning environment were unique, we believe that the results of our natural experiment reveal deficiencies in the current approach and can serve as a call for meaningful change. Taken as a whole, students expressed that they believed cheating was more common after the transition to online learning when there was more pressure and opportunity to cheat and it was easier to justify cheating. Whereas it seems natural to focus on ways to prevent cheating if higher education is forced to continue testing in the online environment, we would suggest that the discussion should probe much deeper. If the integrity of students falters and crumbles when face-to-face monitoring is absent, the prospect of students maintaining integrity, much less being the human voice for the moral use of information, in the complex professional environment is bleak. Indeed, it is certain that our students will face pressure, have opportunity and find it easy to justify doing the wrong thing in their professional careers. We must prepare them to bring integrity and moral leadership to the decision-making process even when these factors are present – no, especially when these factors are present.

The fact that students believed it was possible for cheating to commonly occur should also cause accounting educators to pause. Whereas it may be easier to wring our hands and bemoan the loss of morality in today's students, we would suggest that perhaps it raises some big questions:

- Does the changing availability of information require that we reconsider what we teach and/or what we test?
- Does it make sense to test students over material they can Google?

The natural experiment results suggest that we, as educators, may be failing to require our students to use and apply information, the very skills needed for relevance in the 'Age of Analytics'. Whereas the methods employed to cheat may have varied from student to student and with the deterrent practices used by teachers, we would put forth that cheating as traditionally understood becomes much less likely, regardless of the presence of face-to-face monitoring, if we are assessing students on their ability to apply and direct the use of information. On the other hand, testing students over material that can be looked up easily makes cheating very difficult to eliminate. Perhaps rather than trying to think of ways to prevent students from looking up information they don't remember, a needed skill in the workplace, we should instead reconsider whether what we are assessing and how we are assessing it prepares students to lead in the 'Age of Analytics'.

4. Design Principles for Implementing Relevant Ethics Education

Business and accounting programs have operated in a monoculture of ideas about ethics dominated by the neoclassical microeconomic theory of the firm. In this monoculture, the purpose of a corporation is to maximize shareholder wealth. The right thing to do, according to this theory is the thing that maximizes profits. The language of business ethics has been the language of utilitarianism and the cost/benefit analysis. It is a language that translates well into spreadsheets for use in C-suites. The elegance of the consequentialist calculation is grist for the mill that converts humans to data points, Wells Fargo customer consent to an unnecessary formality, Enron losses to off-balance sheet arrangements, WorldCom operating expenses to pre-paid capacity and representational faithfulness to a quaint notion of a bygone era.

When the task is to replace the monoculture that has persisted in business schools, the answer is not to find a better monoculture, but rather to cultivate a diverse ecology of ideas (Mau, 2018). We look to liberal arts education to construct a model for ethics in business and accounting. The difference in approach is illustrated in Figure 6.1 depicting the contrast in convergent and divergent ways of thinking about business and accounting issues of moral significance.

The first triangle represents the way that ethical issues are addressed in an accounting context so as to converge upon an optimal and defensible decision. Accounting problems arise in a complex environment with multiple stakeholder interests. We typically teach students to accumulate data from multiple sources. Then we equip students with applicable frameworks to address the issue including relevant authoritative accounting standards, codes of conduct and analytical tools. The emphasis is on predicting the consequences that are likely to arise and measuring the impact of each. Students learn to apply those tools to produce an answer that will stand up to scrutiny, perhaps even in a multiple-choice format. In a real-world setting, the solution would be implemented and the information system would capture information on its performance for the next iteration of the processing model.

The second triangle represents the divergent process typical of a liberal arts approach to addressing ethical issues. In the early phase, the emphasis is on understanding the problem and the constructs that we use to represent the ideas involved. The process of considering ethical perspectives may actually broaden the scope of the problem as we grapple with its complexity. The output of the process may be multiple solutions,

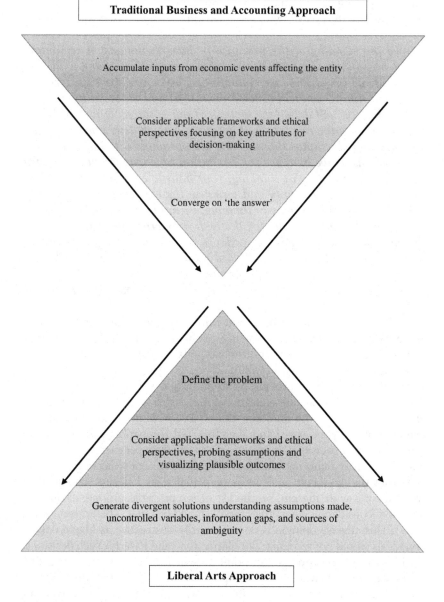

Figure 6.1 Contrasting Approaches to Problem Solving

each with desirable and undesirable attributes and subject to uncertainty due to variables that are uncontrolled in the process. The emphasis in the classroom would be on the inclusiveness of the process and quality of the logical reasoning.

Designer Bruce Mau addressed accounting educators at the 2018 Annual Meeting of the American Accounting Association. He concluded his remarks with the following exhortation:

> *We are standing at the precipice of two revolutions: A revolution of possibility and a revolution of negation. Accountants will help decide which of these we embrace because you will set the terms of our decisions. You will provide the insight and the visibility into our future. You will define the metrics of our sustainable way of life. If we embrace the revolution of negation, we will deny science, we fall back on reductionist thinking and cut our world into falsely discreet problems. If we embrace the revolution of possibility, we will need your comprehensivist thinking, your holistic ecosystem design, and your ability to quantify and visualize the challenges and possibilities we face. In this way of thinking, I want to argue that everything counts. I want to argue for the end of externalities. I want you to push accounting to a higher order of complexity and lead the way to understanding what we will need to accomplish in order to have a future that we and our children can be proud of*
>
> *(Mau, 2018, min. 54)*

Mau (2018) is arguing for divergent thinking, rather than a reductionist or convergent approach, to solving problems. Employing a divergent approach to ethics issues requires students to develop or draw upon thinking and decision-making skills.

A practical education provides tools and skills to function in a complex environment. A liberalizing education forces us to grapple with constructs that may generate more questions than answers. It may introduce factors that are not easily measured and, therefore, not compatible with traditional ways of making decisions. It involves classical ethics perspectives and questions of what is right, just and fair. Whereas such constructs are essential to disrupt the monoculture of ideas perpetuated by business schools, they are last, by a wide margin, on the list of six priorities among accounting educators considering what ethics topics should be taught (Blanthorne et al., 2007). This adverse opinion is not necessarily obstructive as liberal education ideals would not recognize popularity as a valid basis for such decisions.

This may be an appropriate point at which to clarify our intentions by issuing a call toward a liberal approach to accounting ethics education. We do not insist that it is the only way or even the best way in all circumstances to introduce ethics in the curriculum. We seek to provide encouragement for those who question whether the positive science of neoclassical microeconomic theory that has dominated our institutions is addressing the right questions and serving our students' and society's long-term best interest. This approach probably works best in a dedicated three-hour course on ethics.

For programs in which a serious effort at integrating ethics across the curriculum is undertaken, the Giving Voice to Values (GVV) curriculum has achieved acclaim in industry, executive education and traditional accounting programs. Christensen, Cote and Latham (2018) provide evidence of the effectiveness of the GVV approach integrated across four courses. Miller, Shawver and Mintz (2020) and Shawver and Miller (2017) report on the effectiveness of the GVV approach in accounting classrooms. The GVV approach is featured in three separate chapters in the companion volume to this text. The GVV approach is relatively simple to implement compared to the level and type of preparation that it would take to get comfortable with over 2,000 years of classical perspectives on ethics. As such it might be reasonable to train some or all accounting faculty to implement a GVV module in traditional accounting courses. The GVV approach is designed to produce demonstrable results in the near-term and equip students and professionals with skills and tools that they can use to apply to situations in which their gut reaction provides an unambiguous feeling on the right thing to do.

Mau's (2018, min. 24) first design principle in his list of 24 ideas to guide his teams is, "First inspire. Design is leadership. Lead by design". The GVV curriculum is founded on an inspirational principle, to give those who know what they should do the voice through which they can live and speak their values (Gentile, 2012). The approach may be especially appealing to those who hold the view that classical ethical perspectives provide the tools to rationalize whatever choice is most appealing at the moment. To take such a dim view of classical perspectives, however, is to deny the value of rigorous consideration of ethics to accountants who are training to move into positions with considerable impact on distributive justice in our society. There are those among us, although they may be outliers, who find inspiration in the classical ethical perspectives and the liberalizing approach. Let us give them permission to inspire our students to confront big questions and complicated answers.

5. Conclusion

In writing about science education Arons (1973) shared the following insight that may be equally true in the context of today's accounting curriculum:

> *Wider understanding of science will be achieved only by giving students a chance to synthesize experience and thought into knowledge and understanding. Such a chance is not available in the deluge of unintelligible names and jargon precipitated at unmanageable pace and volume in so large a proportion of our college courses, and it is not available in the absence of humanistic, historical, or philosophical perspectives within those courses.*
>
> *(Arons, 1973, p. 769)*

Indeed, in today's 'Age of Analytics', it is critical that accountants bring synthesis and perspective to the table. It is no longer adequate to train competent calculators and classifiers and urge them to have integrity. Relevance demands that today's students be able to apply and guide the use of information with integrity.

Almost 100 years ago, long before bots or artificial intelligence, Cross (1922) wrote about the concept of the palimpsest, a parchment or tablet upon which traces of the original text remain although it has been effaced and written over, to describe the value of the liberal education in the context of professional training:

> Life is a parchment with a double text; the one bold, compelling, the other faintly traced upon the page, but full of the philosophy, the hidden meaning, that makes life worth the effort which one must put forth to earn the means to live. Thus, I return to 'palimpsest'. The external and practical courses college students are obliged to take to fit themselves for their particular jobs in a physical world will become the visible blackletter text on the parchment. Beneath this text, if they plan their education wisely, liberally, will lie faintly visible the words of wisdom which will be their key to living happily and fully in a world of mind and spirit above the no less real world of meat and drink and raiment. Those whose education is such a palimpsest will find themselves able in imagination to take wing and poise balanced high above earth's confusion, and to flash their thoughts through time and space while their hands toil and their bodies sweat in the relentless here and now. In education the straight line is neither the shortest, the safest, nor the surest way. Take the longer, the liberalizing way.
>
> (Cross, 1922, p. 352)

We conclude by inviting accounting educators to consider the importance of supplying the faint, but enduring, imprint over which our students will write their stories. The bold-face type will chronicle accomplishments, promotions and badges of competency earned as they upskill to the latest technology. If we do our jobs well, the stories will have depth and meaning that will transcend the age in which they were written.

References

Appiah, K. A. (2020). *If My Classmates Are Going to Cheat on an Online Exam, Why Can't I?* Retrieved July 8th, 2020, from www.nytimes.com/2020/04/07/magazine/if-my-classmates-are-going-to-cheat-on-an-online-exam-why-cant-i.html

Arons, A. B. (1973). Toward Wider Public Understanding of Science. *American Journal of Physics*, 41(6), 769–782.

Association to Advance Collegiate Schools of Business (AACSB). (2018). *Accounting Standards*. AACSB-International. Retrieved July 21st, 2020, from www.aacsb.edu/accreditation/standards/accounting

Blanthorne, C., Kovar, S. E., & Fisher, D. G. (2007). Accounting Educators' Opinions About Ethics in the Curriculum: An Extensive View. *Issues in Accounting Education*, 22(3), 355–390.

Choo, F., & Tan, K. (2008). The Effect of Fraud Triangle Factors on Students' Cheating Behaviors. *Advances in Accounting Education*, 9, 205–220.

Christensen, A., Cote, J., & Latham, C. K. (2018). Developing Ethical Confidence: The Impact of Action-Oriented Ethics Instruction in an Accounting Curriculum. *Journal of Business Ethics*, 153(4), 1157–1175.

Coffey, S. S. (2020a). *Our Proposal to Evolve CPA Licensure*. Retrieved July 8th, 2020, from https://blog.aicpa.org/2020/01/our-proposal-to-evolve-cpa-licensure.html#sthash.M7OhU8cA.68Cx9EET.dpbs

Coffey, S. S. (2020b). *Another Step Closer to Evolving CPA Licensure*. Retrieved July 8th, 2020, from https://blog.aicpa.org/2020/05/another-step-closer-to-evolving-cpa-licensure.html#sthash.y2xRwDAE.WHV0N0Ip.dpbs

Cressey, D. R. (1973). *Other People's Money*. Montclair, NJ: Patterson Smith.

Cross, E. A. (1922). Palimpsest. *The North American Review*, 216(802), 347–352.

Gentile, M. (2012). *Giving Voice to Values: How to Speak Your Mind When You Know What Is Right*. New Haven, CT: Yale University Press.

Harari, Y. N. (2019). *21 Lessons for the 21st Century*. New York: Vintage.

Heilweil, R. (2020). *Paranoia About Cheating Is Making Online Education Terrible for Everyone*. Retrieved July 8th, 2020, from www.vox.com/recode/2020/5/4/21241062/schools-cheating-proctorio-artificial-intelligence

Kidwell, L. A., & Kent, J. (2008). Integrity at a Distance: A Study of Academic Misconduct Among University Students on and Off Campus. *Accounting Education: An International Journal*, 17(Supplement), S3–S16.

King, C. G., Guyette, Jr. R. W., & Piotrowski, C. (2009). Online Exams and Cheating: An Empirical Analysis of Business Students' Views. *The Journal of Educators Online*, 6(1), 1–11.

Kubena, B. (2020). Louisiana Colleges Address Grades, Cheating as Classes Go Online after Coronavirus Closures. *The Advocate*. Retrieved July 8th, 2020, from www.theadvocate.com/baton_rouge/news/coronavirus/article_ba562fe4-7051-11ea-8324-5f8eeaecfca1.html

Mau, B. (2018). *Awakening*. Paper presented at the 2018 American Accounting Association Annual Meeting, Washington DC, USA. Retrieved July 21st, 2020, from https://aaahq.org/Meetings/2018/Annual-Meeting/Video-Gallery

Melati, I. N., Wilopo, R., & Hapsari, I. (2018). Analysis of the Effect of Fraud Triangle Dimensions, Self-Efficacy, and Religiosity on Academic Fraud in Accounting Students. *The Indonesian Accounting Review*, 8(2), 189–203.

Miller, W. F., Shawver, T. J., & Mintz, S. M. (2020). Measuring the Value of Integrating GVV Into a Standalone Accounting Ethics Course. *Journal of Accounting Education*, 51, 1–19.

Shawver, T. J., & Miller, W. F. (2017). Moral Intensity Revisited: Measuring the Benefit of Accounting Ethics Interventions. *Journal of Business Ethics*, 141(3), 587–603.

Zimmerman, J. (2020). Coronavirus and the Great Online Learning Experiment. *The Chronicle of Higher Education*. Retrieved July 8th, 2020, from www.chronicle.com/article/Coronavirusthe-Great/248216/

Appendix
Survey Sent to Accounting Students

We are attempting to gather data in order to improve the student learning experience in the online environment. Academic integrity is one aspect of the online environment that we are hearing about from students. As such, we would like your opinion. The Southeastern handbook identifies the following behaviors as examples of academic integrity issues:

The use of unauthorized material, communication with fellow students during an examination, attempting to benefit from the work of another student and similar behavior that defeats the intent of an examination or other class work

For simplicity, we will refer to academic integrity violations as "cheating" in the questions that follow.

We are not collecting any personally identifiable information. The demographic and experimental data that we collect will be reported in aggregate only. You are under no obligation to complete this survey. You may opt out at any time by simply exiting the survey. We are aware of no risks or benefits to you from participating. Your participation is greatly appreciated and may result in benefits to the program, however.

1. In your opinion, before classes were moved to an online format how common was cheating in this class?

   Mark only one oval.

                         1   2   3   4   5
   Virtually nonexistent   Widespread throughout the class

2. In your opinion, after classes were moved to an online format how common was cheating in this class?

   Mark only one oval.

                         1   2   3   4   5
   Virtually nonexistent   Widespread throughout the class

3. In your opinion, before moving to an online environment, how much pressure to engage in academic integrity violations did students perceive?

Mark only one oval.

	1	2	3	4	5	
No pressure						Extreme pressure

4. In your opinion, after moving to an online environment, how much pressure to engage in academic integrity violations did students perceive?

Mark only one oval.

	1	2	3	4	5	
No pressure						Extreme pressure

5. In your opinion, before moving to an online environment, how much opportunity to engage in cheating did students perceive?

Mark only one oval.

	1	2	3	4	5	
No opportunity						Unlimited opportunity

6. In your opinion, after moving to an online environment, how much opportunity to engage in cheating did students perceive?

Mark only one oval.

	1	2	3	4	5	
No opportunity						Unlimited opportunity

7. In your opinion, before moving to an online environment, how hard/ easy was it for students to rationalize or justify cheating in this class?

Mark only one oval.

	1	2	3	4	5	
Extremely hard						Extremely easy

8. In your opinion, after moving to an online environment, how hard/ easy was it for students to rationalize or justify cheating in this class?

Mark only one oval.

	1	2	3	4	5	
Extremely hard						Extremely easy

9. In your opinion, did the university's grading accommodations (pass/ fail and withdrawal policy) make cheating less likely or more likely?

Mark only one oval.

	1	2	3	4	5	
Far less likely						Far more likely

10. To what extent does cheating give you concern about fairness in grading?

Mark only one oval.

	1	2	3	4	5	
Not at all concerned						Concerned a great deal

11. To what extent does cheating give you concern about the value of your degree?

    Mark only one oval.

	1	2	3	4	5	
Not at all concerned						Concerned a great deal

12. Please provide any comments regarding academic integrity issues in the online environment. Of particular interest are any changes that you noted when classes moved online.

13. Do you have any suggestions as to how we can do better with regard to academic integrity?

Part 2

Giving Voice to Values

Making Ethics Real

7 Giving Voice to Values

Operationalizing Ethical Decision-Making in Accounting

William F. Miller & Tara J. Shawver

Mary Gentile's 'Giving Voice to Values' (GVV) curriculum is a relatively new and exciting addition to the tools available to accounting professors for teaching ethics. The overarching goal of the offering is to increase the likelihood that a person will take purposeful action when they encounter an ethical issue (Gentile, 2010). The curriculum has been adopted by over 1,000 organizations across the globe primarily due to the ease with which it can be implemented as a stand-alone training module and/or integrated into an existing ethics training program. The offering includes discipline-specific cases so it can be adopted in virtually any industry or profession. After personally testing its effectiveness on nearly a thousand undergraduate accounting students over the last five years, we find it effective not only in increasing the likelihood that students will act on their values but also in increasing student confidence and providing them with skills needed to effectively deal with the ethical issues they are likely to encounter once they enter the accounting profession. We also believe it increases students' critical thinking skills, develops a questioning mindset (professional skepticism) and makes it less likely they will subordinate their own judgment to others like a supervisor, organization or client.

The GVV offering is described as a post decision-making (Gentile, 2010) framework because the focus is on acting once an issue is encountered. One of the underlying assumptions of the GVV offering is that most people recognize an unethical practice when encountered, so GVV focuses on what to do next. This is very different than the typical approach to teaching ethics. Most ethical decision-making models incorporate the four parts of Rest's (1986) ethical decision-making model: ethical sensitivity, moral reasoning, moral judgment and moral action. Rest's model typically entails the teaching of ethical theories, ethical decision-making models and moral development, requiring the instructor to have a background in ethics to teach it. Gentile (2010) does not consider GVV to be an ethical decision-making model. However, some suggest that whereas it might not be the intent of GVV to increase a person's ability to recognize an ethical issue or to think and act ethically, it may very well do that too (Edwards & Kirkham, 2013; Shawver & Miller, 2018).

There is a clear need for an offering like this. Most unethical practices go unreported, or when they do get reported, they often are not elevated within the organization to the appropriate party to ensure that the situation is rectified. Gentile (2010) contends that whereas most people recognize unethical practices when they see them, they fail to take action at that point because they don't know how, don't want to get involved, don't know who to report it to, lack the confidence to and/or are fearful of the repercussions if they do so. She contends that it is very easy for a person to rationalize not reporting an issue.

Central to the GVV curriculum are what Gentile (2010) describes as 'common reasons and rationalizations' that people use not only in deciding not to report an unethical practice but also in justifying the unethical decisions and practices to themselves and others. There are four common reasons and rationalizations that Gentile (2010) identifies and a fifth specific to the accounting profession identified by Mintz and Morris (2014), as shown in Table 7.1.

The GVV curriculum is centered on ways to overcome these common excuses, whether self-prescribed or used by others. The curriculum also recognizes, and takes into account, the uniqueness of the individuals involved in the dilemma. For instance, whereas some people may be extroverts, others may be introverts: whereas some people may be more outgoing and very comfortable speaking to others, some people may be shy and not comfortable talking with others. Unfortunately, unethical practices are so common that all accounting graduates will likely encounter multiple ethical dilemmas over the course of their careers. The curriculum includes a self-assessment students can complete to help them understand their individual strengths and weaknesses in regard to interacting with others. It also includes a set of tools (what Gentile, 2010, calls

Table 7.1 GVV Reasons and Rationalizations

Type	Justification
Expected or standard practice	Everybody does it. It's nothing new; we have been doing it this way for a very long time. It really is standard practice. It's expected (of me, you, the organization, the industry).
Materiality	This is not a big deal. The impact of this action is not material. It doesn't hurt anyone.
Locus of responsibility	It's not my job (or yours) to question this; I'm just following orders here (and so should you). It's company policy.
Locus of loyalty	It is in the best interest of the boss, the department, the company. If the practice stops then there will be negative ramifications: I know this isn't quite fair to the customer, but I (you, we) don't want to hurt my (your/our) direct reports/team/boss/company.
It's a one-time request	We really need this and I (you) need to just let it go this one time. Everything will be fine moving forward and so I (you) should ignore it this one time.

'levers') to maximize the likelihood they will not only speak up when an ethical issue is encountered but also be able to successfully stop the unethical practice from continuing. A description of common levers is shown in Table 7.2.

Table 7.2 Examples of GVV Levers (Tools)

Lever	Description/Example
Ask for help	Remember, you are never alone. We all have numerous resources available to call upon for help and advice: co-workers, colleagues, mentors, professional organizations, hotlines, etc. Accounting-specific avenues and required codes of conduct should be covered in the course that GVV is integrated into (like section 2.130.020 of the AICPA code of conduct).
Find allies	Recognize that you do not necessarily have to tackle or resolve the issue by yourself. Seek others in the organization to help you report or resolve the issue. Allies can be used to help jointly address the issue or simply referred to when discussing the issue with your supervisor. For example: 'I understand what you are saying, but I am still uncomfortable with this, let's walk down the hall and ask X (the boss's colleague or boss) what they think'. The mere mention of bringing others into a situation might bring it to resolution.
Identification of risk: consider both short- and long-term consequences	Many issues are created from only considering short-term consequences (which might all be positive). The decision maker might not be aware of the negative long-term consequences or the risks surrounding their actions, so identifying them as a point of discussion might provide an avenue by which to reverse a course of action.
Research the topic	Identify authoritative support by reviewing company policies, procedures and codes of conduct, as well as those of the profession for the parties involved (e.g., the AICPA code of conduct). Being able to cite specific guidance when addressing the issue can be quite persuasive.
Provide solutions rather than complaints	To minimize defensive or negative reactions to raising an issue, it is better to present a solution to a problem, rather than to complain about a problem.
Consider what is unique about you or the situation that you can use to your advantage	If a new employee, you can broach the discussion by using that to your advantage. For example: 'I know I am new, so I probably just don't understand why we do X in that way. Can you help me to understand it?'
Identify the impact of the issue on both primary and secondary stakeholders	Identification of consequences to both primary and secondary stakeholders may provide another avenue for discussion. Often time people do not consider the potentially far-reaching effects of their actions to secondary stakeholders.
Highlight the benefits of the proposed solution	A discussion of benefits or advantages of the solution can be used as a way to persuade the decision maker to follow your suggestion.

Shawver and Miller (2018)

The GVV curriculum does not promote a combative stance when it comes to acting on one's values. It promotes a methodology to rationally discuss an unethical practice and successfully resolve it through persuasion. The GVV methodology complements the reporting requirements for members of the American Institute of Public Accounting (AICPA) and the Institute of Management Accountants (IMA). Both the AICPA and the IMA require its members to report ethics violations to their immediate supervisor. If reporting to that person does not resolve the matter, the member must continue up the natural reporting chain of command for their position until they reach the audit committee of the board of directors. If after reporting the matter to the board it is not resolved, the member cannot report the matter externally without breaching the confidentiality standard that both the AICPA and the IMA have. Under the AICPA standard, even if a member decides to resign their position, that does not absolve them of their obligation to the profession to try to resolve the underlying ethical issue.

Through the use of GVV it is hoped that the matter can be brought to resolution long before the accountant makes it up the entire reporting chain. However, the member needs to be prepared to do just that. The GVV methodology fits the accounting profession's code of conduct like a glove. The steps in the GVV methodology are shown in Table 7.3.

1. Implementation of GVV Into an Accounting Class

All the curricular materials needed to integrate GVV into an accounting class as well as more general information about GVV is available for free online.[1] Shawver and Miller's (2018) book is also a great resource for anyone who wants to integrate GVV into their accounting classes.

The GVV materials provide instructors the flexibility to choose which cases and topics they want to use for the courses they teach. We have integrated the GVV curriculum into our required courses, Financial Accounting and Advanced Financial Accounting and one elective, Accounting Ethics. In our Advanced Financial Accounting course, we dedicate three weeks of the semester (approximately 20% of the course) to the GVV module. We have modified our approach several times over the last five years and will discuss what we believe to be the most effective way to integrate the curriculum next.

The GVV module we incorporate includes videos, assigned readings, lecture and discussion. The University of Texas at Austin has integrated the GVV into their college of business curriculum. They created a series of eight 3- to 5-minute videos that provide all the background the student needs to know about GVV prior to it being introduced in class. These videos can be found online.[2] They include the following topics:

- Introduction to GVV
- GVV Pillar 1 Values

Table 7.3 The Steps in the GVV Methodology

Steps	Description/Example
Identify the main arguments, reasons and rationalizations you will need to address.	Why might you be inclined to not speak up? If you don't speak up, will you be failing to live up to the AICPA, IMA or other code of conduct? Will you be subordinating your own judgment by failing to act? Are your reasons and rationalizations valid? If you do report the issue, what reasons and rationalizations do you think you will hear? Are they valid?
What's at stake for the key parties, including those who disagree with you? What's at stake for you?	Identify all the risks associated with the ethical dilemma you have encountered to both primary and secondary stakeholders. Make sure to identify both the short- and long-term consequences should the practice not be stopped. Many unethical practices are unintentionally put in place originally because of a failure to recognize the risk to all stakeholders or the long-term consequences of an action.
What levers can you use to influence those who disagree with you?	In addition to the risks identified in the prior step, identify all the levers you have at your disposal to help you evaluate the issue and fully prepare prior to your reporting it. See Table 7.2 for a list of common levers you might consider. Then, avail yourself of these levers.
What is your most powerful and persuasive response to the reasons and rationalizations you need to address?	Imagine reporting this issue to your boss or other person of authority. For each reason and rationalization that you have already identified, identify your best response. Think through what a conversation about the topic might be like. Your boss says X (a reason and rationalization you identified) and you say Y (what you think will overcome that excuse). In other words, in this step you are thinking through the conversation that needs to be had when the issue is reported. This step should incorporate the levers you have previously identified.
To whom should the argument be made? When and in what context?	More likely than not, through the process of completing the previous steps you will have identified where you want to start and with whom you want to discuss the matter. You need to decide if its best to have an initial one-on-one meeting with that party or parties, or perhaps you will decide to discuss the issue with someone else (a colleague). You need to decide the who, what, when and where of the meeting. You also need to think about possible next steps if you are not able to resolve the issue at this first meeting. Have a plan. Think through how the person or persons you are going to meet with might react and be prepared for various alternatives.
Report the issue.	The five steps here are designed to prepare you for your meeting and give you confidence that you will be successful in resolving the issue.

- GVV Pillar 2 Choice
- GVV Pillar 3 Normalization
- GVV Pillar 4 Purpose
- GVV Pillar 5 Self-Knowledge and Alignment
- GVV Pillar 6 Voice
- GVV Pillar 7 Reasons and Rationalizations

When we first started to implement GVV, we assigned readings on each of these topics for our students to complete before our first lecture on the material. We have found that the students are much more likely to watch the videos than they are to complete the readings. The videos aren't lengthy, and the students have commented that they are fun to watch. We recommend that the material be covered before the first lecture as it then provides instructors more time in class to concentrate on the actual application of GVV to specific cases.

We have each student read and complete an individual written reflection using 'A Tale of Two Stories' (Gentile, 2010) in class. This case first requires students to think about and share an experience where they have previously encountered an ethical issue and spoken up. The case then requires students to think about and share an experience where they have encountered an ethical issue but failed to speak up. The questions answered and discussed in class with this exercise are:

When the student spoke up:

- What did you do, and what was the impact?
- What motivated you to speak up and act?
- How satisfied are you? How would you like to have responded? (This question is not about rejecting or defending past actions but rather about imagining your ideal scenario.)
- What would have made it easier for you to speak/act?

  - Things within your own control.
  - Things within the control of others.

When the student did not speak up:

- What happened?
- Why didn't you speak up or act? What would have motivated you to do so?
- How satisfied are you? How would you like to have responded? (This question is not about rejecting or defending past actions but rather about imagining your ideal scenario.)
- What would have made it easier for you to speak/act?

  - Things within your own control.
  - Things within the control of others.

We then have the students read the mini case 'A Billing Bind' (Gentile, 2010) and complete the first five steps of the GVV methodology by answering these questions:

- What are the main arguments you are trying to counter? That is, what are the reasons and rationalizations you need to address?
- What is at stake for the key parties, including those who disagree with you?
- What levers can you use to influence those who disagree with you?
- What is your most powerful and persuasive response to the reasons and rationalizations you need to address? To whom should the argument be made? When and in what context?

This assignment, like the first exercise, is completed in class and provides students with needed practice in applying the GVV methodology to a real case. It also provides the instructor with the opportunity to solidify the concepts the students would have heard about during the videos they watched: GVV terminology, self-assessment, shared/universal values, common reasons and rationalizations, levers and so on. The billing bind case is great for this and engages the students in a scenario that they can easily imagine finding themselves in. The case deals with an accounting intern being asked by her supervisor to overbill for her work. Whereas our students complete the two assignments during class, there is nothing preventing a professor from assigning them to be completed outside of class and then just having the discussion in class. Therefore, there is flexibility as to the amount of in-class time that you might dedicate to GVV.

We include both individual and group assignments surrounding four specific cases that we selected for inclusion in our Advanced Financial Accounting class. There are many cases available to choose from (with more being published regularly). So, again, an instructor has great flexibility as to what to include if they choose to integrate GVV into one or more of their classes. We have the students form groups of three or four and then randomly assign each group one of the following four cases (copies of the full cases can be found online):[3]

- Jeff Salett – From the Top, Sort of (Request of Controller to not follow GAAP)
- Student Privileges with Strings Attached (Request of an intern to breach university software licensing rules)
- The New Associate (Request to allow/ignore a breach of CPA firm independence)
- The Part-time Job with Full-time Challenges (Uncovering fraud and being asked to not report it)

When we first implemented GVV into our 'Advanced Financial Accounting' classes, we had each student individually analyze each of the three cases not assigned as part of their group project by responding to the following four questions in writing:

- What would motivate you to speak up and act or to stay silent?
- What are the arguments you would try to counter?
- What would you do and who would you talk to?
- What do you hope will happen and what will you do if it does not?

However, we then modified our GVV implementation by adding an additional six questions to encourage reflection and discussion surrounding reporting up the chain of the management hierarchy as prescribed by the AICPA and the IMA.

- What concerns would you have if you discussed this situation with an internal manager who is your direct supervisor?
- What concerns would you have if you discussed this situation with a Chief Financial Officer (CFO), Chief Executive Officer (CEO) or member of the board of directors?
- What concerns would you have if you discussed this situation with someone outside the organization?
- How can you minimize your concerns if you discussed this issue with an internal manager who is your direct supervisor?
- How can you minimize your concerns if you discussed this issue with a CFO, CEO or member of the board of directors?
- How can you minimize your concerns if you discussed this issue with someone outside the organization?

There are two benefits of incorporating these individual assignments: the students are provided more opportunity to practice with GVV and they come to class prepared to evaluate and participate in the discussion of each group case.

The group assignment requires the application of the entire GVV methodology to the cases assigned. Each group must answer and turn in a written response to the first five questions of the GVV methodology on their assigned case. They need to decide how to bring the case to resolution using the GVV methodology and role play that solution to the entire class. Each group creates the characters needed to effectively resolve the case and turn in a written copy of their scripted role play. A standard rubric (Appendix A) is used by both the professor and the student audience members to evaluate the group's analysis. Students are asked to fill out the evaluation immediately following the performance and that is followed by a class discussion of the performance as well. The discussion often results in a much deeper understanding of the case and identifies additional ways in which the case could have been brought to resolution. A detailed description of the individual and group assignments can be found in Appendix B.

Whereas we find a great deal of benefit in implementing GVV in our Advanced Financial Accounting courses, we realize there may be resistance in doing so by others due to the amount of course time it takes. The use of role play is additive and supported by a line of research surrounding performative ethics. However, there is still benefit to be gained from integrating GVV without the role-play assignment. We integrated GVV into an Introduction to Financial Accounting course and we did not include role play. Instead, we modified the individual assignment to have each student respond to the first five questions of the GVV methodology in writing. We then discussed the responses to each of those questions in class. This enables GVV to be implemented and cuts in half the in-class time dedicated to it.

Students report that they really enjoy the GVV module and pre-post tests have shown that the material does increase student confidence and the likelihood they will report and try to resolve an ethical issue when encountered. We are greatly encouraged by this. We have observed a much greater depth of student engagement, participation and discussion of cases when we apply the GVV methodology than when we have used other decision-making models. One of the great things about the GVV methodology is that it is designed for ease of use and modification. We have modified cases, case questions and/or added questions to particular cases to get at specific concepts that we want to cover. To demonstrate this, we have written the following case and incorporated the questions that we wanted addressed, versus only the standard GVV methodological questions. Teaching notes for this case are also included.

2. Accounting for Values: A CFO's Dilemma

2.1. Abstract

You are the CFO of Lockheed Martin, hold both a Certified Management Accountant (CMA) certification and a Certified Public Accountant (CPA) license and since 2015 have been instrumental in the company experiencing an 81% increase in total stockholder return, a 10% increase in the annual dividends and a $2 billion increase in net earnings. One of the governments with which Lockheed Martin does business is Saudi Arabia. On October 2nd, 2018, *Washington Post* reporter Jamal Khashoggi was brutally murdered and dismembered inside the Saudi Arabian consulate in Istanbul Turkey. The company's historical position has been to follow the lead of the USA Government and continue to do business with customers unless the USA Government prohibits it. Students are provided both the company's and the IMA's codes of conduct to determine potential violations. This case provides students the opportunity to analyze and explore real values conflicts they may encounter in their future careers.

2.2. The Company

Lockheed Martin has annual revenues of $51 billion and is ranked 58th in the 2018 Fortune 500. They employ over 100,000 employees (roughly 92.8% are USA based), working in the areas of aeronautics, missiles and fire control, rotary and mission systems and space. Sixty-nine percent of Lockheed Martin's revenue comes from the USA Government, 30% from International Customers and 1% from USA Commercial and other clients (Lockheed Martin Corporation, 2018b). Sixty-three percent of the international revenue comes from the USA Government effectively selling Lockheed Martin's products to foreign governments (indirect sales revenue), with the remaining 37% of foreign sales being made directly (Lockheed Martin Corporation, 2018a).

Per Lockheed Martin's 2018 fact sheet (Lockheed Martin Corporation, 2018b), the four product areas referenced earlier are described as follows:

Aeronautics ($20.1 billion revenue): designs, engineers and creates the world's most advanced aircraft, including the world's only fifth-generation multi-role stealth fighter – the F35. Aeronautics is also the home of Skunk Works – one of the nation's preeminent rapid solution providers.

Missiles and Fire Control ($7.2 billion revenue): develops and produces electric, optic and smart munitions systems and is the pioneer in the field of high-performance missile, missile defense, ground, vehicle and rocket technology. It is the home to Lockheed Martin Energy, which develops and implements bio, wind and tidal energy systems.

Rotary and Mission Systems ($14.2 billion revenue): designs, manufactures and services and supports military and civil helicopters, naval and radar systems and provides world-class systems integration, training and logistics. It is home to Lockheed Martin's autonomous systems, cyber security C4ISR and electronic warfare systems.

Space ($9.5 billion revenue): creates technologies that power exploration, connectivity and security from space. Major programs include GPS III and secure communications, human and robotic exploration of deep space, strategic deterrence and missile defense and commercial communications and remote sensing.

Lockheed Martin's Mission: we solve complex challenges, advance scientific discovery and deliver innovative solutions to help our customers keep people safe.

Lockheed Martin's Vision: be the global leader in supporting our customers' missions, strengthening security and advancing scientific discovery.

Lockheed Martin's Values: do What's Right, Respect Others, Perform with Excellence.

Lockheed Martin takes being ethical and maintaining an ethical culture very seriously, utilizing the core values identified earlier as the foundation of their code of conduct. Every Lockheed Martin employee must sign an agreement that they have received and will abide by the Lockheed Martin Code of Conduct (Lockheed Martin, 2017). The Lockheed Martin Code of Conduct has integrated Mary Gentile's GVV program (Lockheed Martin Corporation, n.d.) into it and every employee must participate in annual ethics training. The GVV program provides individuals with the confidence and tools necessary to report an ethical issue when it is encountered. Lockheed Martin demands that every employee question and report issues that they deem to be potentially in violation of or in conflict with their core values.

One of Lockheed Martin's ethical standards surrounds the protection of human rights which states in part: we are committed to good citizenship, which includes the protection and advancement of internationally recognized human rights (Lockheed Martin, 2017).

2.3. The Dilemma

You are the CFO of Lockheed Martin, hold both a CMA certification and CPA license and since 2015 have been instrumental in the company experiencing an 81% increase in total stockholder return, a 10% increase in the annual dividends and a $2 billion increase in net earnings.

One of the governments with which Lockheed Martin does business is Saudi Arabia. They have done so since 1965, with signed deals totaling $900 million for delivery in 2019 and 2020 (Zillman, 2018). In addition, there is a proposal to supply Saudi Arabia with Lockheed Martin's Thaad Air Defense System for $15 billion (Capaccio & Flatley, 2018).

On October 2nd, 2018, *Washington Post* reporter Jamal Khashoggi was brutally murdered and dismembered inside the Saudi Arabian consulate in Istanbul Turkey. Over the next couple of weeks as facts about the murder slowly came to light, you learned that the USA CIA concluded that the murder was planned and executed at the behest of the highest levels of the Saudi Government. During this same time, reporters, members of the public and some employees began questioning whether Lockheed Martin should continue to do business with Saudi Arabia. You know the company needs to take a position and are certain that, during the next earnings call with investors and analysts, the question is bound to come up (let alone at any public or private event that you or any member of the executive team attends).

Calls by the public to stop doing business with certain countries are nothing new. In fact, there have been calls to stop doing business with Saudi Arabia over alleged human rights violations associated with Saudi airstrikes in Yemen, which killed thousands of civilians and human rights violations of their own citizenry (Human Rights Watch, 2017). Historically, Lockheed Martin's position, like that of its primary competitors, has been to simply follow the USA Government's lead: as long as the USA Government allows sales to a particular country, then Lockheed Martin will do business with them. In the past, you have had no issues supporting this position. Lockheed Martin, like its primary competitors, relies on the USA Government for most of its revenue. The maximization of shareholder return demands keeping customers happy.

Supporting your and the company's past position is a section in Lockheed Martin's code of conduct dealing with conducting international business with integrity. In part, the anti-boycott provision states "Do not engage in or support restrictive international trade practices or boycotts not sanctioned by the USA Government" and "Do not enter into an agreement, provide any information or take any action that would cause Lockheed Martin to refuse to deal with potential or actual customers, suppliers or others in support of an illegal boycott" (Lockheed Martin, 2017, p. 30).

However, as the facts about Khashoggi's murder have come out, you have started to question whether this position is still valid (as have members of your family and friends). Last night at the dinner table, your 17-year-old son asked how you could continue to sell arms to Saudi Arabia as it effectively condones murder. You explained the company's position. But your son then asked you something that gave you pause and about which you have been unable to stop thinking. He simply asked if there were any circumstances other than a USA Government restriction on sales that would cause Lockheed Martin to stop doing business with a customer? You did not have an answer for him and told him that you need to think about that. The next day at work, you have a meeting with the CEO to discuss the upcoming earnings call and, more specifically, Lockheed Martin's position on doing business with Saudi Arabia. In preparation for that meeting you review the company code of conduct (Lockheed Martin, 2017). One of the last pages (page 37) of the company's code of conduct identifies the steps you should take when you think you are dealing with an ethical issue, as shown in Exhibit 7.1.

Exhibit 7.1 Lockheed Martin Code of Conduct (Page 37)

Do What's Right	*Respect Others*	*Perform with Excellence*

Ask Yourself . . .	We Take Action
✓ Have I considered all the risks? ✓ Who gains from this and who could lose? ✓ Does this sound too good to be true? ✓ Why is this bothering me? ✓ How would this look to our customer or supplier?	**WE SET THE STANDARD** • We use the Voicing Our Values techniques to put our values into practice. • We address values conflicts and potential violations of law or policy when they arise. • We make ourselves aware of warning signs that our values are at risk.

✓ How would I feel if my family or friends knew what I was doing?

✓ Do I have valid data that may lead to a different decision?

✓ Is this fair and honest?

✓ Does my leadership know?

✓ What are the consequences of this solution?

✓ Do I need to ask more questions for a clearer picture?

WHY WE DO IT

- The integrity of the Corporation relies on each of us taking responsibility for living our values.
- Values conflicts are a normal occurrence in the work environment and must be resolved.
- Becoming familiar with warning signs helps us identify and correct potential problems before they grow.

POLICIES

- CPS-001 Ethics and Business Conduct
- CPS-718 Disclosures to the United States Government
- CPS-730 Compliance with Anti-Corruption Laws
- CRX-021 Internal Investigations

In addition, you review your obligations to the accounting profession by reviewing both the IMA and the AICPA codes of conduct, as shown in Exhibits 7.2 and 7.3.

Exhibit 7.2 IMA Statement of Ethical Professional Practice Effective July 1, 2017

Principles

IMA's overarching ethical principles include honesty, fairness, objectivity and responsibility. Members shall act in accordance with these principles and shall encourage others within their organizations to adhere to them.

Standards

IMA members have a responsibility to comply with and uphold the standards of Competence, Confidentiality, Integrity and Credibility. Failure to comply may result in disciplinary action.

I. Competence

1. Maintain an appropriate level of professional leadership and expertise by enhancing knowledge and skills.

2. Perform professional duties in accordance with relevant laws, regulations and technical standards.

3. Provide decision support information and recommendations that are accurate, clear, concise and timely. Recognize and help manage risk.

II. Confidentiality

1. Keep information confidential except when disclosure is authorized or legally required.
2. Inform all relevant parties regarding appropriate use of confidential information. Monitor to ensure compliance.
3. Refrain from using confidential information for unethical or illegal advantage.

III. Integrity

1. Mitigate actual conflicts of interest. Regularly communicate with business associates to avoid apparent conflicts of interest. Advise all parties of any potential conflicts of interest.
2. Refrain from engaging in any conduct that would prejudice carrying out duties ethically.
3. Abstain from engaging in or supporting any activity that might discredit the profession.
4. Contribute to a positive ethical culture and place integrity of the profession above personal interests.

IV. Credibility

1. Communicate information fairly and objectively.
2. Provide all relevant information that could reasonably be expected to influence an intended user's understanding of the reports, analyses, or recommendations.
3. Report any delays or deficiencies in information, timeliness, processing or internal controls in conformance with organization policy and/or applicable law.
4. Communicate professional limitations or other constraints that would preclude responsible judgment or successful performance of an activity.

Resolving Ethical Issues

In applying the Standards of Ethical Professional Practice, the member may encounter unethical issues or behavior. In these situations, the member should not ignore them, but rather should actively seek resolution of the issue. In determining which steps to follow, the member should consider all risks involved and whether protections exist against retaliation. When faced with unethical issues, the member should follow the established policies of his or her organization, including use of an anonymous reporting system if available. If the organization does not have established policies, the member should consider the following courses of action:

- The resolution process could include a discussion with the member's immediate supervisor. If the supervisor appears to be involved, the issue could be presented to the next level of management.
- IMA offers an anonymous helpline that the member may call to request how key elements of the IMA Statement of Ethical Professional Practice could be applied to the ethical issue.
- The member should consider consulting his or her own attorney to learn of any legal obligations, rights and risks concerning the issue. If resolution efforts are not successful, the member may wish to consider disassociating from the organization.

IMA (2017)

Exhibit 7.3   AICPA Code of Professional Conduct (Selected Sections)

Preface: Applicable to All Members
0.100 Overview of the Code of Professional Conduct

.01 The AICPA Code of Professional Conduct (the code) begins with this preface, which applies to all members The term member, when used in part 1 of the code, applies to and means a member in public practice; when used in part 2 of the code, applies to and means a member in business; and when used in part 3 of the code, applies to and means all other members, such as those members who are retired or unemployed.

.02 A member may have multiple roles, such as a member in business and a member in public practice. In such circumstances, the member should consult all applicable parts of the code and apply the most restrictive provisions.

0.300.020 Responsibilities

.01 Responsibilities principle. In carrying out their responsibilities as professionals, members should exercise sensitive professional and moral judgments in all their activities.

.02 As professionals, members perform an essential role in society. Consistent with that role, members of the American Institute of Certified Public Accountants have responsibilities to all those who use their professional services. Members also have a continuing responsibility to cooperate with each other to improve the art of accounting, maintain the public's confidence and carry out the profession's special responsibilities for self-governance. The collective efforts of all members are required to maintain and enhance the traditions of the profession.

0.300.030 The Public Interest

.01 The public interest principle. Members should accept the obligation to act in a way that will serve the public interest, honor the public trust and demonstrate a commitment to professionalism.

.02 A distinguishing mark of a profession is acceptance of its responsibility to the public. The accounting profession's public consists of clients, credit grantors, governments, employers, investors, the business and financial community and others who rely on the objectivity and integrity of members to maintain the orderly functioning of commerce. This reliance imposes a public interest responsibility on members. The public interest is defined as the collective well-being of the community of people and institutions that the profession serves.

.03 In discharging their professional responsibilities, members may encounter conflicting pressures from each of those groups. In resolving those conflicts, members should act with integrity, guided by the precept that when members fulfill their responsibility to the public, clients' and employers' interests are best served.

.04 Those who rely on members expect them to discharge their responsibilities with integrity, objectivity, due professional care and a genuine interest in serving the public. They are expected to provide quality services, enter into fee arrangements and offer a range of services – all in a manner that demonstrates a level of professionalism consistent with these Principles of the Code of Professional Conduct.

Preface: Applicable to All Members

.05 All who accept membership in the American Institute of Certified Public Accountants commit themselves to honor the public trust. In return for the faith that the public reposes in them, members should seek to continually demonstrate their dedication to professional excellence.

0.300.040 Integrity

.01 Integrity principle. To maintain and broaden public confidence, members should perform all professional responsibilities with the highest sense of integrity.

.02 Integrity is an element of character fundamental to professional recognition. It is the quality from which the public trust derives and the benchmark against which a member must ultimately test all decisions.

.03 Integrity requires a member to be, among other things, honest and candid within the constraints of client confidentiality. Service and the public trust should not be subordinated to personal gain an advantage.

Integrity can accommodate the inadvertent error and honest difference of opinion; it cannot accommodate deceit or subordination of principle.

.04 Integrity is measured in terms of what is right and just. In the absence of specific rules, standards, or guidance or in the face of conflicting opinions, a member should test decisions and deeds by asking: 'Am I doing what a person of integrity would do? Have I retained my integrity?'. Integrity requires a member to observe both the form and the spirit of technical and ethical standards; circumvention of those standards constitutes subordination of judgment.

.05 Integrity also requires a member to observe the principles of objectivity and independence and of due care.

AICPA (2016)

2.4. Questions

Before responding to these questions, please read, familiarize yourself with and be prepared to refer to the IMA, AICPA and Lockheed Martin Codes of Conduct. The complete Lockheed Martin Code of Conduct can be found online.[4]

- One of the core principles of the GVV methodology is to identify all the risks associated with a given issue. That principle is reflected in the series of questions identified on page 37 of Lockheed Martin's code of conduct. The IMA code of conduct also states that to determine the course of action to take in resolving an ethical decision, members should identify all the risks involved. Please identify the risks to both Lockheed Martin and you both in continuing to do business with Saudi Arabia and in no longer doing business with them.
- Do you agree with Lockheed Martin's historical position regarding following the lead of the USA Government? Why or why not. How do the facts of the current case impact this answer (if at all)? In your response, please address the concept of legality versus ethicality.
- Draft a response to your son's question.
- Lockheed Martin's code of conduct notes how common values conflicts are in business. Are there any conflicting values in this case? If so, identify them and discuss how you would go about resolving those conflicts.

- As the CFO of Lockheed Martin, what are your ethical obligations in this case under the IMA code of conduct? Does Lockheed Martin's code potentially conflict with that of the IMA?
- As the CFO of Lockheed Martin, what are your ethical obligations in this case under the AICPA code of conduct? Does Lockheed Martin's code potentially conflict with that of the AICPA?
- Does continuing to do business with Saudi Arabia impact your integrity or that of the company? Please explain why or why not.

3. Teaching Notes

3.1. Accounting for Values: A CFO's Dilemma

This case provides an opportunity to explore corporate governance issues and the responsibilities that senior accounting executives have to create and maintain an ethical culture. Examination of the details in the case will uncover value conflicts. Examples of values included in IMA's Statement of Ethical Professional Practice are honesty, fairness, objectivity and responsibility. IMA describes these as 'overarching ethical principles. Examples of overarching principles in the AICPA Code of Professional Conduct include serving the public interest, integrity, objectivity, independence and due care. Examination of the details of the case will enable students to recognize that often times ethical dilemmas have no clear right or wrong answer; however, they must be able to identify the possible courses of action, outcomes and consequences before selecting their 'best' solution.

Appropriate settings for this case include:

- A college-level financial accounting, management accounting, finance or business ethics course
- A graduate-level accounting or business ethics course
- IMA chapter continuing educational program

3.2. Questions

Question 1: One of the core principles of the GVV methodology is to identify all the risks associated with a given issue. That principle is reflected in the series of questions identified on page 37 of Lockheed Martin's code of conduct. The IMA code of conduct also states that to determine the course of action to take in resolving an ethical decision, members should identify all the risks involved. Please identify the risks to both Lockheed Martin and you both in continuing to do business with Saudi Arabia and in no longer doing business with them.

The risks to the company of following the USA Government's lead include continued and or growing public outcries to stop doing business with the Saudi Government, employee discontent with some personnel opting to quit, degradation of the existing ethical corporate culture resulting in an increase in ethical lapses and shareholder discontent resulting in a loss of share value. Exploration of this issue can incorporate a discussion of inherent biases and people's tendency to underestimate risk. The discussion of these risks should incorporate a discussion of the concept of 'tone at the top'. A code of conduct is only as good as the actions which senior management takes. The adage of actions speaking louder than words comes to mind. Whereas the code of ethics might dictate certain behaviors, employees model their behavior after the actions of their managers. In this case, if following the government's lead is viewed as unethical, it sends a message that following the code of conduct is optional, which will likely result in ethical lapses in other areas of the business. Of all of the corporate risks, this one may be largest with negative long-term results.

The individual risk to the CFO of following the USA Government's lead is a loss of personal integrity; loss of respect by family, friends and employees; and a potential violation of the IMA code of conduct. In effect, the CFO could be viewed as subordinating their own judgment to that of their employer or of a customer.

The risk to the company of deciding not to do business with Saudi Arabia is the loss of future revenue from the USA Government. With so much of Lockheed Martin's revenue dependent on keeping the USA Government happy, they need to be very careful about what they do and how they go about it. Prior to any action being taken, a great deal of communication with the USA Government about this issue would be needed to determine the magnitude of the risk to the company and their revenue stream.

The risk to the CFO over deciding to not do business with the Saudis could include the loss of his or her job should the decision result in a loss of revenue from the USA Government.

> Question 2: Do you agree with Lockheed Martin's historical position regarding following the lead of the USA Government? Why or why not. How do the facts of the current case impact this answer (if at all)? In your response, please address the concept of legality versus ethicality.

The case analysis requires students to put themselves in the position of the CFO of Lockheed Martin. The answers to this question are likely to vary greatly from strong support for continuing to do business with Saudi Arabia to discontinuing business altogether. Discussion of the details of this case will allow students to explore the maximization of shareholder return demands and to gain an understanding that the CFO has a leadership position from which he or she may need to make recommendations and support decisions where values conflicts exist.

The facts of this case also provide the opportunity for a discussion of the definition of 'being ethical'. This discussion should include whether the fact that something is legal means that it is also ethical. The same question can be applied to whether following a corporate code of conduct or policy means that you are also being ethical. An example that students often bring up is that of the confidentiality restriction contained in the IMA code of conduct. Following that policy can result in unethical practices going unchecked. Similarly, students might bring up laws which appear unethical, like a three strikes law that can result in long-term incarceration for a minor third offense. Given this case deals with the USA Government, the discussion surrounding this concept can be quite wide and varied.

Question 3: Draft a response to your son's question.

The 'Giving Voice to Values' methodology identifies four categories of typical reasons and rationalizations that people will use to justify their actions or reasoning (Gentile, 2010):

- Standard Practice – everybody does it (all of our competitors operate the same way);
- Materiality – it's not a big deal, or there is little risk to doing it (risks to continuing to do business with the Saudi's are much lower than refusing to do so);
- Locus of Responsibility – it's not my job or your job so don't worry about it (the USA Government determines who we do business with, not us);
- Locus of Loyalty – it's in the best interest of the company or in my or your best interest (not doing business with the Saudi's will result in a significant loss of revenue). Discussion surrounding this question will be quite varied and responses may fall into all of the above categories whether you are incorporating the GVV methodology into the course or not.

The approach of drafting a response to the CFO's son will allow students to consider the aforementioned common reasons and rationalizations that may be influencing the CFO and other executives in the company. More importantly, it will allow them to identify levers (tools they have available to them) and craft counterarguments to the identified reasons and rationalizations. For example, common levers include seeking advice, building a coalition, reframing the issue, identifying authoritative support, identifying risks, addressing the impact of change and proposing benefits of a solution.

In this situation, the CFO should recognize that he or she is not alone and there are plenty of people available to help both within and outside the organization: friends, family, colleagues, co-workers and professional organizations like the IMA. The CFO can seek out others in the organization to help determine under what circumstances the company would actually stop doing business with a customer. Discussing issues with others can often identify positions that were not considered before. For example, maximizing revenue (short-term justification) can often be reframed toward potential long-term consequences (loss of shareholder value or loss of integrity) that counter the short-term benefits. Further, the CFO can use both the Lockheed Martin and IMA codes of conduct in determining the best response to his son. The class discussion surrounding this issue might lead to a discussion of changing or clarifying the Lockheed Martin code of conduct to address the CFO's son's question and the arguments that could be used to persuade the executive team to do so.

> **Question 4: Lockheed Martin's code of conduct notes how common values conflicts in business actually are. Are there any conflicting values in this case? If so, identify them and discuss how you would go about resolving those conflicts.**

This question encourages students to describe the competing values and specifically address the overarching ethical principles as defined by the IMA in the Statement of Ethical Professional Practice: honesty, fairness, objectivity and responsibility. Each student should be able to select from these values and determine the ones that are most important to them. Next, review the standards described by the IMA in the Statement of Ethical Professional Practice: competence, confidentiality, integrity and credibility. Each of these describes responsibilities of the CFO. For example, a CFO should exhibit competence in providing accurate, clear, concise and timely information. A CFO must provide decision support information and recommendations to the CEO and the Board of Directors that recognize and help manage risk. Finally, a CFO must perform professional duties in accordance with relevant laws, regulations and technical standards. Lockheed Martin's position on doing business with Saudi Arabia is not illegal; however, it may be in conflict with their protection of human rights standard. Discussions can explore the benefits of following the law and how it may be in Lockheed Martin's best interest to exhibit leadership in the industry by highlighting the importance of human rights and spearheading change.

Under the integrity standard, the CFO is expected to communicate with business associates to avoid apparent conflicts of interest and must abstain from engaging in or supporting any activity that might discredit the profession. The CFO is responsible for advising all parties of any potential conflicts of interest and to refrain from engaging in any conduct that would prejudice carrying out duties ethically. Students may argue that it is in the best interest of Lockheed Martin's management to continue to do business with Saudi Arabia by pursuing a profit motivation. After all, if Lockheed Martin decides not to do business with the Saudi Government, the Saudi Government most likely would procure the weapons elsewhere. However, the CFO has a responsibility to contribute to a positive ethical culture and place integrity of the profession above personal interests. Discussions may identify that buyers could be located from governments that are more closely aligned with Lockheed Martin's company values. Further, ending business relationships with Saudi Arabia may contribute to a more positive ethical culture at Lockheed Martin.

Under the credibility standard, the CFO is responsible for communicating information fairly and objectively and for providing all relevant information that could reasonably be expected to influence an intended user's understanding of the reports, analyses or recommendations. As previously discussed, by identifying the potential benefits and risks of continuing business with Saudi Arabia, the CFO exhibits credibility.

A discussion surrounding loyalty to company is bound to emerge as well. As noted in the response to the previous question, loyalty can be used as an excuse to justify an action. The value of loyalty can often times be in conflict with other values.

> Question 5: As the CFO of Lockheed Martin, what are your ethical obligations in this case under the IMA code of conduct? Does Lockheed Martin's code potentially conflict with that of the IMA?

In applying the Standards of Ethical Professional Practice, students may identify that they should not ignore the values conflicts that they have identified but rather should actively seek resolution of the issue. When faced with this issue, the student may identify that they should continue to follow the established policies of Lockheed Martin which would support continuing a business relationship with the Saudi Government. After all, the majority of their foreign revenue is generated indirectly through the USA Government. However, if the CFO wishes to create organizational change, they should discuss the value conflicts with the CEO and the Board of Directors.

> Question 6: As the CFO of Lockheed Martin, what are your ethical obligations in this case under the AICPA code of conduct? Does Lockheed Martin's code potentially conflict with that of the AICPA?

The Principles of the Code of Professional Conduct of the American Institute of Certified Public Accountants (AICPA) express the profession's recognition of its responsibilities to colleagues, to clients and as keepers of the public trust. Section 2.300.040 Integrity identifies that integrity is measured in terms of what is right and just. In the absence of specific rules, standards or guidance or in the face of conflicting opinions, a member should test decisions and deeds by asking: "Am I doing what a person of integrity would do? Have I retained my integrity?" Answers to these questions are likely to generate significant discussion.

In addition, the topic of subordination can be discussed. If it does not come up, the instructor should ask whether the CFO is subordinating their own judgment to that of the USA Government and whether that is allowed or not. Integrity requires a member to observe both the form and the spirit of technical and ethical standards; circumvention of those standards constitutes subordination of judgment: subordination of Judgment by a Member in Business "prohibits a member from knowingly misrepresenting facts or subordinating his or her judgment when performing professional services" (AICPA, 2016). This section provides guidance in regard to who the member should report ethical concerns to in an effort to resolve the issue. This standard requires the member to first discuss the issue with their direct supervisor. If they are unsatisfied with the outcome of that conversation, they are required to report the issue to an "appropriate higher level of management within the organization". Examples of appropriate reporting outlets moving up the chain of command include senior management, the audit committee or equivalent, the board of directors or the company's owners (AICPA, 2016). If they cannot resolve the issue to their satisfaction, they could consider resigning.

Question 7: Does continuing to do business with Saudi Arabia impact your integrity? Explain, why or why not.

An organization's integrity and ethical values reflect the commitment of the CEO and other members of top management to adhere to their own company ethical standards. The ethical tone set by top management helps to create their corporate culture. This culture influences how employees act and may impact feelings of their own individual integrity. This question will likely generate much discussion surrounding codes of conduct and personal integrity when organizational values conflict with personal values. This discussion can include wanting to have a good fit between your personal values and those of the company that you work for.

Notes

1. http://store.darden.virginia.edu/giving-voice-to-values; www.GivingVoiceTo Values.org
2. https://ethicsunwrapped.utexas.edu/series/giving-voice-to-values

3. https://store.darden.virginia.edu/giving-voice-to-values
4. www.lockheedmartin.com/content/dam/lockheed-martin/eo/documents/ethics/code-of-conduct.pdf

References

American Institute of Certified Public Accountants (AICPA). (2016). *Code of Professional Conduct*. Retrieved June 2nd, 2020, from www.aicpa.org/content/dam/aicpa/research/standards/codeofconduct/downloadabledocuments/2014december15contentasof2016august31codeofconduct.pdf

Capaccio, A., & Flatley, D. (2018). Lockheed's $15 Billion Saudi Deal at Risk after Khashoggi Death. *Bloomberg*. Retrieved June 2nd, 2020, from www.bloomberg.com/news/articles/2018-10-24/lockheed-s-15-billion-saudi-deal-at-risk-after-khashoggi-death

Edwards, M. G., & Kirkham, N. (2013). Situating 'Giving Voice to Values': A Metatheoretical Evaluation of a New Approach to Business Ethics. *Journal of Business Ethics*, 121(3), 1–19.

Gentile, M. C. (2010). *Giving Voice to Values: How to Speak Your Mind When You Know What's Right*. New Haven, CT: Yale University Press.

Human Rights Watch. (2017). *Saudi Arabia Events of 2016*. Retrieved June 2nd, 2020, from www.hrw.org/world-report/2017/country-chapters/saudi-arabia#

Institute of Management Accountants (IMA). (2017). *IMA Statement of Ethical Professional Practice*. Retrieved June 2nd, 2020, from www.imanet.org/-/media/b6fbeeb74d964e6c9fe654c48456e61f.ashx

Lockheed Martin. (2017). *Code of Ethics and Business Conduct*. Retrieved June 2nd, 2020, from www.lockheedmartin.com/content/dam/lockheed-martin/eo/documents/ethics/code-of-conduct.pdf

Lockheed Martin Corporation. (2018a). *2017 Annual Report*. Retrieved June 2nd, 2020, from www.lockheedmartin.com/content/dam/lockheed-martin/eo/documents/annual-reports/2017-annual-report.pdf

Lockheed Martin Corporation. (2018b). *Lockheed Martin Fact Sheet*. Retrieved June 2nd, 2020, from www.lockheedmartin.com/content/dam/lockheed-martin/eo/documents/2018-lockheed-martin-fact-sheet.pdf

Lockheed Martin Corporation. (n.d.). *Voicing Our Values 2019*. Retrieved June 2nd, 2020, from www.lockheedmartin.com/en-us/who-we-are/ethics/ethics-awareness-training.html

Mintz, S., & Morris, R. (2014). *Ethical Obligations and Decision Making in Accounting: Text and Cases* (3rd ed.). New York: McGraw-Hill Education.

Rest, J. R. (1986). *Moral Development: Advances in Research and Theory*. New York: Praeger.

Shawver, T. J., & Miller, W. F. (2018). *Giving Voice to Values in Accounting*. London: Routledge.

Zillman, C. (2018). *Lockheed Martin CEO Says She'll 'Follow the Government's Lead' in Selling Arms to Saudi Arabia*. Retrieved June 2nd, 2020, from http://fortune.com/2018/11/05/lockheed-martin-ceo-saudi-arms-deal-trump-khashoggi/

Appendix A
GVV Role Play Grading Rubric

Case: _____ Presented by: _____

Your classmates will provide feedback on your case and role-play presentation. They will answer the following questions to provide each team with feedback:

    a. What is your immediate response to the team's strategy and 'script'?

    b. If you were the target of this response, how do you think you would react?

    c. Can you offer suggestions to the team to improve this response?

Grading Scale: On a ten-point scale, the team is scored on the extent to which the criteria are met. The scale is as follows: 10 exceeds all expectations, 7–9 meets most expectations, 4–6 satisfactorily meets some expectations, 1–3 inadequately meets expectations, 0 does not meet expectations at all.

Criteria	Rating
The team shall identify (recognize) and present the ethical issues in the case.	
The team will present possible solutions and the consequences of each (evaluation of pros/cons).	
The team shall make a decision and present the best possible alternative solution.	
The team presents several reasons and rationalizations for this behavior.	
The team presents several arguments and realistic counterarguments.	
The team includes relevant sources (i.e., codes of conduct, laws) to support the counterarguments.	
The team demonstrates an understanding of professional knowledge.	
The team demonstrates an understanding of professional and social responsibility.	
The team delivery techniques (posture, gesture, eye contact, vocal expressiveness) make the presentation interesting.	
The team was prepared, well organized and the presentation was compelling and memorable.	

Appendix B
Assignments Detail

Individual Assignment (Standard GVV Implementation)

Each student will complete an individual assignment about each case (four total cases) that answers the following questions. These questions should be answered prior to the scheduled group presentation for each case.

- What would motivate you to speak up and act or to stay silent?
- What are the arguments you would try to counter?
- What would you do, and who would you talk to?
- What do you hope will happen, and what will you do if it does not?

Individual Assignment (Modified GVV Implementation)

Each student will complete an individual assignment about each case (four total cases) that answers the following questions. These questions should be answered prior to the scheduled group presentation for each case.

1. What would motivate you to speak up and act or to stay silent?
2. What are the arguments you would try to counter?
3. What would you do, and who would you talk to?
4. What do you hope will happen, and what will you do if it does not?
5. What concerns would you have if you discussed this situation with an internal manager who is your direct supervisor?
6. What concerns would you have if you discussed this situation with a CFO, CEO or member of the board of directors?
7. What concerns would you have if you discussed this situation with someone outside the organization?
8. How can you minimize your concerns if you discussed this issue with an internal manager who is your direct supervisor?
9. How can you minimize your concerns if you discussed this issue with a CFO, CEO or member of the board of directors?
10. How can you minimize your concerns if you discussed this issue with someone outside the organization?

Group Case Analysis

Each team must answer the following questions (turn in hardcopy):

- What are the main arguments, *reasons and rationalizations* you need to address?
- What's at *stake* for the key parties, including those who disagree with you? What's at *stake* for you?
- What *levers* can you use to influence those who disagree with you?
- What is your most *powerful and persuasive response* to the reasons and rationalizations you need to address?
- To whom should the argument be made? When and in what context?

Role-Plays

- Each team will work together to script a response to the ethical problem.

  - This hardcopy script must be turned in.

- Each team acts out the script in class.

  - Create people as needed to interact with.
  - Act out what each person might say or do.
  - What would you do?
  - Who would you talk to?
  - How would they respond?
  - How is the dilemma resolved?

8   Incorporating Behavioral Ethics and Organizational Culture Into Accounting Ethics

Steven M. Mintz & William F. Miller

Ethical decision-making models have been used to teach ethics to accounting students for many years. These models rely heavily on philosophical reasoning methods to evaluate and make judgments to resolve ethical dilemmas. Past models have used a rather rigid systematic approach whereby the ethical issues are identified, stakeholder interests are analyzed, alternative courses of action are determined, alternatives are then evaluated and a decision is made. A deficiency in each of these models is the failure to recognize the influence of behavioral ethics and relevant elements of the culture of organizations that are integral parts of carrying out ethical decisions with ethical behavior. The purpose of this chapter is to develop a broader model that incorporates these factors in the context of the PLUS[1] Ethical Decision-Making Model.

The model addresses the following behavioral issues:

1) Whether ethical issues are framed in a way that influences the ethical analysis.
2) The role of bounded ethicality whereby one's ability to see the ethical dimensions of a problem are constrained by forces such as self-interest.
3) Whether ethical fading exists whereby the ethical issues take a back seat to self-interest and cause ethical blind spots to emerge.
4) How ethical blind spots influence the way decisions are made.
5) How to deal with self-serving bias that leads to self-deception and placing self-interest above the interests of others, which in the accounting profession would be the public interest.

Finally, the implementation of the decision includes a search for supporters who can counteract pressures within the organization to deviate from ethical norms, principles and values. Each of these factors are discussed more fully later.

The PLUS Ethical Decision-Making Model developed through the Ethics Resource Center, the research arm of the Ethics & Compliance Initiative (ECI), overcomes the deficiencies of previous models by incorporating ethics filters that provide structure for considering how organizational culture influences ethical decision-making. The mnemonic PLUS stands for policies within the organization, legal and regulatory issues facing the organization, universal principles and values of the organization and self or one's personal definition of right, good and fair (Ethics & Compliance Initiative, n.d.).

Taken together, the influence of behavioral ethics and integration of PLUS filters provide a foundation for a broader perspective on ethical decision-making that incorporates important factors that are insufficiently accounted for in traditional ethical decision-making models. The point is no matter how proficient one is in using ethical reasoning to resolve ethical dilemmas, it is unlikely to change the outcome of a decision unless behavioral factors are addressed and corporate culture is considered in making ethical decisions.

Ethical decision-making models traditionally used to teach ethics to accounting students are explained in the next section. We follow with a discussion of behavioral ethics and then explore organizational culture and how focus on key organizational variables can enhance ethical decision-making. The next section explains the PLUS model. We then describe the key components of a new model developed in this chapter and demonstrate how it can be used to teach ethics to accounting students by applying the model to the ethical dilemma faced by Betty Vinson (discussed in the Section Application of the PLUS Model), the former director of corporate reporting at WorldCom. We conclude with final observations about the benefits of the new model.

1. Ethical Decision-Making Models

The first model discussed in the literature was developed by Langenderfer and Rockness (1989). The model describes an eight-step decision-making process to be used with case analyses of ethical dilemmas faced by professional accountants. It relies heavily on norms, principles and values to evaluate the consequences of alternative actions on stakeholders, the individual and the company. Around the same time, the American Accounting Association published cases developed by May (1990). These cases provide a useful resource to aid in the integration of ethics into the accounting curriculum.

The decision-making model of Langenderfer and Rockness (1989) is presented in Exhibit 8.1.

Langenderfer and Rockness (1989) point out that ethical discussions at the philosophical level need to be strengthened through practical considerations related to rights and responsibilities. This means factors such as the values and standards of practice in the accounting profession need to be considered as in the Mintz and Morris (2017) model described later.

The authors also suggest it may be useful to discuss the ethical issues with a trusted advisor just prior to decision-making. However, this step

Exhibit 8.1 Langenderfer and Rockness's (1989) Ethical Decision-Making Model

Steps	Descriptive Criteria
What are the facts?	Describe the scope of the problem. Refer to industry standards and other pertinent information.
What are the ethics issues and who are the stakeholders in this case?	Identify the ethics issues, stakeholders and competing interests.
What are the norms, principles and values in this case?	Consider how these norms, principles and values influence individuals, the company and society.
Identify alternative courses of action.	List the available alternatives of what can and cannot be done.
What is the best course of action that is consistent with the norms, principles and values?	Evaluate all possible courses of action with respect to norms, principles and values.
What are the consequences of each possible course of action?	Evaluate the potential consequences of alternatives on the stakeholders.
If appropriate, discuss the alternatives with a trusted person to help gain greater perspective regarding the alternatives.	N/A
What is the decision?	Balance the consequences against norms, principles and values and select the best alternative.

comes too late in their model, just before making the decision. Instead, discussions with a trusted advisor should occur earlier to help formulate possible alternatives and later on, if necessary, to counteract pressures to deviate from norms, principles and values. The PLUS model addresses these issues when they can make a difference.

Rest's (1986) Four-Component Model of Moral Behavior takes a different approach by identifying four behavioral considerations for resolving a moral problem: moral awareness, moral judgment, moral motivation and moral character. Moral development links to moral awareness, or spotting the ethical issues and moral judgment or reasoning through the ethical issues using principles, norms and values. Moral motivation and moral character complete the process.

Thorne's (1998) model of ethical decision-making advances the discussion of ethics by incorporating virtue considerations. It also links to Rest's (1986) model of moral behavior. Thorne (1998) conceives of moral development as integral to moral awareness and judgment and virtue as integral to moral intent and moral behavior. Exhibit 8.2 describes the relationship between Rest's (1986) and Thorne's (1998) models and ethical decision-making.

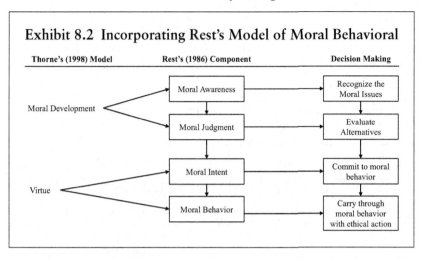

Exhibit 8.2 Incorporating Rest's Model of Moral Behavioral

Following on Thorne's (1998) model, Mintz and Morris (2017) developed an integrated ethical decision-making process that includes both philosophical reasoning and virtue considerations whereas introducing elements of behavioral ethics and organizational culture. The behavioral considerations reflect ways to counteract differences of opinion in the organization. Mintz (2019) points out that the organizational considerations include:

Virtues are characteristic traits of behavior that promote ethical decision-making. *Moral virtues* govern one's feelings, attitudes and moral sentiments and include, for example, friendliness or courtesy, temperance or self-control and truthfulness and courage. Both truthfulness and courage are key elements of ethical behavior for accountants because they enable objective decisions to be made and carried through with integrity. The exercise of moral virtue depends on *intellectual virtues* (i.e., although processes broadly stated) including the ability to deliberate about the proper course of action and apply knowledge to each situation encountered. Virtues are important to accounting professionals because they align with principles of professional behavior including independent thought and action, objective judgment, acting with integrity and maintaining professional skepticism. Accounting professionals should be guided by virtue to make decisions consistent with their public interest obligation. As Libby and Thorne (2007) point out in their study of auditor virtue, intellectual virtues are critical to the role of auditors because they influence an individual's actions. These virtues include integrity, truthfulness, independence, objectivity, dependability, being principled and healthy skepticism (Libby & Thorne, 2007).

Following on Thorne's (1998) model, Mintz and Morris (2017) developed an integrated ethical decision-making process that includes both philosophical reasoning and virtue considerations whereas introducing elements of behavioral ethics and organizational culture. The behavioral considerations reflect ways to counteract differences of opinion in the organization. Mintz (2019) points out that the organizational considerations include:

1) Identifying the effects of an ethical dilemma on the employees, management and the organization
2) Evaluating whether legal issues exist and their effects on the organization
3) Finding supporters in the organization to strengthen the chosen decision and help to counteract those detractors with opposing points of view.

Exhibit 8.3 describes the key components of ethical decision-making, including descriptive criteria and examples taken from the Mintz and Morris (2017) model. Elements of organizational culture have been added and are italicized.

Exhibit 8.3   Mintz and Morris's Integrated Ethical Decision-Making Process*

Components	Descriptive Criteria	Examples/Considerations
Identification of the dilemma	Identify the ethical and professional issues	GAAP, auditing standards, AIPCA Code, IMA ethical standards
	Identify the stakeholders	Investors, creditors, employees, management, the organization
Ethical judgment	Identify alternatives	What can and cannot be done
	Determine whether legal issues exist	Laws, SEC regulations
	Which ethical reasoning methods apply?	Teleology, Deontology, Virtue
	What steps can be taken to resolve the conflict?	*Consider talking to key people within the organization for advice*
Ethical motivation	Evaluate the likely outcomes if specific actions are taken	⌈ What are the possible consequences of alternative actions? What is the consensus view of alternatives? ⌊
	Consider whether anyone's rights are at stake	*Does the organizational culture impinge on anyone's rights?*
	How do intellectual virtues motivate ethical action?	What characteristic traits of behavior influence decision-making?
	Evaluate social and organizational pressures and effect on ethical decision-making	*Identify supporters in the organization to help counteract opposing points of view*
Ethical action	Decide on a course of action	Meet the public interest obligation
	⌈ Be prepared to counteract reasons and rationalizations to deviate from ethical action What steps can be taken to ⌊ strengthen the position?	⌈ *Enlist the help of supporters to respond to opposing points of view* *Reframe the issue if necessary, to influence detractors to* ⌊ *change their position*

*Exhibit 8.3 is adapted from page 77 of Mintz and Morris, 2017. Ethical Obligations and Decision Making in Accounting: Text and Cases. New York: McGraw Hill Education ©. That is also what is in the list of references.

2. Behavioral Ethics

Behavioral ethics is the study of why people make the ethical and unethical decisions they do. Instead of focusing on how one ought to behave, as do philosophical reasoning methods, behavioral ethics studies why people act as they do. By understanding the motivations for acting and the limitations on doing the right thing, a decision maker can be better prepared to counteract internal biases (e.g., the self-serving bias), organizational pressures (e.g., the pressure to conform) and situational factors that might otherwise go unnoticed.

Bazerman and Sezer (2016) suggest that behavioral ethicists do not ask decision makers to follow particular values or rules, but rather try to help decision makers to follow more closely their own personal values with greater reflection. Within the broad topic of behavioral ethics lies the more specific topic of bounded ethicality (Chugh, Bazerman & Banaji, 2005). Chugh et al. (2005) define 'bounded ethicality' as the psychological processes that lead people to engage in ethically questionable behaviors that are inconsistent with their own preferred ethics. That is, if the decision makers were more reflective about their choices, they would make a different decision.

Bounded rationality (March & Simon, 1958) and bounded awareness (Chugh & Bazerman, 2007) are cognitive shortcomings that run parallel to bounded ethicality and may prevent the decision maker from taking the action they would choose with greater awareness. In other words, psychological limitations, such as perceptual awareness, might cause the decision maker to miss the ethical cues.

Bounded rationality and bounded awareness address the ways in which we use information to make decisions. Much of the research on bounded rationality deals with how people misuse and mis-integrate the information that is part of their cognitive mind (Bazerman & Sezer, 2016). Some researchers have argued that people have 'bounded awareness' that prevents them from focusing on readily available and relevant data. Bounded awareness leads people to overlook important, accessible and perceivable information during the decision-making process (Chugh & Bazerman, 2007). This may occur because of a decision bias such as a framing bias (i.e., perception of the ethical issues). Kern and Chugh (2009) show that framing of information influences ethical judgments. This is important because moral perception, recognized by Rest (1986) and Thorne (1998), influences whether ethical understanding and ethical motivation will lead to making ethical choices.

Misguided goals can cause people to focus too much on their own needs and blind them to the ethical aspects that seem unrelated to the goal (Moore & Gino, 2013; Ordonez, Schweitzer, Galinsky & Bazerman, 2009; Tenbrunsel, Wade-Benzoni, Messick & Bazerman, 2000). This is a manifestation of 'ethical blind spots' or the gaps between our intended and actual behavior. In other words, what we should do and what we actually do may be different because of these cognitive limitations (Bazer-man & Tenbrunsel, 2011). The blind spots exist for a variety of rea-sons, including self-interested motivations (like pleasing the boss) which exert undue pressure at the time of the decision increasing the likelihood that these outside influences negatively affect ethical decision-making. In effect these pressures might cloud the ethical issues and cause them to fade in the background.

Tenbrunsel and Messick (2004) define the term 'ethical fading' as the process by which the moral colors of an ethical decision fade away and become void of moral implications, which implies educating individuals on moral principles helps only if they are aware of the ethical coloration of decisions. The authors argue that self-deception is the root of ethical fading (Tenbrunsel & Messick, 2004). Self-deception in this sense leads to clouding of the ethical issues thereby impairing the decision maker's ability to perceive the ethical issues.

Messick and Bazerman (1996) define 'self-deception' as being unaware of the processes that lead us to form our opinions and judgments. Such deception involves masking the truth, the lies that we tell to and the secrets we keep from ourselves (Bok, 1989). Tenbrunsel and Messick (2004) state that decision makers need to acknowledge the pervasiveness of self-deception and its role in unethical decision-making. They argue that self-deception is instrumental in the process of ethical fading (Ten-brunsel & Messick, 2004).

One reason self-deception occurs is errors in perceptual causation. This may occur because the focus of decision-making is on individuals rather than systems, self-interested motives in the assignment of blame and a blurred moral responsibility where acts of omission occur (Messick & Bazerman, 1996). Individuals may focus on a person rather than a sys-tem, such as organizational culture, to resolve problems. This is short sighted because the way in which an organization is run and how differ-ences of opinion are handled can influence ethical behavior and if those at the top eschew values, norms and principles then the systems can't be trusted and unethical behavior may occur.

Mintz and Morris (2020) point out that some people fall victim to self-serving biases in their decision-making, leading them to gather, process and even to remember information in a way that advances their own interest and supports preexisting views. Whereas people can readily notice how the self-serving bias might affect others' decisions on ethical matters, they may be blind to the ethical dimension and how it affects their own decision-making. "This kind of ethical blindness occurs because we fail to perceive or think about the ethical issues and contextual factors blinds us to right and wrong" (Mintz & Morris, 2020, p. 61).

Self-interested motives are a common cause of unethical behavior. Putting one's own interest ahead of internal and external stakeholders causes problems, especially in a field such as accounting where the public interest is paramount. Individuals may have a blind spot where the public is concerned because doing what is best for the public may mean doing what is most harmful to one's own self-interest.

3. Organizational Culture

Behavioral ethics are influenced by organizational culture because the way we perceive the ethical issues and act on them depends on whether the culture supports ethical decision-making. A culture that promotes retaliation against whistle-blowers is less likely to lead to ethical decision-making than one that is open to expressing ethical concerns within the organization. The key is to put into place organizational systems that encourage bringing matters of concern to appropriate parties.

Dunham and Pierce (1989) discuss organizational culture as being comprised of three elements: structure, processes and people which impact an individual's ethical decision-making. According to Bowen (2004), to be ethical, an organization must have an organizational culture that values ethical decision-making. She suggests that an organization's culture can positively or negatively impact the value placed on ethical decision-making both at the individual and organizational level. Many suggest that an organization's culture is a central factor influencing employee ethical behavior (Goddard, 1988; Hoffman, Moore & Fedo, 1983; Robin & Reidenbach, 1987; Soutar, McNeil & Molster, 1994; Vitell & Hidalgo, 2006).

Organizational culture influences decision-making because strategies, procedures and guidelines and organizational systems create the landscape for ethical decision-making. It also determines whether ethical fading exists whereby the moral dimension of an ethical decision fades away because of self-deception. Individuals can behave in a self-interested manner and disguise the moral implications of a decision whereas still believing they are ethical people. This is a manifestation of ethical blind spots where the decision one wants to make is different than the decision that is made because of internal pressures and organizational systems that do not support ethical behavior. By having ethical policies and processes in place and an ethical culture that promotes ethical decision-making, behavioral and cognitive limitations can be kept in check.

Ethical decisions are impacted by many different factors beyond individual values, such as the actions of one's peers, the ethical tone set by organizational management, codes of conduct, organizational policies, practices and norms and societal norms as well. Jones (1991) points out that organizational systems may cause unethical (or ethical) behavior despite acting with the best intentions.

Elango, Paul, Sumit and Shishir (2010) recommend that corporations develop a positive ethical culture, including both ethical training and monitoring. Beu and Buckley (2004, p. 80) state "the most powerful form of accountability has to be more than a code of ethics and more than just words – the underlying culture of the organization, starting with its leadership, has to live by an internalized ethical code" (setting the tone at the top). They argue that organizational culture and systems affect ethical decision-making more than the decision maker's individual characteristics/values. This is why errors in perceptual causation may lead to self-deception in decision-making.

Multiple studies suggest a positive correlation between rewarding unethical behavior and the duration and frequency with which it occurs – creating a vicious circle (Lindsay, Lindsay & Irvine, 1996; Nill & Schibrowsky, 2005; Trevino & Nelson, 1995). These studies suggest that internal organizational structures, like compensation plans, often end up rewarding unethical behavior. Knowing the systems do not support ethical (or might even promote unethical) decision-making early on might help resolve the conflict. Having short-term goals like maximizing reported profits can unintentionally promote and result in unethical behavior (Badaracco & Webb, 1995; Harvey, 2000; Nash, 1990). In fact, Kish-Gephart, Harrison and Trevino (2010) suggest that concentrating on short-term goals to the exclusion of ethical issues is likely to produce a culture that supports unethical conduct. A form of self-deception may result because short-term decisions tend to focus on individual interactions, such as going along with a superior's demands, rather than using the organizational systems to counteract these pressures.

Valentine, Godkin and Vitton (2012) suggest encouraging ethical reasoning among employees by building workplace characteristics that are known to enhance overall corporate ethics. This sentiment is also echoed by Valentine and Hollingworth (2012). It is important that organizations pay attention to universal ethical principles and the values of the organization to create a positive organizational culture that promotes ethical decision-making as suggested by the PLUS model discussed next.

From an accounting perspective, the culture of an organization should promote the values of the accounting profession including independence, integrity, objectivity and professional skepticism. Douglas, Davidson and Schwartz (2001) in their study of ethical decision-making of accountants suggest that an organization's ethical culture may be the greatest deterrent of unethical behavior. An organization's ethical culture has been found to impact auditors' ethical decision-making (Douglas et al., 2001; Ponemon, 1992; Windsor & Ashkanasy, 1995). Sweeney, Arnold and Pierce (2010), conclude that job-related pressures to act are the greatest negative influence on auditor decisions. They suggest that greater emphasis needs to be placed on deterring organizational pressures (through punishments for unethical behavior and rewards for ethical behavior). The perception that ethical behavior is rewarded has been found to have greater impact on ethical decision-making then the perception that unethical behavior is punished (Trevino, Weaver, Gibson & Toffler, 1999; Weaver, Trevino & Cochran, 1999).

The Institute of Management Accountants (IMA) is The Association of Accountants and Financial Professionals in Business. The IMA revised its *IMA Statement of Ethical Professional Practice* in 2017 to directly address the ethical obligation of internal accountants to "contribute to a positive ethical culture and place integrity of the profession above personal interests" (IMA, 2017, p. 3). This is important because following these standards helps to counteract errors in perceptual causation that can lead individuals to emphasize self-interest without regard to organizational culture. The standards go further in stating that members of the IMA should not ignore ethical issues, "but rather should actively seek resolution of the issue" by following established policies of the organization, "including use of an anonymous reporting system if available" (IMA, 2017, p. 4). More will be said about this in the Betty Vinson situation (discussed in the Section Application of the PLUS Model).

The adoption of an ethical decision-making model for an organization's employees to follow would appear to be a critical first step in answering Valentine et al.'s (2012) call for a positive ethical culture. Unfortunately, the vast majority of existing decision-making models do not appear to explicitly incorporate the three essential elements surrounding corporate culture identified by Dunham and Pierce (1989): structure, processes and people.

4. The PLUS Ethical Decision-Making Model

The PLUS Model is based on a seven-step process described next. The word PLUS refers to ethics filters that bring ethical considerations and implications of the decision for the individual and organization to the forefront. The mnemonic PLUS refers to four considerations that apply to the analysis in steps 1, 4 and 7 of the decision-making process as follows:

P = Policies
L = Legal
U = Universal
S = Self

The PLUS decision-making model was developed by the Ethics & Compliance Initiative of the Ethics Resource Center. A description of each filter and its role in decision-making follows (ECI, n.d.).

Policies. Is it consistent with organizational policies, procedures and guidelines?
Legal. Is it acceptable under applicable laws and regulations?
Universal. Does it conform to universal principles and the values of the organization?
Self. Does it satisfy my personal definition of right, good and fair?

The PLUS model is based on two underlying assumptions:

1)   Every employee needs to be empowered to make decisions consistent with their position and responsibilities.
2)   Every decision needs to be tested against the organization's policies (the 'P' factor), applicable laws and regulations (the 'L' factor) as well as organizational definitions of what is right, fair, good and acceptable (the 'U' factor).

It is not enough to simply determine whether a decision is in violation of a prescribed code of conduct, regulation, law or corporate policy; the person making the decision must also ensure they are not subordinating their own judgment or impairing their own value system, which are elements of the 'S' factor.

The advantage of the PLUS model is it relies heavily on organizational ethics and encourages ethical behavior by creating awareness of behavioral factors that might create barriers to ethical decision-making. This is important because no matter how good one's ethical judgment may be, ethical decision-making is not likely to occur unless support for the position exists in the organization as suggested by the Mintz and Morris (2017) model described in Exhibit 8.3 and in the IMA Standards. A summary of the seven-step model follows.

4.1. Step 1 – Define the Problem

Determine why a decision is necessary and identify the desired outcome(s). This helps to clearly state the problem and where to look for alternatives to resolve it. PLUS factors are considered to ensure the problem is identified in the context of organizational policies, laws, principles and personal values. Behavioral considerations play a role as well because the way in which ethical issues are perceived influences one's own definition of what is right, good and fair. Accounting rules and regulations should be addressed to ensure they are incorporated into the decision-making process.

4.2. Step 2 – Seek Out Relevant Assistance, Guidance and Support

Identify the available resources within the organization to help resolve the problem. This helps to define the guidelines and individuals within the organization that may help to resolve the problem. Organizational culture has an important role to play in this step as does the code of ethics and the internal controls. The IMA standards suggest the following to resolve ethical conflicts: discuss the matter with one's immediate superior unless they are involved in which case present it to the next level of management; contact the IMA anonymous helpline to discuss how to apply the standards to the resolve the ethical issue; consult "one's own attorney to learn of any legal obligations, rights and risks concerning the issue" (IMA, 2017, p. 4).

4.3. Step 3 – Identify Available Alternative Solutions to the Problem

Consider all relevant solutions to avoid the dichotomy of one choice versus another (i.e., either this or that). The way alternatives are identified has a lot to do with the way moral issues are perceived and whether ethical fading has a role to play in that perception.

4.4. Step 4 – Evaluate the Identified Alternatives

PLUS factors are considered including the role of organizational systems. Organizational systems, such as whether internal controls support ethical decision-making, influence whether alternatives can be implemented. In addition, systems like internal reporting mechanism can affect to whom reports of differences of opinion should be made.

This step uses decidedly consequence-based criteria. Positive and negative consequences are evaluated with fact-based consequences weighed more heavily because the expected outcome is more likely to occur. The PLUS factors are an integral part of the evaluation to supplement outcomes-oriented considerations, which are teleologically based, along with universal principles, such as deontology and virtue ethics as represented by organizational values. The ethical analysis may be limited if ethical blind spots exist or self-interest is placed ahead of the interest of the stakeholders.

4.5. Step 5 – Make the Decision

After evaluating all the alternatives, it is time to decide on a course of action. The reasons for choosing one alternative over the others should be explained. At this stage, pressures may exist within the organization that influence the decision maker to place their own interests, as colored by organizational pressures, ahead of stakeholder needs and what the ethical action should be.

4.6. Step 6 – Implement the Decision

Putting the decision into effect is essential to changing the situation and resolving the problem identified. Organizational pressures need to be addressed at this stage and supporters sought out to strengthen the chosen course of action.

4.7. Step 7 – Evaluate the Decision

A determination has to be made whether the decision fixes the problem identified. Questions to ask are: did it go away? Did it change

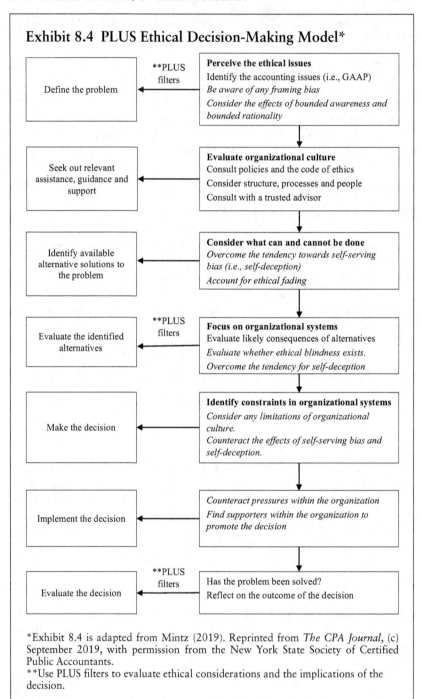

Exhibit 8.4 PLUS Ethical Decision-Making Model*

Define the problem ← ****PLUS filters**

Perceive the ethical issues
Identify the accounting issues (i.e., GAAP)
Be aware of any framing bias
Consider the effects of bounded awareness and bounded rationality

Seek out relevant assistance, guidance and support ←

Evaluate organizational culture
Consult policies and the code of ethics
Consider structure, processes and people
Consult with a trusted advisor

Identify available alternative solutions to the problem ←

Consider what can and cannot be done
Overcome the tendency towards self-serving bias (i.e., self-deception)
Account for ethical fading

Evaluate the identified alternatives ← ****PLUS filters**

Focus on organizational systems
Evaluate likely consequences of alternatives
Evaluate whether ethical blindness exists.
Overcome the tendency for self-deception

Make the decision ←

Identify constraints in organizational systems
Consider any limitations of organizational culture.
Counteract the effects of self-serving bias and self-deception.

Implement the decision ←

Counteract pressures within the organization
Find supporters within the organization to promote the decision

Evaluate the decision ← ****PLUS filters**

Has the problem been solved?
Reflect on the outcome of the decision

*Exhibit 8.4 is adapted from Mintz (2019). Reprinted from *The CPA Journal*, (c) September 2019, with permission from the New York State Society of Certified Public Accountants.
**Use PLUS filters to evaluate ethical considerations and the implications of the decision.

appreciably? Is it better now, or worse, or the same? What new problems did the solution create? In making these determinations, it is important to incorporate the PLUS factors to ensure the solution conforms to organizational policies, laws and regulations, universal principles and values adopted by the organization.

The 'S' component of the PLUS factor is a feature of the decision-making process that requires further explanation. To implement the 'self' factor, the decision maker should consider whether the solution satisfies one's personal definition of right, good and fair. It means that individuals should understand how their values influence decision-making to ensure the decision reflects those values. We can liken personal values to the virtues incorporated in the models of Thorne (1998) and Mintz and Morris (2017) and that reflect principles of professional behavior.

Exhibit 8.4 shows how the PLUS filters influence steps in the decision-making model. We expand on the model to incorporate behavioral and psychological considerations that can influence how those filters are applied in making ethical decisions. These factors are italicized in the exhibit. Exhibit 8.4 combines elements of the PLUS model with the organizational factors discussed by Mintz (2019) and as included in the Mintz and Morris model (2017).

5. Application of the PLUS Model

There are many real-life examples of behavioral limitations in accounting that foster self-deception and unethical decisions. To demonstrate the effectiveness of the model in Exhibit 8.4, we use it to analyze the ethical dilemma faced by Betty Vinson in the WorldCom fraud by looking back and analyzing her actions and what she might have done differently if elements of the model were applied.

The $11 billion accounting fraud at WorldCom led to the imprisonment of Bernie Ebbers, the CEO and Scott Sullivan, the CFO, for masterminding the fraud. Investors collectively lost over $30 billion as a result of improper accounting and financial reporting. The company paid $500 million to investors to settle civil fraud lawsuits.

Betty Vinson, the director of corporate reporting at WorldCom, claimed she was pressured by superiors to make fraudulent entries in the books, got caught up in the fraud and could not find a way out. Her superiors ignored her concerns about improper accounting. She continued to record false entries to satisfy her superiors who were intent on meeting or exceeding financial analysts' earnings expectations. Vinson felt her job was on the line if she did not help to carry out the fraud. She thought about resigning but did not, choosing instead to rely on statements by Sullivan that her participation in making false entries was a one-time request. These assurances clouded her judgment and made it difficult to see the full scope of the ethics issues and she deceived herself into thinking everything would be all right in the end. Persistent requests to keep the fraud going even when she knew it was wrong were a product of bounded ethicality.

Vinson failed to seek out advice or bring her concerns to others in the company who may have helped clarify the issues and provide support other than her superiors who went along with Sullivan. Most notably, Vinson did not contact Cynthia Cooper, the director of internal auditing, who was ultimately responsible for blowing the whistle on the financial fraud. Vinson's ordeal illustrates how cognitive limitations and organizational systems can lead an otherwise ethical person to do wrong things.

The fraud was accomplished primarily in two ways:

1) Capitalizing 'line costs' for interconnectivity with other telecommunications companies as depreciable assets thereby expensing them over the useful life rather than recording them as operating expenses and charging the full amount incurred each year to income of that year.
2) Inflating revenues with bogus accounting entries from 'corporate unallocated revenue accounts'. These were amounts recorded as operating revenue after the close of a quarter to meet earnings estimates. They were, however, nonrecurring amounts that should have been recorded in a non-operating revenue account.

A summary of the facts introduced at trial appear in Exhibit 8.5.

Exhibit 8.5 WorldCom Fraud

Betty Vinson was one of five former WorldCom executives who pleaded guilty to fraud. At the trial of Bernie Ebbers, Vinson said she was told to make improper accounting entries because Ebbers did not want to disappoint Wall Street. Vinson testified that "I felt like if I didn't make the entries, I wouldn't be working there" (Pulliam, 2003, p. A1). She also drafted a resignation letter in 2000, but ultimately decided to remain with the company. It was clear from her testimony that she felt uneasy with the accounting at WorldCom.

Vinson said that she took her concerns to Scott Sullivan the chief financial officer, who told her that Ebbers did not want to lower Wall Street expectations. Asked how she chose which accounts to alter, Vinson testified, "I just really pulled some out of the air. I used some spreadsheets" (Pulliam, 2003, p. A1). Vinson came up with the techniques to manipulate the numbers and another accountant, Troy Normand, saw to it that the books and records of the company had been changed.

Both Vinson and Normand reported to Buford Yates, Jr., the Director of General Accounting at WorldCom. Yates reported to David F. Myers, WorldCom's controller, who in turn reported to Sullivan. So, four accounting officials got caught up in the fraud, all unwilling to reject Sullivan's demands to manipulate the numbers. Each indicated they were pressured by Sullivan to go along with the fraud.

Vinson's lawyer urged the judge to sentence Vinson to probation, citing the pressure placed on her by Ebbers and Sullivan. According to the testimony, she reported her concerns to senior management who assured her recording the entries had been approved at the highest levels and all would be well as long as problems were dealt with as directed.

On December 6, 2002, the SEC reached an agreement with Vinson about her role in the WorldCom fraud and suspended her from appearing or practicing before the Commission as an accountant. In its enforcement release, the SEC alleged that: "At the direction of WorldCom senior management, Vinson and other WorldCom employees caused WorldCom to overstate materially its earnings in contravention of GAAP for at least seven successive fiscal quarters, from as early as October 2000 through April 2002" (SEC, 2002, p. 2). The overstatement included improperly capitalized line costs to overstate pre-tax earnings by approximately $3.8 billion. The SEC agreement went on to say: "Vinson knew, or was reckless in not knowing, that these entries were made without supporting documentation, were not in conformity with GAAP, were not disclosed to the investing public, and were designed to allow WorldCom to appear to meet Wall Street analysts' quarterly earnings estimates" (SEC, 2002, p. 2).

On August 5, 2005, US District Judge Barbara S. Jones sentenced Vinson to five months of jail and five months of house arrest, saying she was taking into account Vinson's cooperation with prosecutors and her subordinate role in the crime. Judge Jones said that although Ms. Vinson "was among the least culpable members of the conspiracy" and acted under extreme pressure, "that does not excuse what she did" (Young & Searcey, 2005).

The facts of the WorldCom case and Vinson's role in hiding the fraud are discussed here in the context of Exhibit 8.4. We examine what Vinson could have done or would have done had she been more in tune with behavioral factors and organizational influences that limited ethical decision-making.

5.1. Step 1 – Define the Problem

Vinson defined the problem as WorldCom needing to meet Wall Street earnings expectations. She was pressured by Sullivan to book false entries to satisfy the desire of Ebbers to hit earnings targets. Her ability to see the ethical issues clearly was affected by limits in perceptual awareness due to bounded ethicality and the inability to see through the demands of Sullivan and do what she knew was the right thing – to refuse to make the false entries that violated Generally Accepted Accounting Principles (GAAP). In failing to see through the ethical cloud of a superior's pressure, Vinson violated Securities and Exchange Commission (SEC) regulations and the AICPA Code of Professional Conduct (AICPA, 2016) that prohibits subordinating one's judgment to a superior in deciding accounting issues.

Whereas Vinson was uncomfortable in making the requested entries, the way she framed the problem blocked her ability to fully appreciate the magnitude of the decision she was making. The problem was framed very narrowly through the lens of satisfying Sullivan and Ebbers and not the public interest. As a result, Vinson did not act on her own values, even though she knew what she was asked to do was improper.

5.2. Step 2 – Seek Out Relevant Assistance, Guidance and Support

Vinson knew GAAP was being violated by capitalizing line costs instead of expensing them. Rather than following the ethical standards of the accounting profession and refusing to become involved, she gave in to the culture at WorldCom that called for putting the interests of the company above all else. Had she sought out advice and supporters sensitive to her position, such as Cooper, the WorldCom fraud might have been stopped in its tracks.

Vinson's mindset influenced the way in which she dealt with the problem. She acted as if she was all alone in the fight against fraudulent accounting. However, there were other resources to use. In addition to the GAAP rules and rules of conduct in the AICPA Code, Vinson could have taken her concerns directly to the audit committee of the board of directors. Even though the board and audit committee were basically detached from financial reporting matters, leaving them to Sullivan and Ebbers, had she gone to Cooper early on, they, together, could have approached the audit committee with their concerns. Finding others in the organization to support one's view is a step consistent with the IMA standards that members should use all internal processes at their disposal to resolve ethical issues. Moreover, there is strength in numbers when dealing with unethical conduct of others.

5.3. Step 3 – Identify Available Alternative Solutions to the Problem

If she had discovered her own biases, Vinson would have been better equipped to identify alternative solutions to the problem that supported ethical decision-making. Along these lines, she should have been sensitive to the existence of ethical fading (minimizing the importance of her own personal values). She needed to find a way to counteract the weak corporate culture but was unable to do so because of cognitive biases.

Vinson considered three alternatives: making the requested entries, refusing to make the requested entries and resigning. As previously mentioned, she did not consider reporting the matter to Cooper or the audit committee. Vinson fell victim to self-serving bias, reasoning that she needed to go along with the fraud to save her position. Having dismissed accounting rules and ethical standards in step 1, Vinson was unable to make a strong argument to superiors and use the rules and regulations to strengthen her position. This could have opened up a fourth option, to take her concerns to Cooper and, if necessary, the audit committee.

5.4. Step 4 – Evaluate the Identified Alternatives

Vinson did not thoroughly evaluate the alternatives because she was not fully aware of the scope of ethical issues including the psychological processes that prevented her from identifying and dealing with perceptual biases. She fell victim to a weak corporate culture that placed self-interest above properly reporting the line costs.

Evaluation of the alternatives requires the application of the PLUS filters to the options identified. Vinson knew that the accounting rules and ethical standards were violated and both she and WorldCom could be subject to legal consequences. She suffered from ethical blind spots and wound up acting in a way that was inconsistent with her personal values. Vinson deceived herself into thinking the problem would somehow go away or at least be contained.

What follows is a brief ethical analysis of the options using universal principles of teleology, deontology and virtue.

5.5. Option 1 – Book the Requested Entries

Organizational systems to consider at WorldCom include the code of conduct, accounting policies and procedures, internal controls and internal audit reporting mechanisms. Vinson should have evaluated how the systems influenced the options identified. As previously stated, she did not rely on the internal auditors to support her position, a step that would have helped to combat ethical blind spots. In addition, an ethical analysis using universal principles and values would have provided support for refusing to record the entries.

A utilitarian analysis requires balancing the benefits and harms of alternative options. By recording the requested entries, Vinson was serving the interests of WorldCom, as identified by Sullivan and Ebbers and manipulating the financial results to meet earnings estimates. The harms of doing so were significant and clearly outweighed the benefits; that is, investors and creditors received false and misleading financial statements. In addition, the legal consequences of the way the line costs were accounted for opened WorldCom to regulatory scrutiny and Vinson to legal jeopardy.

Vinson should have considered the broader picture rather than focus on short-term results. The investors and creditors have a right to receive accurate and reliable financial statements and the accountants and auditors, including Vinson, have an ethical obligation to satisfy those rights under deontology. A universality perspective calls for considering how other accountants in a similar situation would have recorded the line costs under GAAP. A long-term perspective could have strengthened her position by emphasizing that sooner or later the manipulated results would catch up with WorldCom because, with each passing year, more and more falsified entries were needed to keep the deception going.

5.6. Option 2 – Refusing to Make the Entries

This option overcomes all the harms identified in option 1 but raises others including the loss of her job. Vinson was told to be a team player and record the false entries. She was not supported by higher-ups in the accounting function, including Buford Yates, the Director of General Accounting and David Myers, controller, both of whom reported to Sullivan and went along with the fraud. This made it more difficult to drum up support for her position. There is no indication that WorldCom had an anonymous reporting outlet for Vinson to follow.

Sullivan pressured Vinson into thinking the manipulation was short-term. Vinson felt she could ride it out. Had she looked at the situation through psychological processes and what the demands were doing to her ethical self, Vinson would have decided it was best to refuse to record the entries. There were no assurances it would be a short-term request. The problem was once she agreed to go along with the fraud, Vinson began the slide down the proverbial ethical slippery slope and it would become more difficult with each passing quarter to stand up to the pressure imposed by Sullivan. Perhaps she felt constrained in contacting Cooper because she already had begun the slide. This is why seeking out a trusted advisor and supporters at the earliest stages of decision-making is so important – to give clarity to the issues.

By refusing to make the entries, Vinson would have been true to herself and followed her values, not allowing ethical blind spots to influence her decision. The benefits of this option include doing what Vinson knew was the right thing to do, maintaining her integrity by refusing to subordinate her judgment to that of superiors, doing what was best for the stakeholders and placing the integrity of the accounting profession above personal interests, which is consistent with the IMA standards.

Moreover, refusing to record the entries would have shielded her from legal consequences.

5.7. *Option 3 – Resigning*

Refusing to record the entries probably would have led to her firing, but it would have been an act of conscience. It would have been an action true to her sense of self as envisioned in the PLUS factors. It would have been an act of integrity because Vinson would have refused to subordinate her judgment to superiors. Still, it would not have protected stakeholder interests as much as refusing to go along with improper financial reporting, which is a proactive step.

Whereas it is true others in the organization may have taken her place and recorded the false entries, Vinson could have raised the red flag by resigning and, at the same time, reporting her action to the audit committee. Under the AICPA Code and IMA standards, when differences of opinion exist on accounting matters, the accountant should report them up the chain of command. Moreover, resigning a position does not necessarily alleviate the accountant's ethical responsibility to report improper accounting to regulatory authorities. Vinson should have sought legal advice if she had contemplated such steps.

Vinson decided out of self-interest not to resign. She weighed keeping her job as more important than having truthful financial statements and protecting the stakeholders. She allowed psychological pressures to dictate what became an unethical action. By resigning, Vinson would have maintained her integrity, protected her reputation and likely avoided legal consequences. She would have resigned after expressing her concerns and walked away with her head held high.

5.8. *Option 4 – Trying to Convince Vinson's Superiors to Properly Report*

Whereas the facts of the case indicate that Vinson did ask Sullivan about the entries, there is little evidence that she had tried to convince him to properly report the line costs. Given that Troy Normand, Yates and Myers also remained silent about the fraud under pressure from Sullivan, Vinson had little choice but to go to Cooper or the audit committee to elicit their help in convincing Sullivan of the problems with the way line costs were accounted for. At a minimum, having a conversation with one or the other would have given Vinson the opportunity to explore the matter further and perhaps gain new insights.

The virtue of integrity requires a commitment to do the right thing regardless of personal consequences. Vinson did not have the courage of her convictions and, even though she was against the improper reporting, she did not have the cognitive skills to fight off the pressures and failures in the organizational systems she faced.

Option 4 meets each of PLUS filters. Reporting the matter to Cooper and/or the audit committee is consistent with GAAP and would have shielded Vinson from legal consequences. It benefits the stakeholders and fairly represents their interests. In the short run it may have harmed the company for failing to meet earnings expectations but benefitted it in the long run by not getting involved in a vicious cycle of manipulation. Moreover, Vinson would have acted in a way that was consistent with her values.

5.9. Step 5 – Make the Decision

Vinson allowed her self-interests to dictate her decisions. She valued keeping her job above all else. She deceived herself into thinking the problem was less severe than it really was. She underestimated the costs of going along with the fraud. Cognitive biases created a barrier to ethical decision-making, focusing on her own position and not that of the investors and creditors. She had an ethical blind spot with respect to behaving in her perceived self-interests without regard to moral values. Her actions were not consistent with what she knew the right thing to do was thereby failing to apply the 'S' factor in the PLUS model in the evaluation steps.

5.10. Step 6 – Implement the Decision

Unable to find supporters in the accounting area, Vinson felt she had no choice but to go along with the fraud. Her decision had consequences for WorldCom and made the job of Cooper more difficult. No one was reporting the fraud to Cooper, which raises questions whether organizational systems were working as intended. Cooper's role was to make sure the financial reports conformed with GAAP and to prepare WorldCom for the external audit. Had she been informed by Vinson, Cooper would have begun a thorough investigation of the matter in advance of the audit, which is exactly what she did in the end.

The highest ethical value in the accounting profession is integrity. Integrity means acting in accordance with what an accountant knows is right. It also means to not subordinate ethical judgment to superiors who want to act out of self-interest. Vinson's actions fell short in this regard because of cognitive limitations and the failure to consider psychological processes that influenced behavior and the way organizational systems worked.

5.11. Step 7 – Evaluate the Decision

Once a decision has been made, the next step is follow-up, to consider whether it solved the problem and, if not, whether other steps may be warranted. The PLUS factors allow for a post-decision-making perspective and may call for additional action. Vinson should have reflected on the fact that she went along with the fraud and contrary to what she had hoped, Sullivan continued to ask her to manipulate the financial results. Reflection could have led her to the tough decision of refusing to go along but ethical blind spots and a corrosive organization culture created barriers to ethical action.

It is important to reflect on a decision after the fact to evaluate any behavioral factors that may have been ignored, such as bounded ethicality, ethical blind spots and self-serving bias. Steps should be taken to deal with these perceptual limitations, so the next dilemma is better understood and the results are consistent with ethical decision-making. Moreover, there needs to be a better understanding of how organizational culture affects ethical behavior and how organizational systems can be changed to advance ethical decision-making.

6. Conclusions

The model presented in Exhibit 8.4 and discussed in the case of Betty Vinson illustrates how both behavioral and organizational culture influences the way in which decisions are made. The model goes beyond previous ones used in accounting education that, for the most part, restrict the analysis to accounting rules and regulations and philosophical reasoning methods. In reality, many financial frauds occur because of an inability to spot the ethical issues, setting aside or ignoring the ethical issues for the sake of preserving self-interests and being blinded to psychological pressures that can negatively influence ethical decision-making. This occurs by deceiving oneself into thinking the request to go along with improper accounting is a one-time event thereby allowing short-term beneficial effects of manipulated financial reporting to overwhelm long-term ethical decision-making and by not understanding whom to go to in the organization for support. Exhibit 8.4 provides a holistic approach to ethical decision-making that considers all dimensions of an ethical dilemma and provides a systematic way to develop an effective game plan to resolve unethical accounting before it infects the financial reporting process. The public interest is well-served by the model because it places the burden on individual behavior and organizational systems, rather than relying mainly on ethical reasoning methods that can be used to rationalize one approach or another without regard to whether the culture of the organization will support the ethical choice. Accounting educators can use the model along with case studies to deal with psychological processes and organizational systems, such as those that led Vinson to engage in ethically questionable behaviors. It is a hands-on approach that overcomes the limitations of traditional ethical decision-making models.

Note

1. The PLUS decision-making model was developed by the Ethics & Compliance Initiative of the Ethics Resource Center: www.ethics.org/resources/free-toolkit/decision-making-model/

References

American Institute of Certified Public Accountants (AICPA). (2016). *Code of Professional Conduct*. Retrieved June 2nd, 2020, from www.aicpa.org/content/dam/aicpa/research/standards/codeofconduct/downloadabledocuments/2014december15contentasof2016august31codeofconduct.pdf

Badaracco, J., & Webb, A. (1995). Business Ethics: A View From the Trenches. *California Management Review, 37*(2), 8–25.

Bazerman, M. H., & Sezer, O. (2016). Bounded Awareness: Implications for Ethical Decision Making. *Organizational Behavior and Human Decision Processes, 136*, 95–105.

Bazerman, M. H., & Tenbrunsel, A. E. (2011). *Blind Spots: Why We Fail to Do What's Right and What to Do About It*. Princeton, NJ: Princeton University Press.

Beu, D., & Buckley, M. (2004). Using Accountability to Create a More Ethical Climate. *Human Resource Management Review, 14*, 67–83.

Bok, S. (1989). *Secrets*. New York: Vintage Books.

Bowen, S. (2004). Organizational Factors Encouraging Ethical Decision Making: An Exploration Into the Case of an Exemplar. *Journal of Business Ethics, 52*(4), 311–324.

Chugh, D., & Bazerman, M. H. (2007). Bounded Awareness: What You Fail to See Can Hurt You. *Mind & Society, 6*(1), 1–18.

Chugh, D., Bazerman, M. H., & Banaji, M. R. (2005). Bounded Ethicality as a Psychological Barrier to Recognizing Conflicts of Interest. In D. A. Moore, D. M. Cain, G. Loewenstein, & M. H. Bazerman (Eds.), *Conflicts of Interest: Challenges and Solutions in Business, Law, Medicine, and Public Policy* (pp. 74–95). New York: Cambridge University Press.

Douglas, P., Davidson, R., & Schwartz, B. (2001). The Effect of Ethical Orientation on Accountants' Ethical Judgments. *Journal of Business Ethics, 34*(2), 101–121.

Dunham, R., & Pierce, J. (1989). *Management*. Glenson, IL: Scott, Foresman and Company.

Elango, B., Paul, K., Sumit, K., & Shishir, P. (2010). Organizational Ethics, and Ethical Intentions in International Decision Making. *Journal of Business Ethics, 97*(4), 543–561.

Ethics & Compliance Initiative (ECI). (n.d.). *Seven Steps to Ethical Decision Making*. Retrieved June 2nd, 2020, from www.ethics.org/resources/free-toolkit/decision-making-model/

Goddard, R. (1988). Are You and Ethical Manager. *Personnel Journal, 67*(3), 38–47.

Harvey, J. (2000). Reinforcing Ethical Decision Making Through Organizational Structure. *Journal of Business Ethics, 28*, 43–58.

Hoffman, W., Moore, J., & Fedo, D. (1983). *Corporate Governance and Institutionalizing Ethics*. Toronto: Lexington Books.

Institute of Management Accountants (IMA). (2017). *IMA Statement of Ethical Professional Practice*. Retrieved June 2nd, 2020, from www.imanet.org/-/media/b6fbeeb74d964e6c9fe654c48456e61f.ashx

Jones, T. (1991). Decision Making by Individuals in Organizations: An Issue-Contingent Model. *The Academy of Management Review*, 16(2), 366–395.

Kern, M. C., & Chugh, D. (2009). Bounded Ethicality: The Perils of Loss Framing. *Psychological Science*, 20(3), 378–384.

Kish-Gephart, J., Harrison, D., & Trevino, L. (2010). Bad Apples, Bad Cases and Bad Barrels: Meta-Analytic Evidence About Sources of Unethical Decisions at Work. *Journal of Applied Psychology*, 95(1), 1–31.

Langenderfer, H., & Rockness, J. (1989). Integrating Ethics Into the Accounting Curriculum: Issues, Problems and Solutions. *Issues in Accounting Education*, 4(1), 66–67.

Libby, T., & Thorne, L. (2007). The Development of a Measure of Auditors' Virtue. *Journal of Business Ethics*, 71(1), 89–99.

Lindsay, R., Lindsay, M., & Irvine, B. (1996). Instilling Ethical Behavior in Organizations: A Survey of Canadian Companies. *Journal of Business Ethics*, 15(1), 393–407.

March, J. G., & Simon, H. A. (1958). *Organizations*. Oxford: Wiley.

May, W. W. (1990). *Ethics in the Accounting Curriculum: Cases & Readings*. Sarasota, FL: American Accounting Association.

Messick, D. M., & Bazerman, M. H. (1996). Ethical Leadership and the Psychology of Decision Making. *Sloan Management Review*, 37(2), 9–22.

Mintz, S. (2019). A New Approach to Teaching Ethical Decision Making to Accounting Students. *The CPA Journal*, 9, 36–41.

Mintz, S., & Morris, R. (2017). *Ethical Obligations and Decision Making in Accounting: Text and Cases* (4th ed.). New York: McGraw Hill Education.

Mintz, S., & Morris, R. (2020). *Ethical Obligations and Decision Making in Accounting: Text and Cases* (5th ed.). New York: McGraw Hill Education.

Moore, C., & Gino, F. (2013). Ethically Adrift: How Others Pull Our Moral Compass From True North, and How We Can Fix It. *Research in Organizational Behavior*, 33, 53–77.

Nash, L. (1990). *Good Intentions Aside: A Manager's Guide to Resolving Ethical Problems*. Boston, MA: Harvard Business School Press.

Nill, A., & Schibrowsky, J. (2005). The Impact of Culture, the Reward System, and Perceived Moral Intensity on Marketing Students' Ethical Decision Making. *Journal of Marketing Education*, 27(1), 68–80.

Ordonez, L. D., Schweitzer, M. E., Galinsky, A. D., & Bazerman, M. H. (2009). Goals Gone Wild: The Side Effects of Overprescribing Goal Setting. *Academy of Management Perspectives*, 23, 6–16.

Ponemon, L. (1992). Ethical Reasoning and Selection-Socializations in Accounting. *Accounting, Organizations and Society*, 17(3/4), 239–258.

Pulliam, S. (2003). Ordered to Commit Fraud, a Staffer Balked, then Caved: Accountant Betty Vinson Helped Cook the Books at WorldCom. *The Wall Street Journal*. Retrieved June 2nd, 2020, from www.wsj.com/articles/SB105631811322355600

Rest, J. (1986). *Moral Development: Advances in Research and Theory.* New York: Praeger.

Robin, D., & Reidenbach, R. (1987). Social Responsibility, Ethics and Marketing Strategy: Closing the Gap Between Concept and Application. *Journal of Marketing, 51,* 44–58.

Securities and Exchange Commission (SEC). (2002). *In the Matter of Betty L. Vinson, CPA, Respondent. Order Instituting Administrative Proceedings Pursuant to Rule 102(e) of the Commission's Rules of Practice, Making Findings, and Imposing Remedial Sanctions.* Retrieved June 2nd, 2020, from www.sec.gov/litigation/admin/33-8158.htm

Soutar, G., McNeil, M., & Molster, C. (1994). The Impact of the Work Environment on Ethical Decision Making: Some Australian Evidence. *Journal of Business Ethics, 13*(5), 327–339.

Sweeney, B., Arnold, D., & Pierce, B. (2010). The Impact of Perceived Ethical Culture of the Firm and Demographic Variables on Auditors' Ethical Evaluation and Intention to Act Decisions. *Journal of Business Ethics, 93*(4), 531–551.

Tenbrunsel, A. E., & Messick, D. M. (2004). Ethical Fading: The Role of Self-Deception in Unethical Behavior. *Social Justice Research, 17*(2), 223–236.

Tenbrunsel, A. E., Wade-Benzoni, K., Messick, D. M., & Bazerman, M. H. (2000). Understanding the Influence of Environmental Standards on Judgments and Choices. *Academy of Management Journal, 43,* 854–866.

Thorne, L. (1998). The Role of Virtue in Auditors' Ethical Decision Making: An Integration of Cognitive Developmental and Virtue-Ethics Perspectives. *Research on Accounting Ethics, 4,* 291–308.

Trevino, L., & Nelson, K. (1995). *Managing Business Ethics: Straight Talk About How to Do It Right.* New York: John Wiley.

Trevino, L., Weaver, G., Gibson, D., & Toffler, B. (1999). Managing Ethics and Legal Compliance: What Works and What Hurts. *California Management Review, 41*(2), 131–151.

Valentine, S., Godkin, L., & Vitton, J. (2012). Perceived Corporate Ethics and Individual Ethical Decision Making: When in Rome, Doing as the Romans Do. *Journal of Leadership, Accountability and Ethics, 9*(2), 55–67.

Valentine, S., & Hollingworth, D. (2012). Moral Intensity, Issue Importance, and Ethical Reasoning in Operations Situations. *Journal of Business Ethics, 108*(4), 509–523.

Vitell, S., & Hidalgo, E. (2006). The Impact of Corporate Ethical Values and Enforcement of Ethical Codes on the Perceived Importance of Ethics in Business. *Journal of Business Ethics, 64*(1), 31–43.

Weaver, G., Trevino, L., & Cochran, P. (1999). Corporate Ethics Programs as Control Systems: Managerial and Institutional Influences. *Academy of Management Journal, 42,* 41–57.

Windsor, C., & Ashkanasy, N. (1995). The Effect of Client Management Bargaining Power, Moral Reasoning Development and Belief in a Just World on Auditor Independence. *Accounting, Organization and Society, 20,* 701–720.

Young, S., & Searcey, D. (2005). Former Executive at WorldCom Gets 5-Month Jail Term. *The Wall Street Journal.* Retrieved June 2nd, 2020, from www.wsj.com/articles/SB112324869137506086

9   Putting Ethical Dilemmas on Students' 'RADAR'

Joan Lee & Dawn W. Massey

1. Introduction

In recent years, research increasingly has highlighted concern over a shift away from professionalism by accountants, ranging from auditors (e.g., Baud, Brivot & Himick, 2019; Chow, Massey, Thorne & Wu, 2013; Guo, 2016; Shaub & Braun, 2014) to management/industry accountants (e.g., Ashman, 2014; Fiolleau & Kaplan, 2017) to tax professionals (e.g., Dzienkowski & Peroni, 2016; Shafer & Simmons, 2008). Given that organizational leaders face ethical dilemmas practically daily (Moreno, 2011) and accounting leaders face increased pressure to act unethically (CGMA, 2013), as Shaub (2017) highlights, aspiring accounting professionals need to be prepared to address ethical issues in their careers with a professional attitude, regardless of the setting (e.g., audit, corporate accounting, tax). Indeed, as Gaa (1996, p. 23) warns,

> It is not only mistaken, but dangerous, to address ethical issues in accounting as separate and distinct from technical issues. The danger of making this mistake is that both students and practicing accountants may believe that they can be good accountants without considering the ethical aspects of their behavior.

To these ends, a new model – dubbed the 'RADAR' model (for Research, Analyze, Decide, Act, Reflect) – can assist faculty in teaching accounting students to responsibly address ethical dilemmas encountered in an accounting context.

The beginning of this chapter highlights why a new model is needed. The purpose of this new model, the 'RADAR' model, is not only to put ethical issues top of mind for students but also to give them a robust framework they can use to navigate ethical potholes, including knowledge of the forces that bear upon the process. The influence of other ethical decision-making models on the development of the 'RADAR' model is addressed, with justifications drawn by reference to the literature. After a thorough explanation of each of the five factors in the 'RADAR' model, the chapter concludes with insight into its use.

2. Prior Models

Much of the literature in incorporating ethics in accounting draws on seminal models. Rest's (1983) four-component model serves as the basis for Mintz and Morris' (2020, p. 84) "Integrated Ethical Decision-Making Process." The American Accounting Association's (AAA) seven-step model (May, 1990) is drawn from Langenderfer and Rockness' (1989) model,[1] and the American Institute of Certified Public Accountants' (AICPA) Ethics Decision Tree for Certified Public Accountants (CPA) in Business (AICPA, 2015) is similar to that contained in the Institute of Management Accountants' (IMA, 2017) Statement of Ethical Professional Practice. A brief comparison of those models is included in Table 9.1.

All of the models included in Table 9.1 present facets of the process for attending to ethical situations that bear inclusion in any model that students – as aspiring accountants – are taught. However, the formal

Table 9.1 Comparison of Ethics Models used in Accounting

Model 1 Rest/Mintz & Morris	Model 2 AAA/Langenderfer & Rockness	Model 3 AICPA
1. Identify the ethical and professional issues	1. Determine the facts 2. Define the ethical issues and stakeholders	
	3. Identify the major principles, rules and values	1. Determine if an ethics policy can provide guidance 2. If not, review AICPA professional standards for guidance
2. Identify and evaluate alternative courses of action	4. Specify the alternatives	
	5. Compare values and alternatives	
3. Consider the moral intensity of the situation and virtues that enable ethical action to occur	6. Assess the consequences	3. Discuss with counterparty and/or (internal) authority figure
		4. Endeavor to reduce/ eliminate threats to an acceptable level
4. Decide on a course of action consistent with one's professional obligations[2]	7. Make your decision	5. Decide whether to discontinue the relationship with the organization

models conclude once a decision is made, rather than afterward. In so doing, the models imply that ethical decisions and ethical actions equate even though the literature does not support such a 1:1 correspondence (e.g., Jones, Massey & Thorne, 2003; O'Fallon & Butterfield, 2005). Further, the AICPA (2015) model fails to explicitly consider Ethical Sensitivity (also known as Ethical Awareness), suggesting, instead, that all ethical dilemmas are perceived by accountants. Yet the literature is clear that one must perceive an ethical situation in order to properly react to it (e.g., Jones et al., 2003; Massey & Van Hise, 2009; O'Fallon & Butterfield, 2005).

Perhaps most notably, though, each of the models is deficient in incorporating the role of affect in influencing responses to ethical dilemmas. Affect includes "many nonrational factors [that] influence ethical thought and behavior, including context, perceptions, relationship, emotions and heuristics" (Rogerson, Gottlieb, Handelsman, Knapp & Younggren, 2011, p. 614).[3] Affect, which, in addition to contextual factors, also arises from individual factors such as virtue, personality, gender, nationality and education and combines with intellect in influencing responses to ethical dilemmas by professionals such as nurses (Baysal, Sari & Erdem, 2018) and, more saliently, internal auditors (Latan, Chiappetta Jabbour & Lopes de Sousa Jabbour, 2019). Whereas Mintz and Morris (2020) include several contextual factors/situational pressures in their model, they only include one individual factor (i.e., virtue). The AAA (May, 1990) and the AICPA (2015) models include neither contextual factors/situational pressures nor individual factors.

Thus, although the existing models provided a good starting point, none of the models is complete. The 'RADAR' model addresses this issue by providing a single, robust model that not only explicitly acknowledges ethical sensitivity as a precursor to addressing ethical dilemmas in accounting but, more importantly, continues beyond the decision point to the post-decision phase and integrates into the model consideration of a broad range of nonrational individual and contextual factors/situational pressures that address the affective aspect of the process. The 'RADAR' model is introduced in the next section.

3. The 'RADAR' Model

The 'RADAR' model is depicted in Figure 9.1. The acronym 'RADAR' – for Research, Analyze, Decide, Act, Reflect – corresponds to the five core steps in the model, each of which is further described next. As shown in Figure 9.1, the model incorporates ethical sensitivity/awareness via 'Awareness of [the] Moral Issue', which is a prerequisite to the process. In addition, the model includes post-decision steps and also explicitly recognizes the impact of numerous individual and contextual factors/situational pressures that influence one's approach to addressing ethical issues.

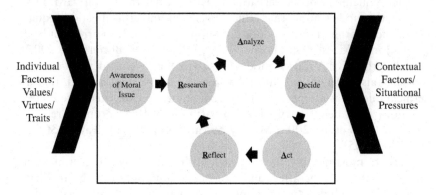

Figure 9.1 The RADAR Model

Lonergan's (1972) writings in the area of human consciousness inform the central tenets of the 'RADAR' model.[4] Lonergan's (1972) work, which is empirically based (Helminiak, Feingold & Donahue, 2020), is chosen because it addresses all aspects necessary to resolve ethical dilemmas encountered in an accounting context. To attend to an issue such as an ethical situation, Lonergan (1972) recognizes four foundational functions (experience, understanding, judgment and decision), each of which is underlain, respectively, by one of four precepts ('Be attentive, Be intelligent, Be reasonable, Be responsible') (Helminiak et al., 2020, p. 8). Taken together, the precepts and functions form the explicit steps in Lonergan's (1972) model.

Lonergan's (1972) first step, 'Be attentive/experience', involves paying attention to one's surroundings, which is needed to perceive ethical dilemmas. As such, it addresses the need to include ethical sensitivity/awareness, which was missing in the AICPA (2015) model.

The second step in Lonergan's (1972) model, 'Be intelligent/understanding', encompasses discovering and exploring possible solutions, whereas the third step, 'Be reasonable/judgment', comprises testing possible solutions and discerning which is best. These steps are consistent with those in the other ethics models commonly used in accounting.

Lonergan's (1972) final step, 'Be responsible/decision', involves deciding and acting in accordance with what one has learned in the prior steps. Unlike the accounting models, which conclude before enacting a decision, the Lonergan (1972) model includes taking action to execute the decision.

Lonergan's (1972) model also is iterative; although presented sequentially here for ease of exposition, once an issue is identified, future steps can result in reversion to prior steps to obtain more information, to identify additional possible resolutions, to re-evaluate possible resolutions and, importantly, to reflect on decisions/actions in order to be ready to face future ethical situations. The notion of reflection, a post-action assessment of the 'goodness' of the outcome(s) and/or how well the process(es) worked, is included in the fifth core step in the 'RADAR' model. It also is included as a post-decision step in the Mintz and Morris (2020) model.

Finally, Lonergan's (1972) approach implicitly fuses affective aspects into the intellectual process. In so doing, Lonergan's (1972) model highlights the importance of individual and contextual factors in influencing the process for attending to ethical situations. Individual factors include values, virtues, traits and any other factors that might lead an individual to view an ethical dilemma from a unique perspective such as age, gender, nationality, education, work experience, prejudices and biases. These individual factors impact both the way in which individuals perceive ethical dilemmas (or if they even perceive them at all) and the way in which they approach the dilemma (e.g., the alternatives they consider might be influenced by these factors). Thus, it is critically important that ethical decision makers are sufficiently self-aware of these factors and 'own their biases' in approaching ethical dilemmas. These factors first influence awareness of the moral issue, but their effects are felt throughout the decision process.

Contextual factors and situational pressures also are considered in the 'RADAR' model. These affect individuals' responses to ethical dilemmas, primarily in the way individuals analyze, decide and act in ethical dilemmas. As stated in Jones' seminal paper, "Specifically, ethical decision-making is issue contingent; that is, characteristics of the moral issue itself, collectively called moral intensity, are important determinants of ethical decision-making and behavior" (Jones, 1991, p. 371). Jones' (1991) moral intensity concept included six different factors: 'magnitude of consequences', 'social consensus', 'probability of effect', 'temporal immediacy', 'proximity' and 'concentration of effect'. The impact of these factors (and other contextual factors such as corporate infrastructure and professional codes) on decision-making has been borne out by Palmer (2013) and Treviño et al. (2014).

Individual and contextual factors and situational pressures may affect whether an individual 'sees' an ethical dilemma and, if so, how it is defined. As noted earlier, Ethical Sensitivity/Ethical Awareness is a prerequisite to ethical decision-making and is included as an essential element in the 'RADAR' model ('Awareness of Moral Issue'). In the context of the 'RADAR' model, this prerequisite is represented as 'Awareness of Moral Issue', and corresponds to Lonergan's (1972) first step, which requires paying attention to, experiencing, one's surroundings, in that one must recognize an ethical dilemma before one can attempt to resolve it.

The letters in the acronym 'RADAR' refer to the five steps at the core of the model. 'Research' is the first of these core steps. It resonates with the part of 'Be intelligent/understanding' in Lonergan's (1972) approach that relates to discovering possible solutions to the dilemma in light of the broad range of stakeholders. It is similar to corresponding steps in the other ethics models used in accounting. In particular, 'Research' is akin to the identification of stakeholders and alternative courses of action aspect of steps 1 and 2 in the Mintz and Morris's (2020) model. It corresponds to steps 2 and 3 – defining the 'stakeholders' and identifying the 'major principles, rules, and values' – in the AAA model (May, 1990) and step 1, determining 'if an ethics policy can provide guidance', in the AICPA (2015) model.

A key tenet in applying the 'Research' aspect of the 'RADAR' model is that all potential solutions should be considered. Often, in ethical dilemmas, there are one or two 'obvious' solutions, usually the polar extreme options, but rarely are these the 'best' options. Broad consideration of all of the various stakeholders affected by the dilemma can lead to alternative solutions.

The first 'A' in 'RADAR' represents 'Analyze'. This step incorporates some of Lonergan's (1972) second step ('Be intelligent/understanding') in that exploring possible solutions might include analysis of the alternatives. It also includes some of the third concept in Lonergan's (1972) model, 'Be reasonable/judgment', which involves testing possible solutions and discerning which is best. Taken together, Research and Analyze correspond also to a part of Mintz and Morris' (2020) second and third steps – namely 'Evaluate alternative courses of action' and 'Consider the moral intensity of the situation and virtues that enable ethical action to occur' – as well as steps 4, 5 and 6 in the AAA model (May, 1990): 'specify the alternatives', 'compare values and alternatives' and 'assess the consequences', respectively.

The next step, the 'D' in 'RADAR', represents 'Decide', which is akin to the 'Make your decision' step in the AAA model (May, 1990), the 'Decide on a course of action consistent with one's professional obligations' step in the Mintz and Morris's (2020) model and 'Decide whether to discontinue the relationship with the organization' step in the AICPA (2015) model. The fourth step in Lonergan's (1972) decision model, 'Be responsible/decision', requires one to decide *and act* based upon what has been learned. These steps are separated in the 'RADAR' model, recognizing that forming moral intention is not sufficient to ensure action upon that intention (e.g., Gentile, 2010). None of the three accounting ethics models introduced earlier explicitly recognizes this critical distinction between intention and action.[5]

The second 'A' in 'RADAR' stands for 'Act'. As noted earlier, in order to emphasize the importance of carrying out a decision that is the outcome of one's deliberations, taking action is recognized as a separate step in the 'RADAR' model. Whereas there is a real risk of failure at each step of the decision process, arguably, the most critical step involves putting one's ethical intention into action because it is one's actions (or inactions) that are ultimately judged as right/wrong. Indeed, Gentile's (2010) peda-gogical approach, Giving Voice to Values, focuses entirely on how to take ethical action once an ethical decision has been made.

The last 'R' in 'RADAR' – 'Reflect' – is what truly distinguishes the model from the other accounting ethics models introduced earlier. Ex-post consideration of the outcome and process enables one to internal-ize the lessons learned in one ethical situation for later use in another. It harkens back to the iterative nature of Lonergan's (1972) model. As well, given the critical importance of integration of intellect and affect in Lonergan's (1972) model, effective reflection includes a primary focus on the affective nature of addressing ethical dilemmas. As such, it allows an individual to consider how various individual and contextual factors and situational pressures impacted the process and, thus, outcome which, in turn, can lead to improved handling of ethical situations in the future.

3.1. Classroom Use

The 'RADAR' model is easily adaptable for use in accounting and accounting ethics classes, both at the undergraduate and graduate levels. Instructors who plan to use 'RADAR' to address ethics cases in the cur-riculum might want to start the term with an exercise to help students recognize their individual traits and personal biases that will, inevitably, affect how they approach ethical decision-making. One way to do this is to consider an ethics case in which the decision maker has a familial/personal connection with the subject of the case. This might involve an owner of a family business who discovers that a relative who is an employee in the business is stealing. Another scenario could be where a manager must choose which workers to lay off during an economic downturn when some of the employees who could be subject to the layoff are personal friends. In each case, students should be challenged to con-sider their personal biases and how those biases affected their decision processes. Questions that might bring this to the surface for the first sce-nario might include: have you ever worked for a family business? If so, do you think all the workers are treated equally in a family business? In the second scenario, questions might include: has anyone in your family ever been laid off? Would you be comfortable turning in a friend who was cheating? These simple scenarios can help students to recognize that their past experiences color the way they approach ethical decision-making. A helpful mantra to repeat throughout the class is 'Own your biases'.

The core of the model itself is fairly self-explanatory and the acro-nym 'RADAR' helps students to remember to 'use their RADAR' when they face ethical dilemmas. The first step in the 'RADAR' model might be considered analogous to other models that ask students to identify the stakeholders. But the 'Research' in 'RADAR' goes beyond identifying all stakeholders. A key facet of using the 'RADAR' model is to research multiple alternative solutions. In case discussion and analysis, students should identify at least three unique alternative courses of action. They should be encouraged to come to well-considered decisions about actions to take. At all times, students should be reminded to be cognizant of not only their own biases (individual factors) but also other external factors/ pressures (contextual factors/situational pressures) that might impact the situation and their perception and handling of it. They also should be encouraged to consider ways they can address the external factors/ pressures, including push back that they might receive, to facilitate their behaving in a manner that comports with the action they decided best.[6]

In order to complete a case analysis using the 'RADAR' model, students must reflect on their analyses of the ethical dilemma and the decisions they made. The impact of individual factors and/or situational factors and pressures (contextual factors) may be more apparent in hindsight. Often, in reflection, students will comment that the case reminded them of a situation faced by a parent or family friend, or perhaps, something they themselves have experienced. Students may recognize that they relied on precedents they had developed in prior cases, precedents that may, or may not, have been appropriate to the instant dilemma.

3.2. Conclusion

The 'RADAR' model presents a comprehensive, unified model for handling ethical dilemmas that can be used with undergraduate or graduate accounting students to assist them with the ethical situations they will face in their careers. Unlike extant accounting ethics models, the 'RADAR' model not only requires ex-ante awareness of the moral issue but also explicitly recognizes the impact on the process of nonrational factors, including individual and contextual factors and situational pressures. It also pushes the student to act on the decision and reflect back on the process and outcome to improve the handling of future ethical situations. The easy to remember acronym, 'RADAR', encourages students to remember to 'Use their RADAR'.

Notes

1. May's (1990) model is based on Langenderfer and Rockness' (1989) eight-step model, subsuming within step 6 ('Assess the consequences'), a step that includes discussing alternatives with a trusted person to gain greater perspective, if appropriate.
2. After deciding on a course of action, Mintz and Morris (2020) recommend reflection to assess the outcome and approach.
3. See also: Jones et al. (2003), O'Fallon & Butterfield (2005), Treviño, Nieuwenboer & Kish-Gephart (2014).
4. Bernard Lonergan was a Canadian Jesuit and philosopher, often referred to as the most significant philosophical thinker of the twentieth century. He is

known as the principal architect of the generalized empirical method, which focused on intellectual reasoning and on the interplay between the subjective and objective. His influential writings have been republished numerous times since his death in 1984.

5. Although step 4 of the Mintz and Morris (2020, p. 84) model is labeled 'Take action', the detailed explanation of it does not ensure that action will be taken. That is, the explanation for the step includes the following bullets:

- Decide on a course of action consistent with one's professional obligations.
- How can virtue (i.e., instrumental virtue) support turning ethical intent into ethical action?
- What steps can I take to strengthen my position and argument?
- How can I counter reasons and rationalizations that mitigate against taking ethical action? Who can I go to for support?

6. Considering possible situational factors/pressures as well as 'push back' and responses can be covered via class discussions, in student write-ups or, as Gentile (2010) suggests, via role-playing.

References

American Institute of Certified Public Accountants (AICPA). (2015). *Ethics Decision Tree: For CPAs in Business*. Retrieved June 2nd, 2020, from www.aicpa. org/content/dam/aicpa/interestareas/professionalethics/resources/ethicsen forcement/downloadabledocuments/ethics-decision-tree-business.pdf

Ashman, J. (2014). *The Professional Obligations of Accountants Involved in Strategic Planning* (Dissertation). Retrieved June 3rd, 2020, from https://oura rchive.otago.ac.nz/handle/10523/4906

Baud, C., Brivot, M., & Himick, D. (2019). Accounting Ethics and the Fragmentation of Value. *Journal of Business Ethics*. Retrieved June 2nd, 2020, from https://doi.org/10.1007/s10551-019-04186-9

Baysal, E., Sari, D., & Erdem, H. (2018). Ethical Decision-Making Levels of Oncology Nurses. *Nursing Ethics*, 26(7/8), 2204–2212.

Chartered Global Management Accountant (CGMA). (2013). *Managing Responsible Business – A Global Survey on Business Ethics*. Retrieved June 2nd, 2020, from www.cgma.org/resources/reports/managingresponsiblebusiness.html

Chow, C., Massey, D., Thorne, L., & Wu, A. (2013). A Qualitative Examination of Auditors' Differing Ethical Characterizations Across the Phases of the Audit. *Research on Professional Responsibility and Ethics in Accounting*, 17, 97–138.

Dzienkowski, J., & Peroni, R. (2016). The Decline in Tax Adviser Professionalism in American Society. *Fordham Law Review*, 84, 2721–2753.

Fiolleau, K., & Kaplan, S. E. (2017). Recognizing Ethical Issues: An Examination of Practicing Industry Accountants and Accounting Students. *Journal of Business Ethics*, 142(2), 259–276.

Gaa, J. (1996). Ethics Research and Research Ethics. *Behavioral Research in Accounting*, 8(Supplement), 12–23.

Gentile, M. (2010). *Giving Voice to Values: How to Speak Your Mind When You Know What's Right*. New Haven, CT: Yale University Press.

Guo, K. (2016). The Institutionalization of Commercialism in the Accounting Profession: An Identity-Experimentation Perspective. *Auditing: A Journal of Practice and Theory*, 25(3), 99–118.

Helminiak, D. A., Feingold, B. D., & Donahue, M. J. (2020). Clarifications About Lonergan's "Authenticity" for Application in Psychology. *New Ideas in Psychology*, 57(April), 1–12.

Institute of Management Accountants (IMA). (2017). *IMA Statement of Ethical Professional Practice*. Retrieved June 2nd, 2020, from www.imanet.org/-/media/b6fbeeb74d964e6c9fe654c48456e61f.ashx

Jones, J., Massey, D., & Thorne, L. (2003). Auditors' Ethical Reasoning: Insights From Past Research and Implications for the Future. *Journal of Accounting Literature*, 22, 45–103.

Jones, T. (1991). Ethical Decision Making by Individuals in Organizations: An Issue-Contingent Model. *The Academy of Management Review*, 16(2), 366–395.

Langenderfer, H., & Rockness, J. (1989). Integrating Ethics Into the Accounting Curriculum: Issues, Problems, and Solutions. *Issues in Accounting Education*, 4(1), 66–67.

Latan, H., Chiappetta Jabbour, C. J., & Lopes de Sousa Jabbour, A. B. (2019). Ethical Awareness, Ethical Judgment and Whistleblowing: A Moderated Mediation Analysis. *Journal of Business Ethics*, 155(1), 289–304.

Lonergan, B. (1972). *Method in Theology*. New York: Herder and Herder.

Massey, D., & Van Hise, J. (2009). Walking the Walk: Integrating Lessons From Multiple Perspectives in the Development of an Accounting Ethics Capstone. *Issues in Accounting Education*, 24(4), 481–510.

May, W. (1990). *Ethics in the Accounting Curriculum: Cases & Readings*. Sarasota, FL: American Accounting Association.

Mintz, S., & Morris, R. (2020). *Ethical Obligations and Decision Making in Accounting: Text and Cases* (5th ed.). New York: McGraw Hill Education.

Moreno, M. (2011). *Ethical Dilemmas: Pressures on Leaders to Walk the Talk* (Dissertation). Retrieved June 3rd, 2020, from https://repository.usfca.edu/cgi/viewcontent.cgi?article=1221&context=diss

O'Fallon, M., & Butterfield, K. (2005). A Review of the Empirical Ethical Decision-Making Literature: 1996–2003. *Journal of Business Ethics*, 59(4), 375–413.

Palmer, D. (2013). The New Perspective on Organizational Wrongdoing. *California Management Review*, 56(1), 5–23.

Rest, J. (1983). Morality. In E. M. Markman, P. H. Mussen, L. Carmichael, & J. H. Flavell (Eds.), *Handbook of Child Psychology. Vol. 3, Cognitive Development* (4th ed., pp. 556–629). New York: Wiley.

Rogerson, M., Gottlieb, M., Handelsman, M., Knapp, S., & Younggren, J. (2011). Nonrational Processes in Ethical Decision Making. *American Psychologist*, 66(7), 614–623.

Shafer, W., & Simmons, R. (2008). Social Responsibility, Machiavellianism and Tax Avoidance. *Accounting, Auditing and Accountability Journal*, 21(5), 695–720.

Shaub, M. (2017). A Wisdom-Based Accounting Ethics Course. *Advanced in Accounting Education: Teaching and Curriculum Innovations*, 20, 181–216.

Shaub, M., & Braun, R. (2014). Call of Duty: A Framework for Auditors' Ethical Decisions. In S. Mintz (Ed.), *Accounting for the Public Interest*. New York: Springer Dordrecht Heidelberg.

Treviño, L. K., den Nieuwenboer, N. A., & Kish-Gephart, J. J. (2014). (Un)Ethical Behavior in Organizations. *Annual Review of Psychology*, 65, 635–660.

Index

Printed in the United States
by Baker & Taylor Publisher Services